# THE FAILURE OF THE HEATH

*Also by Martin Holmes*

THE FIRST THATCHER GOVERNMENT: Contemporary Conservatism and Economic Change

BEYOND EUROPE: Selected Essays, 1989–93

* THATCHERISM:  Scope and Limits, 1983–7

* THE EUROSCEPTICAL READER (*editor*)

* THE LABOUR GOVERNMENT, 1974–9: Political Aims and Economic Reality


* *Also published by Macmillan*

# The Failure of the Heath Government

**Martin Holmes**
*Lecturer in Politics*
*St Hugh's College*
*Oxford*

Second Edition

Published by
MACMILLAN PRESS LTD
Houndmills, Basingstoke, Hampshire RG21 6XS
and London
Companies and representatives
throughout the world

First edition (*Political Pressure and Economic Policy: British
Government 1970–1974*, Butterworths) 1982
Second edition (Macmillan) 1997

ISBN 0–333–71606–X hardcover
ISBN 0–333–71607–8 paperback

A catalogue record for this book is available
from the British Library.

This book is printed on paper suitable for recycling and
made from fully managed and sustained forest sources.

10   9   8   7   6   5   4   3   2   1
06  05  04  03  02  01  00  99  98  97

Printed and bound in Great Britain by
Antony Rowe Ltd, Chippenham, Wiltshire

# Contents

# Acknowledgements

I wish to thank those politicians, civil servants, trade unionists, industrialists, journalists and academics who kindly consented to be interviewed for this book. I am especially indebted to Dr David Butler whose wise and patient advice is no less appreciated 15 years after the original publication in 1982.

My thanks are also due to my superb secretarial assistant, Penelope Whitworth, for the speed, precision and good nature with which she worked.

I would also like to thank the Principal and Fellows of St Hugh's College for providing an atmosphere conducive to scholarship and research. Tim Farmiloe and Sunder Katwala at the publishers handled the manuscript with customary courtesy and efficiency, and I am grateful to them.

Needless to say any errors in the following pages are my responsibility alone.

Martin Holmes
St Hugh's College, Oxford
January 1997

# The Failure of the Heath Government
# Introduction to the Second Edition

When this book was first published in 1982[1] the Heath government was widely accepted to have been a failure. Free-market and Thatcherite critics had long since criticised the U-turns which produced both the economic meltdown of 1973–4 and the two electoral humiliations of February and October 1974. Critics on the left had voraciously assaulted a government which had introduced the social poison of the Industrial Relations Act 1971, waged class war against the miners and exhibited, in Mr Heath's own words, the 'unacceptable face of capitalism'. The Heath government, while the memories were still politically fresh, was associated with the three-day week, five States of Emergency in three and a half years, and the dismal series of power cuts resulting from protracted industrial disputes.

By the late 1990s, however, several studies had emerged which portrayed the Heath government in a much more favourable light. These revisionist works sought to place the 1970–4 Conservative government in an historic context which exonerated Heath from the culpability which both his own party, and his nominal political antagonists on the left, had ascribed to him.[2] Revisionist analyses have been characterised by – even though not necessarily motivated by – anti-Thatcherism. To the opponents of the philosophy, style and policies of 1979–90, the Heath government has acquired the status of a tragic, yet heroic, administration which, albeit unwittingly, paved the way for Thatcherism. On the principle that the enemy of your enemy is your friend, the Heath government has been enlisted in the rollcall of honour of those who opposed the Thatcherite project.

The revisionist defence of Heath falls into three main categories: there was no alternative, practical or ideological, to Heath's U-turns; international economic circumstances were severely adverse; and the Labour governments 1964–70 and 1974–9 were even less successful. As a subtle variation on the revisionist theme it has also been argued that the economic and industrial failures of the Heath government should be offset against the successful entry of Britain into the European Economic Community on 1 January 1973. But how convincing is the revisionist defence? How far is it simply a continuation of the ideological battle against Thatcherism by other means? To evaluate the revisionist case it is necessary to examine it from first principles.

The most frequently cited exculpation is that the Heath government had no option but to abandon its original Selsdon Park policies, because the tide of fashionable intellectual opinion was still favourable to the postwar Keynesian consensus based on a high level of government intervention in the economy. Moreover, it is argued, the requirement of practical politics – based on the concept of what is politically possible – necessitated the U-turns in the absence of any feasible alternative policies. Thus Dennis Kavanagh writes that:

> Ministers and advisers clung to a Keynesian paradigm which was out of date but no credible alternative was available in the early 1970s.[3]

Similarly the same apologist ventures that 'In 1970 incomes policies were not widely regarded as a failure and there was no comprehensive monetarist analysis available at the time.'[4]

Even Edward Heath's fairminded and perceptive biographer, John Campbell, referring to the U-turn on incomes policy, has argued that 'the fact remains that there was near universal support for Heath's approach in 1972, if only he could have pulled it off, and little confidence that the country could be saved from the abyss by any other means'.[5] To Anthony Seldon, 'there was no alternative and acceptable philosophy available which would have provided the intellectual underpinning for an assault on the prevailing orthodoxy of Keynesianism',[6] while Robert Taylor goes as far as to suggest that 'the Conservatives came to power in 1970 without any detailed promise to roll back the frontiers of the state'.[7] The difficulty in assessing such views is that it depends what is meant by 'credible', 'acceptable', and 'comprehensive' alternatives to Heath's U-turns. But although any assessment is inevitably subjective, sufficient evidence existed at the time to indicate the availability of alternatives which had already entered the bloodstream of Conservative politics both before and after the 1970 election. John Charmley has traced this process back to the 1965 Conservative policy document *Putting Britain Right Ahead* so that by 1970, there was 'not much . . . that Thatcherites would cavil at'. But Charmley is correct to argue that 'whilst Heath was good at exposing proto-Thatcherism, he was a good deal less adept at implementing it'.[8] The majority of Conservatives, however, did take seriously the fundamental policy re-appraisal of Opposition and did not expect the next Conservative government simply to continue the policies of its Wilsonian predecessor.

Revisionist critics undervalue the extent of the commitments with which the Heath government took office; they explain away the Selsdon Park disengagement from Keynesian interventionism, rather than explain it. The truth is that the Heath government lost its nerve in 1971–2 because of rising unemployment. Its failure was one of political will rather than a lack of intellectual justifications for its original policy stance. 'When in 1971 unemployment spurted towards the – at that time unthinkable – million mark, [Heath] lost his nerve. . . . Being a man of no fixed ideology he turned in his tracks',[9] is the considered verdict of the late Peter Jenkins, himself no Thatcherite. While it may be correct to argue that Heath never really understood the philosophical derivation of the Selsdon Park policies, that is not the same as saying that no one else understood the intellectual complexities. For one thing the thorough policy review of 1966–70 had produced an intellectual debate which preceded the 1970 Conservative manifesto commitments to promote free-market solutions. For another the supporters of such solutions – the Powellite neo-liberals on economics – vociferously proclaimed their opposition to the U-turns. Nor is it convincing to argue that intellectual alternatives were absent; Milton Friedman's Chicago School theories were well enough known to be castigated by the Keynesians from the late 1960s onwards. In Britain Professor Alan Walters at the London School of Economics, and the free-market thinkers and political free spirits at the Institute of Economic Affairs, had already injected into public debate the economic counter-revolution which finally triumphed after 1979.[10] It performs a signal disservice to historical accuracy to argue, as do the revisionists, that such intellectual and political developments were the consequences of Heath's U-turns rather than the cause of the Selsdon Park approach. As the authoritative historian of the IEA, Richard Cockett, has argued:

> Given their growing influence within the Conservative Party during the 1960s, Edward Heath's victory in the election of 1970 was welcomed by the IEA as his government seemed to hold out, for the first time in post-war British history, the prospect of a significant degree of economic liberalism. Arthur Seldon even voted Conservative for the first time. As well as those Conservative politicians and younger activists who learnt their economic liberalism from the IEA, other Conservatives had also been developing their own critique of the Keynesian consensus, and putting their own alternatives forward within the official Party hierarchy.[11]

What the revisionists underestimate is the extent to which Keynesian thinking had already been intellectually undermined within the Conservative party by 1970; they ignore the original determination to stick to the 1970 manifesto commitments and thereby underestimate the collapse of political will on which the 1972 U-turns depended. This argument has been made by several senior Conservatives who were involved in, or highly sympathetic to, the Selsdon Park approach. In Norman Tebbit's view, 'no one should doubt that at the time of the election in 1970 Ted Heath was committed to the end of [the] corporate consensus and to the new liberal economics. The Selsdon programme fitted well with his earlier battle to end retail price fixing, which was quite wrongly held to have cost the Conservatives the 1964 election'.[12] Sir Keith Joseph's biographer has observed that 'after Selsdon Park the word went out that the party leadership had come down firmly on the side of the free market rather than on that of the interventionist economy . . . Selsdon [Park] took place while Joseph was delivering his series of speeches about the reinvigorating effect on industry of the free market economy'.[13] Similarly, as Nicholas Ridley recounted in his memoirs:

> Ted Heath nevertheless seemed mildly promising. When he took his Shadow Cabinet to the Selsdon Park Hotel . . . and produced the new policies on which he would fight the election, I became enthusiastic. He promised to stop subsidizing industry, to reduce taxation, and to return some nationalized industries to the private sector. He even asked me to chair the small policy group he was setting up to work up the privatization policy. Our small group met frequently, and we soon had a report, which after much fine-tuning I presented to Ted Heath. I attended a Shadow Cabinet meeting at which it was approved, with one or two deletions and additions. Suitably disguised, the policy went into the Manifesto. We won the election of June 1970 and Ted Heath became Prime Minister. I was appointed Parliamentary Under-Secretary at the Ministry of Technology. Geoffrey Rippon was Secretary of

State. All seemed set to embark on the privatization programme and the dismantling of the socialist state . . . Rising unemployment in 1970–1 led him to abandon the Selsdon Park policies upon which he had been elected.[14]

Likewise, David Howell, who played a prominent role in policy formation in the 1960s recalled in a letter to the *Wall Street Journal – Europe* in October 1996 that notions such as privatisation were extensively researched prior to the 1970 election victory. Howell writes that:

In the mid-60s, with the Conservatives in opposition, I was charged with setting up the Conservative Party's Public Sector Research Unit, to find ways of unraveling the state sector and, in particular, the nationalized utilities. Drawing on American ideas and particularly on those of Louis Kelso, as set out in his book, *The Capitalist Manifesto*, I introduced the concept of privatization to the British political vocabulary for the first time in 1969, in my pamphlet 'A New Style of Government'. We also urged the widespread adoption of worker and consumer shareholding in privatized concerns.[15]

The Heath government was not lost for an alternative to its U-turns; simply sticking to its original policy would have sufficed. Rather, the Heath government explicitly rejected its original policy, not because of any antagonistic intellectual tidal wave, but because of the political fear that rising unemployment would prove electorally disastrous. Jim Prior, while ideologically sympathetic to Heath, admits that:

In January 1972, although the jobless total adjusted for seasonal factors remained below one million, the unadjusted overall total exceeded that. The Commons had to be suspended during the Prime Minister's Questions following Labour's furious protests. This in itself did not shake Ted, but he utterly despised and detested the pre-war Conservative governments, who had tolerated between two and three million unemployed. It was therefore no surprise in which direction Ted decided our economic policy should go when he now had to choose between tolerating a continued high level of unemployment, in the hope that this would keep some control over wage claims and inflation – or trying to run the economy with a higher level of output and growth, and seeking some other means of control over wage and price increases.[16]

It is certainly true as the respected journalistic commentator Hugo Young has argued, that the U-turns were 'in line with the kind of compromises commonplace in the 1960s in the face of economic disaster or union militancy. *But from a government that had made extravagant pledges to do the opposite, they were bewildering concessions* [emphasis added]'.[17] The main feature of the U-turns was their stark political brutality. That their economic effectiveness proved elusive is equally clear.

It is a delicious irony, which the revisionists downplay, that unemployment, as a direct consequence of the U-turns, was higher in February 1974 than when the government took office in June 1970. Moreover it can be argued that the Thatcher government also faced the wrath of the Keynesian establishment, including the famous 364 dissenting economists, to the same extent as the Heath government.[18] The difference lay not in the absence of a coherent free-market set of policies, 1970–4, but in the political determination to stick to them. As

Dell has observed of Heath, 'nothing is more infectious than panic and of all the varieties of panic, none is more infectious than Prime Ministerial panic'.[19]

The second argument advanced by the revisionists is that international economic circumstances severely disadvantaged the Heath government which was unlucky to be affected by external shocks of such magnitude as the collapse of the Bretton Woods system and the 1973-4 oil price explosion. Revisionists extend a charitable interpretation of external events 1970-4 in contrast to most historians and commentators who have not cited external misfortune to exculpate Anthony Eden at Suez, Harold Wilson's 1967 devaluation of the pound, or James Callaghan's 1976 IMF application. The Heath government has received a disproportionately sympathetic treatment on account of international economic turbulence beyond its immediate control. Campbell comments that 'it was the "oil shock" which wrecked Heath's government . . . the oil crisis . . . both dealt the miners a winning hand and strengthened their willingness to play it'.[20] In Seldon's view, 'the balance of exogenous factors ran powerfully against the government',[21] the consequence of which was that 'international developments caused profound difficulties, including the collapse of the dollar and the end of the Bretton Woods system . . . '[22] Alec Cairncross shares the same view observing that 'Heath was conspicuously out of luck. The world boom of 1972-3 coincided at just the wrong time with his own little boom. He had no North Sea oil to free him from balance of payments difficulties.'[23]

Such analyses offer a spirited, but ultimately unconvincing, defence of Heath. The collapse of the Bretton Woods system, which led to the floating of the pound in June 1972, helped rather than hindered Heath's macro-economic strategy of Keynesian reflation. It enabled the Heath government to experience a growing balance of payments deficit without facing the intractable problems of over-valuation which had bedevilled Attlee in 1949, Eden in 1956 after Suez, and Wilson between 1964 and the eventual devaluation in November 1967. The exchange rate could take the strain in a way which had not been politically possible – even if economically sensible – in the Bretton Woods system. The enforced disintegration of the fixed exchange rate regime liberated the pound from the straitjacket which Rab Butler had identified twenty years before at the time of the ROBOT plan.[24] It would have been preferable to have floated the pound in 1952 – or during 1964-7 – to enable British industry to regain competitiveness after years of artificial overvaluation; but better late than never in 1972. Heath's reflationary strategy only got as far as it did before imploding because of the removal of the balance of payments constraint. Moreover, unlike the 1949 and 1967 formal devaluations, Heath did not suffer political opprobrium and loss of governmental authority because the 1972 floating was forced upon him by external events. Far from damaging his government this external shock was a positive blessing, a stroke of good fortune.

Although the same cannot be said for the 1973 OPEC energy crisis – subsequently quadrupling the price of oil – the Heath government handled its impact poorly. Revisionists cannot argue persuasively that bad luck rather than bad judgement was to blame. The oil crisis is an unconvincing alibi for a government whose economic strategy had already long since come off the rails. The oil crisis occurred well over a year after the monetary and budgetary meltdown had generated the inflationary take-off. According to the economic historian Nicholas Woodward, 'not only was the economy given a major stimulus, but that stimulus was applied over an extremely short period. The outcome was that in 1973 the economy exhibited all the signs of overheating.'[25] Additionally, in contrast to the hindsight verdicts of the revisionists, Heath himself did not cite the oil crisis as the external shock which derailed his strategy, arguing as late as November 1973 that 'the prospects and opportunities for British industry are more exciting and more solidly based than at any time since the Second World War'.[26] Indeed it was Heath's failure to grasp the oil crisis as the alibi the revisionists claim it to be, which produced the entrenched stubbornness of the fatal fruitless negotiations with Joe Gormley and his colleagues. But far from bemoaning his bad luck – and changing his negotiating strategy – Heath obliviously soldiered on, trapped by the logic of his self-imposed incomes policy rigidities. Moreover the worst effects of the oil crisis were delayed until 1974–5 when the massive cumulative extent of the transfer of wealth to the OPEC countries was fully appreciated. If any government can offer the consequences of the Yom Kippur war as an excuse for economic underperformance it is the Wilson government 1974–6, not the Heath government 1970–4. The fact that Heath initially envisaged both his dash for growth and his incomes policy stipulations as outside the consequences of the oil price increase is sufficient proof to refute the revisionist argument that externally generated bad luck destroyed his negotiating authority with the miners and broke the back of his government.

Additionally, it can be argued that the Heath government did not make the best of the favourable international economic climate between 1970 and 1973 which, according to the authoritative study of European growth by Crafts and Toniolo, was part of a longer-term 'Golden Age' of prosperity from 1945.[27] If this 'Golden Age' came to an end in 1973 following the oil crisis it occurred at the end of the Heath government, which suggests that the years 1970–3 were a missed opportunity to undertake the necessary Selsdon Park reforms when international financial constraints did not pose an external impediment. Indeed Heath's inheritance from Wilson in 1970 was in stark contrast to the three-day-week incipient stagflation he bequeathed to Wilson in 1974. In the context of the time, as Cairncross argues, the Wilson government had overcome its economic crises by 1970.[28]

Wilson, moreover, worked carefully in conjunction with his Chancellors of the Exchequer particularly in 1969–70 when he did not seek to second guess Roy Jenkins' fiscally prudent stewardship. Heath, by contrast, was distrustful of the Treasury, not because of economic policy, but because of its lukewarm attitude to EC membership on account of the increased balance of payment burden. Heath foisted economic policy U-turns on a reluctant and politically weak Chancellor, Anthony Barber, who kept his well-founded doubts to himself. The 'Barber boom' was in reality the Heath boom. The outcome was that 'the country was . . . to pay the costs of having a Chancellor without a political base or strong convictions of his own, blown hither and thither by a dominant Prime Minister with an apocalyptic vision, and bound to his office by a sense of loyalty to his colleagues and his party rather than to the nation he is employed to serve'.[29] Heath unbalanced the proper constitutional convention regarding relations between Number 10 and Number 11, in contrast to the Labour governments of the period; not surprisingly the corrosion of the economic policy process helped to produce the downward spiral which culminated in the winter of 1973–4.

The third revisionist defence of Heath seeks to contrast the favourable record of 1970–4 with the alleged failures of the 1964–70 and 1974–9 Labour governments. To M. A. Young:

'Wilson governed on the basis of political expediency . . . [the Heath administration made] . . . a brave attempt to reinvigorate a flagging economy and restore confidence in a political system the Wilson government had done much to demean. . . . Despite his own classless image Wilson had shown himself either unwilling or unable to prevent [sectional] interests from exercising an effective veto over any of his government's more positive proposals. *In Place of Strife* had recognised the unions' economic importance; its abandonment revealed the strength of their power.[30]

But as this author has already argued, in *Contemporary Record*,[31] Mr Young seeks to rubbish the 1964–70 Wilson government and by contrast to portray Heath as a great improvement; Wilson was dominated by 'sectional interests', unlike Heath who sought to preserve one nation. In reality the Wilson government had sought to restrict trade union abuses of power and only a backbench rebellion, orchestrated in Cabinet by James Callaghan, had prevented Barbara Castle's *In Place of Strife* proposals from tackling the strike problem. It was Wilson who attacked the 'tightly knit group of politically motivated men' in the 1966 seamen's dispute as well as the power of communist agitators. Heath by contrast presided over a greater period of industrial disruption, imposed five states of emergency – one for a mere overtime ban – and effectively abandoned his Industrial Relations Act, not because of the loss of a parliamentary majority, but to appease the union leaders in the pursuit of incomes policy negotiations. The incessant industrial disruption of the Heath period, caused as much by the absurdities of compulsory wage control, produced the opposite of One Nation Toryism, with the Conservative party fighting the February election on the divisive platform of 'who rules the country'.

A less extreme, and a more intellectually sophisticated, revisionist defence of Heath is advanced by Anthony Seldon who claims that 'to discuss the [Heath] government as a failure would be trite and wrong. The Labour governments of 1964–70 and 1974–9 faced similar difficulties and fared no better.'[32] Judged by the prevailing standards of their day this verdict is not sustainable. The Wilson government left office in 1970 with inflation at 8% and inherited a 16% level in 1974, rising to 27% because of the monetary timelag. Wilson bequeathed a balance of payments surplus and inherited the then largest deficit in British history in 1974. Wilson presided over a steady, if unspectacular, growth rate of 2% in contrast to the 0% growth of the winter of 1973–4, compounded by the three-day week, and industrial turmoil. Moreover, Wilson's 1964–70 administration presided over an era of enlightened social reform by facilitating private members legislation on abortion, divorce reform, homosexual law decriminalisation, and the abolition of capital punishment;[33] the Heath government brought this social tolerance to an end.

The 1974–9 Labour government was less successful than 1964–70 but, nonetheless, its achievements outshine the dereliction of 1970–4.[34] Wilson ended the self-inflicted damage of the miners' dispute with skill and wisdom; Jim Callaghan forced his party to accept the necessity of austerity measures to secure the 1976 IMF loan while protecting the politically sensitive social services and the NHS. It was Wilson who warned that inflation was mother and father to unemployment and Callaghan who launched a devastatingly accurate critique of the limitations of Keynesian economics at the 1976 Labour conference. Although Callaghan could not avoid the destruction of his government amid the chaos of the 'winter of discontent' at least he avoided the imposition of a reduced working week and the declaration of a State of Emergency, unlike Heath in 1973–4. Nor did Callaghan leave himself vulnerable to administrative paralysis by copying Heath's overreliance on a civil service guru of the type of Sir William Armstrong. Callaghan had a general election forced on him by a defeat in Parliament; he did not opt for an election without a clear sense of purpose or a strategy for victory. Heath stubbornly clung to power despite his general election defeat while Callaghan accepted defeat with good grace, refusing to be provoked by 'troops out' militants in his Cardiff constituency and speaking warmly of the historic significance of Britain's first woman Prime Minister.[35] Edward Heath was no Jim Callaghan.

The fourth principal defence of the Heath government cites its success in obtaining membership of the EC which had eluded the Macmillan and Wilson governments. This argument is often used as a mitigating factor for failure in the economic arena. M. A. Young argues that 'Edward Heath firmly believed that . . . membership of the European Community would not only assist his overall policy for sustained economic growth but enhance Britain's influence in the world'.[36] John W. Young considers that 'it is difficult to deny that entry to the EC was a great success for the Prime Minister and the most important step for Britain taken by government'.[37] But the most committed revisionist advocate of Heath's European policy as a triumph is John Campbell, who hails a 'historic achievement'.[38] As well as supporting the principle of EC entry Campbell defends Heath from contemporary political opponents such as Wilson, and those later writing with hindsight, who have argued that the terms of entry were not good enough and that Heath was desperate to join the EC at any price. Thus, Campbell argues that:

> there was always going to be a steep admission fee for Britain, seeking to enter the Community sixteen years after it was founded, just at the moment when the Six had finally completed the financial arrangements that suited them. The fault was Churchill's and Attlee's and Eden's, as well as de Gaulle's, that the price was high. But that price seemed reasonable in 1971. It was based on the expectation, first, of continued economic growth and, second, of a fresh impetus towards closer integration in which Britain and the other new members would be fully involved and hence fully protected. Agriculture was expected to take progressively less of the Community budget, industrial and regional policy – from which Britain would have expected a greater return – progressively more. That the 1971 terms came to appear unreasonable by 1979 – the 1975 renegotiation was largely cosmetic – was due, first, to the 1973 oil shock and the international economic recession, which set back any new Community initiatives by several years, and, second, to Britain's exceptionally poor economic performance in the 1970s, which made her contribution to the Community Budget more burdensome than had been expected in 1971.[39]

Such an interpretation downplays the fact that Heath never intended the negotiations over the terms of entry to fail; he was always prepared to personally intervene to ensure their smooth passage as his accommodating relationship with President Pompidou indicated. Heath was an unconditional supporter of EC membership whereas Wilson's support was conditional upon several economic factors as well as the political balance between friend and foe within his own party. Heath had to give the impression of negotiating toughly because the realities of adversarial politics demanded it. But in reality the terms of entry interested him little – it was the benefits of membership on which he complacently concentrated to the detriment of the terms secured. The consequence of this approach to entry led directly to Labour's renegotiation 1974–5, and to Mrs Thatcher's prolonged challenge to the inequitable budgetary contribution 1979–84. With much justification Heath's successor as party leader has recalled that:

> At the time Ted resolved discussion about the costs of entry by saying that no one was arguing that the burden would be so intolerable that we should break off negotiations. But this whole question of finance should have been considered more carefully. It came to dominate Britain's relations with the EEC for more than a decade afterwards, and it did not prove so easy to reopen. Though the Community made a declaration during the entry negotiations that 'should an unacceptable situation arise within the present Community or an enlarged Community, the very survival of the Community would demand that the Institutions find equitable solutions', the net British contribution quickly grew. The Labour Government of 1974–79 made no progress in reducing it. It was left to me do do so later.[40]

The negotiations were thus 'doomed to succeed'[41] as a consequence of Heath's political will – the one policy which was not subjected to a U-turn – and the willingness of Pompidou to reverse the veto of his predecessor. To Heath, 'the importance of entering the EC [was] to secure a stage on which Britain could be seen to act out a leading, national role in foreign affairs'.[42] The economic minutiae of butter, lamb and agricultural pricing was left to Rippon to negotiate as swiftly as he could with the minimum of domestic political opposition. As George has described, 'Heath attempted . . . to organise the EC as a strong actor in world affairs under British leadership, much as de Gaulle had tried to organise it under French leadership.'[43] Such an approach did not lend itself to genuinely tough negotiations which may have failed.

But even if, for the sake of argument, Heath is credited with terms of entry compatible with British interests, how justified is it to ascribe EC membership to the Heath government alone? Britain joined the EC under the Heath government but not as a result of the parliamentary majority of the Heath government. As the Conservative opponents of EC membership constantly pointed out the Heath government had to rely on the votes of the Labour pro-Marketeers, led by Roy Jenkins, to secure the passage of the legislation. With up to 39 potential Conservative rebels led by Enoch Powell, Heath was fortunate that the Jenkinsites bailed him out. Jenkins and his supporters risked their political careers for the cause in which they believed and displayed courage and principle on a par with the Conservative opponents of EC entry. It was the intervention of the Jenkinsites – and the Liberals – which proved crucial to the legislation by which Britain joined the EC on 1 January 1973.

Cosgrave is right to go as far as to argue that, for the anti-EC Conservatives, the battle was lost almost from the start because 'the government, though there were some worrying moments, was confident that, in a crisis, Jenkins and at least some of his followers would come to their rescue.'[44] Similarly Sir Geoffrey

Howe, speaking on television in 1996, recalled that 'when we joined Europe in 1971, there were 25 people on the back benches throughout that time arguing against it. But we carried it through because we were able to mobilise a substantial part of the Labour party as well.'[45] Labour's growing ideological schism, as recent authoritative analysts such as Jones have argued, came to Heath's aid as the revisionist social democrats regarded Europe as an article of faith. Thus in the early 1970s' climate, 'the pro-European revisionists, who increasingly described themselves as social democrats as a symbol of affinity with Continental social democracy, became publicly identified with the European issue. This conferred the advantage of projecting them as a clearly organised grouping under the acknowledged leadership of Roy Jenkins'.[46] If credit for EC entry is to be apportioned it belongs more appropriately to the Labour rebels than to Heath who risked nothing but the legislation itself. Entering the government lobby was easy enough for Heath and Conservative proponents of EC membership; the Jenkinsites, who colluded with the Tory whips, risked their careers, their party's internal cohesion and their authority within the wider Labour Movement. It began the process which culminated in the 1981 Limehouse Declaration establishing the SDP as a breakaway party as David Owen has acknowledged. As Jenkins' sympathetic biographer has described it, the decision to vote in favour of EC membership in principle 'was Jenkins' finest hour'.[47] To David Owen the five Labour MPs who defied their own whip on the subsequent legislation 'were the true Labour party heroes of Britain's entry into the European Community. We hid behind their bravery and were demeaned.'[48] To simply ascribe EC entry to the Heath government is to ignore the parliamentary arithmetic and the intense pressure under which the Labour pro-Marketeers crucially sustained the legislation. It was good luck rather than good judgement which enabled Heath's government to preside over Britain's entry to the Common Market.

It may, however, also be argued that neither the Heath government nor anyone else deserves credit for taking Britain in. To Eurosceptics EC entry was – and has remained – a matter of regret. However this matter is judged in intellectual terms it is clear that by the 1990s the Conservative party had become divided from top to bottom on the issue of Europe. Moreover, the Eurosceptics have been growing in number and the balance within the party has shifted strongly away from the Eurofanaticism of the Heath administration. Edward Heath's legacy to his own party has been to perpetuate the divide. If EC entry was Heath's greatest achievement at the time, it no longer appears to command the same level of political assent. A new generation of Conservative Eurosceptics look more to Mrs Thatcher's 1988 speech at Bruges than to Mr Heath's espousal of a European destiny.[49] Even some Conservatives, such as Lord Tebbit, who supported Heath enthusiastically in the division lobbies in the 1970s have now, with the benefit of hindsight, changed to the Eurosceptic camp. Increasingly it is those on Labour's Euroenthusiast wing, plus the Liberal Democrats (rather than fellow Conservatives) who regard EC entry in a favourable light.

The growth of Euroscepticism within the Conservative party has partly resulted from the disappointing economic consequences of EC membership especially the operation of the Common Agricultural Policy (CAP), the controversy over the Common Fisheries Policy (CFP), the intrusion of Single Market directives into what Douglas Hurd has called the 'nooks and crannies of everyday life', the long-running feud over Britain's budgetary contribution, and the false god of Exchange Rate Mechanism (ERM) membership for the pound. More significant has been the feeling that Heath deliberately disguised the full extent to which parliamentary sovereignty would be systematically transferred to EC supranational institutions. The 1971 White Paper on EC membership insisted that there would be no question of any erosion of essential national sovereignty as the Common Law would remain the basis of Britain's legal system with the courts continuing to operate as hitherto. But the 1972 Act of accession, in its Clause II, stipulated that EC law should prevail over British law although the extent to which this would occur was downplayed by the government in general and by Heath and his Solicitor-General Sir Geoffrey Howe in particular.[50] The disguising of the ultimate federalist destination of EC membership during the 1970s has left an increasingly bitter taste to the intra-Conservative disputes in the 1990s.

In summary, the revisionist defence of the Heath government has been a long time coming, not least because of the political longevity of Margaret Thatcher, Heath's nemesis. The revisionist case is far from convincing. The arguments that the intellectual climate was too inclement, or that an alternative to the U-turns was not available, cannot withstand serious analysis. It is not difficult to refute the alibi of external economic events beyond the government's control. Nor can Heath be favourably compared – according to the accepted precepts of the postwar Keynesian consensus – to the 1964–70 or 1974–9 Labour governments. Even EC entry is more complicated, less dependent solely on Heath, and more open to question, than at first glance. The truth is that Heath really did leave to his party, to the wider electorate, and ultimately to himself, only the lessons of failure.

# References

1. *Political Pressure and Economic Policy: British Government 1970–4*, Butterworths, 1982.
2. STUART BALL and ANTHONY SELDON, *The Heath Government 1970–4: A Reappraisal*, Longman, 1996; JOHN CAMPBELL, *Edward Heath: A Biography*, Jonathan Cape, 1993; JOHN RAMSDEN, *The Winds of Change: Macmillan to Heath 1957–75*, Longman, 1996; DENNIS KAVANAGH, '1970–4', in *How Tory Governments Fall* A. Seldon (ed.), Fontana, 1996; M. A. Young, 'The One-Nation Government', *Contemporary Record*, November 1989, Vol. 3, No. 2.
3. DENNIS KAVANAGH, op. cit., p. 384.
4. DENNIS KAVANAGH, ibid., p. 385.
5. JOHN CAMPBELL, op. cit., p. 478.
6. STUART BALL and ANTHONY SELDON, op. cit., p. 14.
7. Ibid., p. 157.
8. JOHN CHARMLEY, *A History of Conservative Politics 1900–96*, Macmillan, 1996, p. 183.
9. PETER JENKINS, *Mrs Thatcher's Revolution: The Ending of the Socialist Era*, Jonathan Cape, 1987, p. 60.
10. See also TIM CONGDON, *Reflections of Monetarism*, Edward Elgar, IEA, 1992 for a discussion on this theme.
11. RICHARD COCKETT, *Thinking the Unthinkable: Think-Tanks and the Economic Counter-Revolution 1931–83*, HarperCollins, 1994, p. 200.
12. NORMAN TEBBIT, *Upwardly Mobile: An Autobiography*, Weidenfeld & Nicolson, 1988, p. 94.
13. MORRISON HALCROW, *Keith Joseph: A Single Mind*, Macmillan, 1989, p. 43.
14. NICHOLAS RIDLEY, *My Style of Government*, Hutchinson, 1991, pp. 3–4.
15. *Wall Street Journal – Europe*, 29 October 1996.
16. JIM PRIOR, *A Balance of Power*, Hamish Hamilton, 1986, p. 74.

17. HUGO YOUNG, *One of Us*, Macmillan, 1989, p. 75.
18. See M. HOLMES, *Thatcherism: Scope and Limits 1983–7*, Macmillan, 1989.
19. EDMUND DELL, *The Chancellors*, HarperCollins, 1996, p. 385.
20. JOHN CAMPBELL, op. cit., pp. 561–3.
21. STUART BALL and ANTHONY SELDON, op. cit., p. 17.
22. Ibid., p. 12.
23. SIR ALEC CAIRNCROSS, in STUART BALL and ANTHONY SELDON, op.cit., p. 138.
24. For Butler's justification of ROBOT in terms of Keynesian demand management see LORD BUTLER, *The Art of the Possible*, Hamish Hamilton, 1971, pp. 158–9.
25. NICHOLAS WOODWARD in N. F. R. CRAFTS and N. WOODWARD, (eds), *The British Economy since 1945*, Oxford University Press, 1991, pp. 201–2.
26. *The Times*, 9 November 1973.
27. N. F. R. CRAFTS and G. TONIOLO, *Economic Growth in Europe since 1945*, Cambridge University Press, 1996.
28. ALEC CAIRNCROSS, *Managing the British Economy in the 1960s: a Treasury Perspective*, Macmillan, 1996.
29. EDMUND DELL, op. cit., p. 394.
30. M. A. YOUNG, *Contemporary Record*, op. cit.
31. M. HOLMES, *Contemporary Record*, ibid.
32. STUART BALL and ANTHONY SELDON, op. cit., p. 19.
33. For an excellent account of the 1964–70 administration, see BEN PIMLOTT, *Harold Wilson*, HarperCollins, 1992.
34. See MARTIN HOLMES, *The Labour Government 1974–9: Political Aims and Economic Reality*, Macmillan, 1985.
35. Of Heath's clinging to power in February 1974, JAMES CALLAGHAN in his memoirs, *Time and Chance*, Collins, 1987, p. 293, comments that 'we thought Heath should have resigned forthwith, but he began negotiations with the Liberals'.
36. M. A. YOUNG, op. cit.
37. JOHN W. YOUNG, in STUART BALL and ANTHONY SELDON, op. cit., p. 283.
38. JOHN CAMPBELL, op. cit., p. 363.
39. JOHN CAMPBELL, op. cit., p. 362.
40. MARGARET THATCHER, *The Path to Power*, HarperCollins, 1995, p. 208.
41. This phrase is quoted in JOHN W. YOUNG, in STUART BALL and ANTHONY SELDON, op. cit., p. 267.
42. CHRISTOPHER LORD, *British Entry to the European Community under the Heath Government*, Dartmouth, 1993, p. 46.
43. STEPHEN GEORGE, *Britain and European Integration since 1945*, Basil Blackwell, 1991, p. 53.
44. PATRICK COSGRAVE, *The Lives of Enoch Powell*, Bodley Head, 1989, p. 323.
45. Quoted by ROBERT HARRIS, *Sunday Times*, 15 December 1996.
46. TUDOR JONES, *Remaking the Labour Party: From Gaitskell to Blair*, Routledge, 1996, p. 99.
47. JOHN CAMPBELL, *Roy Jenkins: a Biography*, Weidenfeld & Nicolson, 1983, p. 142.
48. DAVID OWEN, *Time to Declare*, Penguin Books, 1992, p. 189.
49. See, for example, MARTIN HOLMES, *The Eurosceptical Reader*, Macmillan, 1996, chapters 5–8.
50. For a comprehensive analysis of this process see LORD BELOFF, *Britain and European Union: Dialogue of the Deaf*, Macmillan, 1996.

Part I
# The Political Setting

# Chapter 1

# Electoral victory and the 'Quiet Revolution'

*'. . . we shall have to bring about a change so radical, a revolution so quiet, and yet so total that it will have to go far beyond the programme for a Parliament to which we are committed.'*

Edward Heath
Conservative Party Conference 1970

## 1.1  Opposition 1964–1970

For a party that considers itself to be the 'natural governing party' a lengthy spell in Opposition is unlikely to be harmonious. So it proved for the Conservative Party between 1964 and 1970, after 13 unbroken years of office. Two defeats at the polls in two years, the establishment of a 'technological' socialist government committed to modernizing, not revolutionizing, Britain, and three leaders in as many years had left the Conservative Party at its lowest fortunes since the surprise defeat of 1945, a situation not helped by Party Leader Edward Heath who often failed to inspire confidence among either the electorate or the Party faithful. The opinion polls registered a contrast between Mr Wilson's lead over Mr Heath and the Conservatives' lead over Labour, reflecting the public's assessment of the qualities of the two leaders.

Mr Heath had become the first elected leader of the Conservative Party in 1965 defeating Reginald Maudling and Enoch Powell under the new rules regulating the Election of the Party Leader, which replaced the process by which previous leaders had 'emerged'. Mr Heath was also the first Conservative Party Leader since Bonar Law to have been educated at a grammar school rather than at a public school, a break with tradition which, along with Mr Heath's bachelor status, aroused interested speculation at the time but has since almost completely diminished in relevance[1]. First elected to the Commons in 1950 for Bexley, Mr Heath had spent a considerable amount of his parliamentary career in the Whips Office, being Chief Whip from December 1955 to October 1959, a period that included the traumatic events of the Suez crisis in 1956. There followed a seven-month spell as Minister of Labour before he was appointed Lord Privy Seal with Foreign Office responsibilities in 1960. In this capacity Mr Heath had risen to natural prominence by leading the abortive attempt of the Macmillan government to enter the EEC. Thereafter, Mr Heath's dedication to the United Kingdom eventually joining the EEC became an article of faith, earning him the reputation as his Party's most dedicated 'European'. From 1963 up to the defeat of the Conservatives in the General Election of October 1964, Mr Heath was Secretary of State for

Industry, Trade and Regional Development and President of the Board of Trade during which time he pioneered through the Commons, despite considerable back bench resentment, the controversial bill to abolish Resale Price Maintenance. However, as Party Leader since 1965 the difficulty lay in the Conservatives' unaccustomed role as Her Majesty's Opposition, especially following Mr Wilson's election victory in March 1966. As an Opposition leader Mr Heath was naturally at a disadvantage to the Prime Minister but the earnest, grave style of Mr Heath often seemed to the public to be a poor substitute for the flamboyant, headline-catching approach of Harold Wilson. Although both Mr Heath and Mr Wilson were from similar lower middle-class, grammar school and Oxford backgrounds they were politically and temperamentally different. While Mr Wilson retained his identification with his Yorkshire background, Mr Heath was reticent about his early years in Broadstairs as the son of a carpenter. Mr Wilson's outgoing, chatty, some would say gimmicky style of leadership, contrasted with Mr Heath's formal, tense, some would say shy, personal characteristics. In the Commons the gladiatorial-style clashes between the two men were occasionally bitter. Mr Heath's image was precariously built on the title of the Conservatives' 1966 Election Manifesto, *'Action not Words'*, a phrase that did not always draw a favourable comparison between him and Mr Wilson. However, it did accurately portray Mr Heath as a man of decision rather than an ideologist. One of Mr Heath's biographers, Andrew Roth, has argued further that 'Mr Heath cannot be considered an ideologist partly because he does not understand even the ideology he claims to hold'[2].

Despite such difficulties of style, the rehabilitation of the Conservatives' cause lay in the unpopularity of the Labour Government, which trailed the Opposition in the opinion polls – at one stage by 20% – from 1967 to just before the 1970 election. Indeed, the feeling that the Government was doomed at the next election was never as strong in recent British politics as during the dark days of 1968 and 1969. The Opposition's own problems thus tended to reflect policy-making decisions on the assumption of regaining office. Groups like the Monday Club, the Institute of Economic Affairs and the Bow Group, as well as individual MPs, tended to be eager to put forward specific and diverse views. In the winter of 1965/6 Mr Powell and Mr Maudling quarrelled over incomes policy, an issue that reflected the wider division on economic policy between, roughly, the 'interventionists' and the 'free-marketeers'. Mr Powell's inclination to speak on topics other than his Shadow Defence brief was a constant source of irritation to Mr Heath, as was Edward du Cann's independent style of Party Chairmanship. However, in 1967 Mr du Cann was replaced by Anthony Barber, an able and energetic supporter of Mr Heath. Such problems soon seemed unimportant when, in April 1968, Mr Powell was sacked from the Shadow Cabinet by Mr Heath, after making a speech in Birmingham advocating an end to Commonwealth immigration – a speech that provoked instant controversy because of its style and tone. Indeed, it was for the style of its delivery rather than for its content, which was not out of line with official Conservative policy, that Mr Powell was dismissed. Nevertheless the Conservative Party rank and file were dismayed at the manner of Mr Powell's dismissal and some considered Mr Heath's reaction as the more reprehensible. Thenceforth Mr Powell was continually to embarrass Mr Heath, as he pushed his anti-immigration line and attacked Conservative policy towards the EEC to such an extent that he almost appeared to be campaigning for the Party leadership. However, Mr Powell's apologists do point to his late intervention in the 1970 General Election on the Conservatives' behalf as significant in swinging the electorate behind the Party under Mr Heath's leadership.

Although the party turmoils had caught the headlines the policy-making strategy of the Opposition had been more thorough than ever before. It is indeed arguable that the emphasis given to policy making was the most thorough of any Opposition in British politics. This certainly suited Mr Heath's style of leadership in that he preferred the serious, studious approach to policy making through committees to the confrontations with Harold Wilson in the Commons. Mr Heath built up a reputation for thoroughness, organization, and full-time dedication to his post of Party Leader. He was thus invariably better briefed than most of his colleagues and maintained total control over policy making. As Lindsay and Harrington note, 'Heath organized his Opposition team very much as though it were a Government-in-exile. The main advantages of this were that it admitted, and encouraged, detailed examination of policy'[3]. Similarly, Ramsden has noted that, regarding policy formation, '. . . Mr Heath had a more personal monopoly of authority in the Party than any leader since Neville Chamberlain'[4]. Mr Heath himself was Chairman of that Advisory Committee on Policy until November 1968 when Reginald Maudling took over. Wholesale denationalization was ruled out and incomes policy was too sensitive an issue within the Conservative Party so that the main policy-making emphasis was on the reduction of taxation with eventual taxation reform, industrial relations reform and the commitment to Britain's entry to the EEC. The Conservatives' continuing commanding lead over Labour in the polls and impressive by-election successes added urgency to policy formulation. Brendon Sewill, the head of the Conservative Research Department up to the 1970 election victory, has commented that:

> It was widely said that the Conservative Government took office in 1970 with a programme worked out in more detail than attempted by any previous Opposition. I make no apology for that. If a Party wishes to make fundamental changes in society to do so in time for the advantages to become apparent before the next election it is essential for incoming Ministers . . . to know exactly what they want to do[5].

One former Minister recalled that Mr Heath's government was 'more prepared than any before – in Opposition we all studied like billy-o and in the end we were over-prepared'[6]. The emphasis on establishing specific policy priorities was regarded as crucial.

To this end the Shadow Cabinet and its principal advisers met at the Selsdon Park Hotel in January 1970 to discuss policy over a weekend when 'most of the loose ends were tidied up and the priorities established'[7]. The meeting was partly a publicity exercise and partly a genuine attempt to put forward relevant policies that the electorate would not simply identify with 'window-dressing' in an electioneering way. It was these more serious aspects of policy that Harold Wilson dubbed 'Selsdon man' – a derogatory phrase that was to stick long after the actual conference was forgotten. The policy priorities outlined at Selsdon Park were largely the result of the intense policy preparation of the previous four years. In the areas of taxation reform, industrial relations and EEC entry, specific policies had been worked out with the emphasis on a regeneration of British industry and the encouragement of profitability after the constraints of socialism. For Mr Heath, the commitment to reinvigorate the economy was a strong personal one. As one Conservative MP put it, 'Ted had a deeply-rooted resentment to what he saw as the UK's poor economic performance since the war'[8].

## 1.2    The 1970 General Election

To put their policies into effect it was necessary to win the next General Election, something that had seemed to be a matter of course for so long. However, when 18 June 1970 was announced as Polling Day this was by no means certain. In April 1970, for the first time since 1967, the polls showed Labour to have regained the lead. The May municipal elections confirmed a substantial swing to Labour and the temptation for Harold Wilson to opt for a June election, urged on by many in the Labour Party, was impossible to resist. The chief reason for this was that the Labour Government regarded its balance of payments success, which it had so diligently cultivated for six years in office, as a foolproof winner, despite the Conservatives' gamble of concentrating on the issue of rising prices. The Conservative Party manifesto entitled '*A Better Tomorrow*' made the control of inflation the priority for the next administration; 'In implementing all our policies the need to curb inflation will come first. For only then can our broader strategy succeed'[9]. The 1970 Conservative Party manifesto was a forthright document that mixed effective criticism of Labour's record with specific policy commitments on the lines worked out in Opposition. As an electoral document it was effective. However, as the series of policy U-turns emerged in the following two years the manifesto pledges became an embarrassment. One former Minister thought that 'it was too hard'[10], and a back bench MP regarded it as 'much too abrasive'[11]. Douglas Hurd has claimed that the manifesto had 'too many rhetorical questions and too many sentences without the verbs. The abrupt style led to errors of judgement which caused trouble later'[12].

At the beginning of the election campaign, it was clear that the Labour Government would fight the election on the strength of the economy based on the secure foundations of the balance of payments success.

Inflation was the central political issue of the Conservative Party manifesto, the one major weakness in Labour campaign defences. The Conservatives were thus well-advised to make maximum political capital out of this issue. As the 1970 manifesto put it:

> The cost of living has rocketed during the last six years. Prices are now rising more than twice as fast as they did during the Conservative years. And prices have been zooming upwards at the very same time as the

Government has been taking an ever increasing slice of people's earnings in taxation. Soaring prices and increasing taxes are an evil and disastrous combination. Inflation is not only damaging to the economy: it is a major cause of social injustice, always hitting hardest at the weakest and poorest members of the community . . . . Labour's compulsory wage control was a failure and we will not repeat it[13].

Even more damaging of the Wilson Government's pay policy was the manifesto's assertion that 'We utterly reject the philosophy of compulsory wage control'[14]. But despite the concentration on the inflation issue the Conservative campaign had a less than confident start:

At the end of the first week there was little sign that the Conservative campaign was getting across, and Mr Heath invited the shadow cabinet and other senior advisers to drop in for coffee at Albany on Sunday, 7 June. It is plain that they were mutually cheered by the reports from their travels about the country and their own constituencies. It is also plain that they encouraged Mr Heath to press on still more vigorously with the economic theme. But privately many of them had the darkest forebodings about the outcome[15].

Douglas Hurd has noted that the 1970 election 'would have to be a shopping basket election' based on the fact that rising prices, and in particular food prices, were the main issues that worried the electorate[16]. For the Conservatives the problem was getting the message through to the electorate that they could perform better than Labour in reducing inflation. Thus speaking in his Bexley constituency on 30 May, Mr Heath outlined five ways in which a Conservative government would cut prices – by cutting taxes, checking increases in prices and charges of State Industries, controlling government spending, boosting savings and expanding output. Certainly, the issue of prices was closely associated with the Labour Government's Prices and Incomes Policy and Mr Heath did not miss the chance to exploit its unpopularity especially as the Conservative Party manifesto 'utterly rejected the philosophy of wage control'. Similarly, speaking in Birmingham on 4 June, Mr Heath warned that 'If you put a Labour Government back into office you will have your wages frozen for another lengthy period by Act of Parliament'[17].

The Conservative campaign was not fought entirely on rising prices – it was virtually impossible for it to be, if Mr Wilson's claim that the United Kingdom's economy was strong again was not to be challenged. From 8 June until polling day the Conservatives – and the press – shifted the emphasis on to the overall record of the Wilson Government. Mr Heath stated that Labour had got only 'one out of ten' for tests of good economic management. He tried to belittle Labour's balance of payments success. 'Their one success [is] the balance of payments surplus bought by devaluation. One out of ten. No wonder we're bottom of the class in Europe'[18].

Mr Wilson was less enthusiastic about other aspects of economic policy, sticking by his balance of payments success as steadfastly as he had stood by the policies that achieved it. 'Which is stronger, an £800 million deficit or a £600 million surplus?' was the message he preferred to put to the electorate. However, Mr Wilson's theme of the strong economy received a setback when Lord Cromer, a former Governor of the Bank of England, said in a television interview that an incoming government would face a serious inflationary crisis. This claim from a supposedly neutral and authoritative source helped to lend credibility to the Conservatives' warnings that the economy was fundamentally unsound. But, after the four-day national newspaper strike ended on 13 June, the May trade figures of a £31 m deficit obviously helped Mr Heath's campaign on the underlying weakness of the economy, offering 'just enough fleeting chance of success'[19]. Iain Macleod ventured that the 'trade figures show why we are having an election now . . . . The honeymoon after devaluation is over'[20]. In Mr Wilson's view, 'the trade figures showing a £31 m deficit were crucial – the press really got hold of them'[21].

However, the Conservatives' final fling of the campaign was reserved for the prices issue[22]. In his *Diaries of a Cabinet Minister*, Richard Crossman, failing to see the danger for Labour, commented that 'It is clear that the only thing the Tories have to hang on to is the rise in the cost of living and its effect on the pensioners and housewives'[23]. Certainly, the final few days of the campaign did not help Mr Wilson, although one Conservative considered that 'Mr Heath has privately given up days before the election'[24]. As well as the surprising £31 m trade gap, there was further confirmation of the accelerated trend of inflation with the publication of the retail price index[25] and the unemployment figures were the worst for many years. On top of which Enoch Powell's 'Vote Tory' message caught the headlines, and the imagination of some of the electorate. Mr Powell, in his fifth major speech of the campaign, urged his listeners to vote Conservative declaring that the election was 'not about Enoch Powell [but] about you and your future and your children's future and your country's future'[26]. But as one of Mr Powell's biographers points out, 'however much Powell had swayed the electorate the unambiguous victor was the triumphant Mr Heath'[27]. Ultimately, Mr Heath's central issue of rising prices stood the test of the campaign better than Mr Wilson's theme of the strong economy.

On 18 June the country went to the polls and early results soon indicated that a Conservative government was to take office thus confounding the predictions of the opinion polls. Only one poll, that of the Opinion Research Centre, correctly forecast a Conservative victory. That the ORC poll was conducted late in the campaign has been cited as substantial evidence for a late swing to the Conservatives. The £31 m trade gap, and Enoch Powell's appeal to the electorate to vote Conservative, no doubt helped the Conservatives at the eleventh hour, although professional opinion within the Conservative Party based on constituency reports suggested that the campaign had progressively been moving in the Conservatives' favour.

Having won 330 seats the Conservatives had a clear majority of 30 over all other rivals with a national swing of 4.8%. The new Cabinet was named on the evening of 20 June with Iain Macleod as Chancellor, the post he had always coveted and prepared so hard for in Opposition, Reginald Maudling as Home Secretary, Quintin Hogg as Lord Chancellor, and Sir Alec Douglas Home as Foreign Secretary. Among other senior posts, Robert Carr was appointed Secretary of State for Employment and Productivity with the task of implementing the Conservatives' proposals to reform Trade Union law, and Anthony Barber, as Chancellor of the Duchy of Lancaster, was given responsibility for Britain's EEC negotiations. On the steps of Number 10, Downing Street, echoing Disraeli, Mr Heath pledged that 'Our purpose is not to divide but to unite and, where there are differences, to bring reconciliation and create one nation . . .'[28]. Similarly, typifying the mood of his administration, Mr Heath told the Commons: 'The country has had almost six months of almost continuous electioneering . . . and it has now just about had enough of it. The result is clear cut. The game is over'[29]. Mr Heath was not reluctant to re-emphasize the radical nature of his government and '. . . it was widely believed among both his friends and his enemies, that he would be ruthless in carrying out the provisions of his manifesto'[30].

However, the Government did suffer one major setback during the period between the Election victory and the unveiling of the 'Quiet Revolution' at the October 1970 Conservative Party Conference, when on 21 July, while convalescing at his official residence after a successful appendix operation, Iain Macleod died suddenly of heart failure. It is impossible to know for sure how the overall economic policy of the Government would have proceeded had he presided over it as Chancellor. Opinion generally is that Macleod's loss was a blow from which the Heath administration never fully recovered. Macleod's political and intellectual stature was bigger than that not only of his successor but also those of most of his colleagues. Among many tributes in the Commons the Prime Minister spoke of a 'tragedy, not just for his colleagues and the House of Commons, but for the whole country, that he should have died just as he assumed the office for which most of his work in recent years had been a preparation'[31]. One Conservative MP considered Macleod 'basically lazy . . . but he would not have let the Treasury be run from Number 10'[32]. Other Conservatives regarded Macleod's death as a 'grave blow'[33] and as 'the biggest possible tragedy, for he has the stature to stand up to Heath'[34].

## 1.3    The 'Quiet Revolution'

Macleod's political feel and the 'ability to communicate which Ted Heath lacked'[35] was to be especially missed in the years ahead. Macleod's successor was Tony Barber who some believed to be disadvantaged by 'not having prepared himself for the Treasury'[36]. However, although unprepared for the Treasury in 1970, as any successor to Iain Macleod would have been, Mr Barber had had considerable Treasury experience as Economic Secretary to the Treasury, 1959–1962, and as Financial Secretary, 1962–1963. But Mr Barber, by succeeding a man who had died after only a month in office, was destined to receive less than flattering comparisons. Sir Harold Wilson has ventured that '. . . one cannot imagine [Macleod] making some of the errors which his successor, Anthony Barber, contrived . . .'[37].

It was not until the Conservative Party Conference in October 1970 that the radical approach of the Government was articulated by Mr Heath in a speech that launched the phrase the 'Quiet Revolution'. The conference, which was naturally given over to much self-congratulation, was also a personal triumph for Mr Heath who was described by Peter Thomas, the Party Chairman, as

> . . . a leader of outstanding personal courage and tenacity; a man who always said what he believed to be true. The malignity and smears of our opponents and critics never got him down and his confidence in victory never faltered. More than any election in our Party's history this was a personal triumph[38].

Robert Carr spoke of the plans to reform industrial relations law that had already been strongly criticized at the TUC and Labour Party conferences. John Davies, in a widely publicized speech, reiterated the Government's determination to move away from the follies of industrial intervention, promising 'not to bolster up or bale out companies when I can see no end to the process of propping them up'[39]. Mr Davies, scarcely a month in Parliament, had been elevated to the Cabinet Secretary of State for Trade and Industry in the reshuffle caused by the death of Iain Macleod. One Junior minister at the DTI thought that he was 'politically green, trying to run his Department like a business'[40], and a political opponent recalled that 'politically John Davies just wasn't housetrained'[41]. Such criticism is pertinent more to Mr Heath, who promoted him from the back benches, than to Mr Davies himself. Despite considerable experience in the 1960s as the CBI's Director General, Mr Davies was in effect denied the opportunity to acquire the political experience necessary both effectively to run a government department and to discharge his ministerial responsibilities to Parliament. If Mr Davies was indeed Cabinet material then a longer spell on the back benches, preferably over six months, would have considerably assisted his ministerial, as well as a political career.

Tony Barber, Iain Macleod's successor as Chancellor, promised to cut public expenditure, income tax, surtax and SET. However, it was Mr Heath's speech[42] on the final day of the conference that caught the mood of the occasion. The Prime Minister, after criticizing wildly inflationary wage demands, told the conference that:

> We were returned to office to change the course and the history of this nation, nothing else. And it is now this new course which the Government is now shaping.
>
> Change will give us freedom and that freedom must give responsibility. The free society which we aim to create must also be a responsible society . . . . Free from intervention, free from interference, but responsible. Free to make your own decisions, but responsible also for your mistakes. Free to lead a life of your own, but responsible to the community as a whole. This then is the task to which your Government is dedicated. This is the challenge and from it will come opportunity . . . . Opportunity to take our destiny, the destiny of the nation, once again in our own hands . . . .
>
> If we are to achieve this task we shall have to bring about a change so radical, a revolution so quiet, and yet so total, that it will go far beyond the programme for a Parliament to which we are committed and on which we have already embarked.
>
> We are laying the foundations but they are the foundations for a generation[43].

Mr Heath's conference speech was, probably, the best speech he made during his Premiership. This was not because of the policy content, important though that was, but because for the only time as Party Leader Mr Heath had coined a phrase which would become synonymous with, not only the speech itself, but with the new style of leadership and determination to follow a Conservative path radically different from the *status quo* that had been inherited from Harold Wilson. Supporters of Mr Heath's policy reversals have tended to view the 'Quiet Revolution' as a temporary, though embarrassing, phenomenon. But viewed from October 1970 the 'Quiet Revolution' was not intended to be transitory, which makes its subsequent abandonment all the more remarkable.

The clear message of the 'Quiet Revolution' was 'less government and a better quality' with the emphasis on a complete break with the policies and style of the previous administration. Thus there were inevitable changes in Whitehall. Richard Meyjes from Shell and a team of businessmen moved in to set about questioning departmental attitudes to reduce inter-departmental overlapping and wastage. The Central Policy Review Staff (known as the 'Think Tank') was established under the direction of Lord Rothschild to review central policy matters within the Cabinet Office. In mid-October two 'super-ministries', the Department of Trade and Industry, headed by John Davies, and the Department of the Environment, headed by Peter Walker, were created out of a reshuffle of five ministries in a substantial Whitehall reconstruction, which it was rather naively believed would improve the quality of government.

But the 'Quiet Revolution' was intended to go beyond the mere reorganization of Whitehall. It heralded not a 'Selsdon man' in a nineteenth century *laissez-faire* sense – there was no commitment to dismantle the welfare state, for example. Instead it sought to promote a technological, managerial man looking to a European commitment to aid the regeneration of competition in industry and personal initiative in the wealth creating, rather than the wealth distributing, process. As Lindsay and Harrington put it, 'The motto might have been, "keep more of your own money and stand on your own feet"'[44]. It is ironic that opponents of the 'Quiet Revolution', of all political colours, regarded the policies of less governmental control over the economy as a retreat to a former age. This can partly be explained by the intellectual fashions of the time. Lord Blake has pointed out that the Conservatives in 1970 embarked on a course 'which – and this is the key point – did not appear intellectually reputable'[45], to those opinion-formers who were wedded to 'pragmatism' and 'consensus'. However, although the 'Quiet Revolution' may not have appeared to follow the current orthodoxies of consensus politics it was still committed to the mixed economy. What the 'Quiet Revolution' sought to reverse was the steady progression towards a collectivist economy dominated by state regulation. The 'Quiet Revolution' approach was not only about reversing the trends towards collectivism, important though that was; it was also concerned with the modernization of the United Kingdom economy and the reinvigoration of industry and enterprise that were essential if the United Kingdom was to face a European future from a position of industrial strength rather than weakness, a policy to which Mr Heath was personally dedicated more than any other that had been worked out in Opposition.

Thus, the reduction in the levels of taxation, the effective control of inflation and the transformation of Britain's comparatively low rate of economic growth were essential elements in the 'Quiet Revolution' strategy. Far from being backward looking the attempt to reform industrial relations law, despite its failure, was an attempt to drag the trade unions into a new world that would not tolerate outmoded industrial practices and the destruction and danger caused to the economy by industrial militancy. Unlike Harold Wilson's 1964 conception of harnessing the 'white heat of the technological revolution' the 'Quiet Revolution' was prepared to confront every aspect of Britain's poor economic record in the hope of shaping a future that would be, in that regard, radically different from the past. Brendon Sewill has noted that the strategy '. . . was no less an attempt to change the whole attitude of mind of the British people: to create a more dynamic, thrusting, "go-getting" economy on the American or German model; to create not merely new material wealth but also new pride in achievement'[46]. Perhaps such optimism was, with hindsight, misplaced, and, similarly, it was an overstatement to describe the outset of the 'Quiet Revolution' as 'Bliss was it in that dawn'[47]. It did contain some inherent weaknesses – for example that large Ministries are inherently superior to smaller ones, and that legal reforms alone could restructure satisfactorily industrial malpractice – but the overall message and intention of the 'Quiet Revolution' was relevant and appropriate to the United Kingdom in 1970[48].

As well as in the changes in Whitehall the practical effects of 'Quiet Revolution' thinking were evident shortly after the Party conference when Tony Barber presented a comprehensive review of public expenditure to the Commons on 27 October. Sixpence (6d) was cut off the standard rate of income tax from April 1971, corporation tax was cut by 2½% from January 1, charges for school meals and milk were increased, as were prescriptions, to save £32m, and the Industrial Reorganization Corporation was abolished. Investment Grants were abolished to save £670m per annum by 1974/5, being replaced by tax incentives. The Regional Employment Premium, costing £100m per annum, was also to be phased out by 1974 and nationalized industry spending curtailed and the proposed nationalization of the ports was cancelled. The Industrial Expansion Act was to be repealed and the pledge to move from deficiency payments to British farmers to levies on imported food would now be implemented, saving the Exchequer an eventual £150m, and offering the prospect of additional revenue (from levies) in addition. Another £40m of saving would come from reductions in capital spending on minor roads. A further £100m saving was envisaged by shifting financial support for local authority housing from the subsidization of rents to the subsidization of families on the basis of need. Government aid to the Consumer Council, the British Productivity Council and the government research councils was ended or reduced and museum charges were introduced. As well as the cuts in expenditure and the steps to jettison so many of Labour's interventionist institutions the Chancellor announced the provision of an extra £100m for hospitals particularly for the old and the mentally handicapped, and an extra £28m for primary schools, and the introduction of a new scheme, the Family Income Supplement, offering up to £3 per week for the poorest families. The net result, after allowing for the tax allowances to replace investment grants, would be a saving to public funds of £1100m by 1974/5; and the rate of increase in public expenditure between 1971/2 and 1974/5 would be cut from 3.5% per annum to 2.8% per annum.

As Mr Barber stated: 'I believe that the whole House will agree it is right to take action to break out of the depressing cycle of high taxation and low growth which has bedevilled our country in recent years'[49]. Of course, the whole House did not agree. While the Conservatives were delighted, Labour MPs were enraged, to the extent that one Conservative MP described the success of the package as being 'in direct ratio to the annoyance on the Labour benches'[50]. Sir Keith Joseph, the Health Minister, cautiously ventured that '. . . 6d off the standard rate is not enough to transform the country's prospects. But it is a first step, it is a sign of hope'[51].

Both the theory of the 'Quiet Revolution', as announced at the Conservative Party Conference, and the practical measures taken to reform Whitehall and to review radically public expenditure were political-ly controversial – perhaps in strictly political terms, over-ambitious – but in terms of the policy priorities the country required, they represented a considerable step in what Mr Heath and his Ministers believed to be the right direction. The 'Quiet Revolution' represented a mood of optimism and expectation for the Conservative Party in the same way as the creation of the Welfare State, following the 1945 election victory, had represented to the Labour Party the realization of practical socialism. Thus at the outset of the 'Quiet Revolution', Mr Heath optimistically ventured that '. . . over the period of this Parliament I believe that not only the direction of policy, but the attitude of the people will change to such a degree that future generations will look back on these years and say: "This was our launching pad"'[52]. Given Mr Heath's deeply-held desire to improve Britain's economic performance – within a European context where inefficiency would have no place – there is no reason to doubt the sincerity of such a statement. However, as the following chapters will try to demonstrate, it was political pressure on the Government, rather than the inherent deficiencies of policy, that led to the abandonment of the 'Quiet Revolution'. The following chapters, therefore, aim to explain not just the immediate reasons for the policy reversals, but also the political context in which they were made in terms of the difficulty of sustaining the 'Quiet Revolution' policies when they so clearly appeared to contradict the post-war Keynesian consensus to which the Conservative Party, under Mr Heath's leadership, was still committed.

## References

1. Surprisingly there was only one major biography of Edward Heath published before he became Prime Minister: *Edward Heath* by GEORGE HUTCHINSON, Longmans, 1970. Two other biographies emerged in 1972: *Heath and the Heathmen* by ANDREW ROTH, Routledge and Kegan Paul, 1972, and *Edward Heath: Prime Minister* by MARGARET LAING, Sidgwick and Jackson, 1972.
2. A. ROTH, op. cit. (Ref. 1), p. xiv.
3. T. F. LINDSAY and M. HARRINGTON, *The Conservative Party 1918–79*, Macmillan, 1979, p. 249.

4. J. RAMSDEN, *The Making of Conservative Party Policy: The Conservative Research Department since 1929*, Longmans, 1980, p. 237.
5. BRENDON SEWILL in R. HARRIS and B.SEWILL, *British Economic Policy 1970–74: Two Views*. IEA Hobart Paperback No. 7, 1975, p. 31.
6. Interview, Junior Minister.
7. DOUGLAS HURD, *An End to Promises: Sketch of a Government 1970–74*, Collins, 1979, p. 13.
8. Interview, Conservative MP. This comment was typical of many describing Mr Heath's intense commitment to reinvigorate Britain's economy.
9. Conservative Party Manifesto, '*A Better Tomorrow*', 1970.
10. Interview, Cabinet Minister.
11. Interview, David Knox.
12. D. HURD, op. cit. (Ref. 7), p. 21.
13. Conservative Party Manifesto, '*A Better Tomorrow*', 1970.
14. Ibid.
15. D. E. BUTLER and M. PINTO-DUSCHINSKY, *The General Election of 1970*, Macmillan, 1971, pp. 156–7.
16. D. HURD, op. cit. (Ref. 7), p. 20.
17. *The Times*, 5 June 1970.
18. *The Times*, 9 June 1970.
19. D. HURD, op. cit. (Ref. 7), p. 23.
20. *Daily Telegraph*, 16 June 1970.
21. Interview, Sir Harold Wilson.
22. A Gallup Poll on 19 June 1970 gave the Conservatives a 1.5% lead over Labour among women in the electorate and a 2% lead among housewives.
23. R. H. S. CROSSMAN, *The Diaries of a Cabinet Minister: Vol. III*, Hamish Hamilton and Jonathan Cape, 1977, p. 946.
24. Interview, George Hutchinson.
25. The retail price index showed a rise of 2.1 points in April and May.
26. ROY LEWIS, *Enoch Powell: Principle in Politics*, Cassell, 1979, p. 143.
27. DOUGLAS E. SCHOEN, *Powell and the Powellites*, Macmillan, 1977, p. 66.
28. *Sunday Telegraph*, 21 June 1970.
29. *Hansard*, 2 July 1970, Vol. 803, Col. 406.
30. PATRICK COSGRAVE, *The Failure of the Conservative Party 1945–75*, p. 121.
31. *Hansard*, 21 July 1970, Vol. 804, Col. 241.
32. Interview, Conservative MP.
33. Interview, George Hutchinson.
34. Interview, Conservative Party adviser.
35. Interview, David Knox.
36. Interview, Senior Civil Servant.
37. SIR HAROLD WILSON, *Final Term: The Labour Government 1974–76*, Weidenfeld & Nicolson and Michael Joseph, 1979, p. 1.
38. *The Times*, 8 October 1970.
39. *The Times*, 9 October 1970.
40. Interview, Sir John Eden.
41. Interview, Sir Harold Wilson.
42. See DOUGLAS HURD, op. cit. (Ref. 7), Ch. 6, for an entertaining description of how Mr Heath's speeches were prepared.
43. *The Times*, 12 October 1970.
44. T. F. LINDSAY and M. HARRINGTON, op. cit. (Ref. 3), p. 30.
45. Lord Blake in *The Conservative Opportunity* (Ed. by Lord Blake and John Patten), Macmillan, 1976, pp. 3–4.
46. R. HARRIS and B. SEWILL, op. cit. (Ref. 5), p. 30.
47. JOCK BRUCE-GARDYNE, *Whatever Happened to the Quiet Revolution?*, Charles Knight, 1974, p. 5.
48. The Conservative Right have argued that it has indeed stood the test of time well, given the similarity of philosophy and approach to that adopted by the incoming Conservative Government in May 1979.
49. *Hansard*, 27 October 1970, Vol. 805, Col. 51.
50. *Hansard*, 27 October 1970, Vol. 805, Col. 59.
51. *Hansard*, 5 November 1970, Vol. 805, Col. 1391.
52. *The Times*, 13 March 1971.

Part II
# Political Pressure and Economic Policy

# Chapter 2

# The Industrial Relations Act: its origins, operation and consequences

*'The State cannot legalize any act; it can only criminalize acts or leave them alone.'*

Thomas Szasz, *The Second Sin*,
Routledge & Kegan Paul 1974

## 2.1 The 1960s' background

The comprehensive reform of industrial relations law was central to modernizaton of British industry, which the 'Quiet Revolution' sought[1]. In Opposition the commitment to a major reform had been intensified by what the Conservatives regarded as an unnecessary capitulation to trade union power in 1969 when Barbara Castle's *'In Place of Strife'*[2] proposals proved to be abortive. This followed the spectre of a revolt by back bench Labour MPs, supported by several members of the Cabinet and orchestrated by James Callaghan, which forced Harold Wilson and Barbara Castle to abandon legislative plans that may well have assisted Labour's popularity with the electorate. Instead the 'solemn and binding' agreement between Mr Wilson and the TUC General Secretary, Vic Feather, was treated with near-universal cynicism by the public who were becoming increasingly unsympathetic to the growing incidence of strike action. Despite the time-consuming study of the Donovan Commission, 1965–1968, and the *'In Place of Strife'* proposals, Labour left office in 1970 with the problems of Britain's industrial relations structure untackled and with unofficial strikes accounting for over 90% of all strikes. The Conservatives, therefore, could count on considerable public support for any proposals that might reduce the number of strikes, particularly the unofficial strikes that had antagonized public opinion. The Conservatives' proposals thus tended to be 'built up by electoral pressure to be a panacea'[3]. As one industrial relations expert put it, 'The 1960s were the great age of the unofficial strike'[4] with the consequence that the intensification of industrial conflict before the 1970 election victory exacted a considerable influence on the legislation that was finally passed. The section in the 1970 Conservative Party manifesto headed *'A Fair Deal at Work'*[5] left no doubt as to the intentions of introducing legislation, or of the thinking behind it:

> There were more strikes in 1969 than ever before in our history. Already in the first three months of 1970 there were 1134 strikes compared with 718 in the same period last year, when the Labour Government said the position was so serious that legislation was essential in the national

interest. This rapid and serious deterioration directly stems from Labour's failure to carry through its own policy for the reform of industrial relations.

We will introduce a comprehensive Industrial Relations Bill in the first Session of the new Parliament. It will provide a proper framework of law within which improved relationships between management, men and unions can develop. We welcome the TUC's willingness to take action through its own machinery against those who disrupt industrial peace by unconstitutional or unofficial action. Yet it is no substitute for the new set of fair and reasonable rules we will introduce[6].

There is no reason to doubt the sincerity and good intentions behind such plans, nor to question the Conservatives' underlying assumption that abuses of trade union power had increased to an unacceptable level, involving considerable public inconvenience not least to individual trade union members themselves. It is ironic that the Labour Opposition should have launched an attack on the policy of industrial relations reform as 'class legislation' so soon after the similar provisions of '*In Place of Strife*' had been disregarded. However, the new Government's attitude did reflect both the public mood and the tide of informed opinion, which had gradually come round to the view that abuses of trade union power should be legally curbed in the national interest[7]. The *Employment and Productivity Gazette* statistics indicated that 1970 was the worst year for strikes since 1926, figures that strengthened the Government's resolve.

## 2.2  The implementation of the Act

As far as Whitehall reaction was concerned the Conservatives did not come up against opposition in principle to their well-advanced proposals. Whitehall criticism tended to be related to the question of details, to the nuances of emphasis, rather than to matters of fundamental importance. Sir Denis Barnes, Permanent Secretary at the Department of Employment, 1968–1973, has stated that:

> . . . there wasn't identity of view between officials and the incoming Ministers on detail. Nor – and I think this is a point I'd like to make very strongly – was there identity of view within the Department. There was a general acceptance that there was going to be legislation. But within officials there was a range of opinion and there were some who would have preferred no legislation at all, particularly officials who were concerned with the day to day operation of industrial relations, in conciliation and so forth . . . . First of all, I think all officials – I can say this more or less certainly – did not favour a ballot. And I can say it with fair certainty because we did not favour a ballot when it was put in '*In Place of Strife*'. I found it very interesting to see that there was a very distinct cleavage of view between politicians and civil servants over ballots . . . .
> Another thing in which I think there was a difference of opinion – that was the closed shop. I can't remember all the details of this, but I think

officials felt that prohibition or restriction, too severe restriction on the closed shop, was probably going too far; that where employers, managements and the unions had agreed on one and employers thought it suited them and the unions thought it suited them, the officials felt that the arrangement ought to be allowed to stand[8].

A contrary view about the Department of Employment's approach to the legislation was that 'senior civil servants felt that Barbara Castle had been disgracefully treated over '*In Place of Strife*' and took a vendetta against the trade unions becoming too hawkish'[9]. Moran argues, convincingly, that once responsibility for incomes policy had been transferred in the late 1960s to the Department of Employment (& Productivity), the civil servants began increasingly to favour legislative intervention to enforce, or assist with, wage restraint[10]. Similarly, one industrial relations specialist thought Sir Denis Barnes to be 'the leading hawk'[11], and one trade union leader regarded 'Denis Barnes as the architect of it all in my opinion'[12]. While it may be too simplistic to portray Whitehall as totally 'hawkish', it is fair to say that Whitehall opinion, centred on the Department of Employment, was more than receptive to the Conservatives' determination to legislate given the Establishment's political defeat over '*In Place of Strife*'. Whitehall's infamous ability to frustrate the aspirations of governments, of whatever party, certainly did not apply to the Conservatives' plans for industrial relations reform.

It is particularly interesting to mention with regard to the use of ballots that a Conservative Party study group in Opposition, led by Sir Geoffrey Howe to America, noted that 90% of ballots in the United States had favoured strike action. The Conservatives thus came to place considerable hope in the use of cooling-off periods before ballots were taken[13]. In this way they expected the Industrial Relations Act to play an economic role, whereby inflationary wage demands would be de-escalated and militancy curbed during the cooling-off period[14]. This line of argument, despite its naïve optimism, was often advanced. Mr Heath, for example, betrayed the belief that controlling inflation and controlling disputes were inseparable when he said that:

> No Government in its senses wishes to intervene in the details of bargaining between employer and employee. But no Government worthy of the name can abdicate its responsibility to make sure that the consumer and the community as a whole are protected. At no time is this responsibility more important than at a time when rising prices are still causing hardship to those least able to meet them – hardship which can only be made worse by inflationary wage settlements. That is why this Government cannot and will not allow the interests of the community as a whole to be ignored and forgotten[15].

In general terms, therefore, the Act was expected to put a brake on the sort of unofficial action in support of unreasonable wage claims that added to inflationary pressure[16]. In this context, the Act genuinely wished to strengthen the trade union leadership in relation to the power of the shop stewards as it had emerged in the 1960s. As Mr Carr put it, the real need was '. . . to strengthen the authority of the democratically elected trade union leadership'[17]. Brendon Sewill has noted that '. . . nothing was done to reduce the force of *official* [my emphasis] strikes. Indeed the "right to strike" was positively expressed in legislation for the first time in history'[18]. Thus the Conservatives 'wanted the Act to give trade union officers greater incentive to impose authority . . . the underlying philosophy was to make the union officers behave like the officers of the 1950s – like Deakin or Bevin'[19].

But the TUC was wary of the Government's whole outlook, a misunderstanding that was not helped by the absence of constructive criticism or consultation between the Government and the TUC. Mr Carr has since stated that:

> . . . the unions wouldn't consult. We produced a consultative document (in October 1979). And they then took this view because I had said that there were certain pillars central to this Bill, which we could not compromise. Perhaps that was, with the wisdom of hindsight, an unwise thing to say . . . . By and large they said 'we are opposed and we are not even going to talk about it'. I'm afraid this was maintained not only in public but in private[20].

Sir Geoffrey Howe, who drafted the Industrial Relations Bill, has also noted that Mr Carr

> . . . had very little option but to present the broad shape of it as he did, and say these are the areas in which we intend to make definite provision, not come and talk to us about how we do it. We didn't really have much expectation that they would come, although for my part I should very much have wished they had . . . there was no willingness on their side to come forward[21].

Thus, although it was the view of some Ministers that 'the union *leaders* privately liked the proposed legislation'[22], the lack of consultation and outright public opposition of the TUC was quickly seized upon by the militant shop-floor opponents, and before the Industrial Relations Bill was unveiled on 3 December 1970, the SU Carburettor plant at Birmingham had been brought to a standstill by an unofficial strike against the proposed legislation. This was the first strike, and by no means the last, of its kind. The Bill itself contained two surprises for the Opposition. Firstly, instead of being taken in a 50-strong Standing Committee, consideration of the Bill was to be conducted on the floor of the House. Secondly, the 'teeth' of the Bill provided for large unions to be liable to pay compensation up to £100 000 to aggrieved firms for breaking the new rules for conduct on industrial relations. The other main provisions of the Bill covered most aspects of industrial relations. A strengthened Registrar of trade union and employers' organizations was established to control and supervise implementation of the rules of those organizations. Collective agreements were to be presumed legally binding unless they contained a written provision to the contrary. A list of 'unfair industrial relations practices' was drawn up, commission of which would entail loss of freedom from liability of action and for which offenders could be ordered to pay compensation. A new Industrial Relations Court with the status of the High Court was established, together with the Industrial Tribunals, to deal with all offences under the Bill. The Secretary of State was empowered to apply to the National Industrial Relations Court (NIRC) for an order for a cooling-off period of up to 60 days where a strike would create a serious risk to the community and the national economy. Similarly, the Minister could ask for an order for a secret ballot if he doubted that the threatened strike action was supported by a majority or if there was a threat to national security, to the economy, or to the safety of a substantial portion of the community. A statutory right for an individual to belong or not to belong to a union and safeguards against unfair dismissal were 'the least contentious part of the Act'[23].

Pre-entry closed shops were made void but 'agency shops', in which a union was represented and financially supported by all the employees except conscientious objectors, were permitted. The Commission on Industrial Relations (CIR) was placed on a statutory basis and given power to formulate new agreements that could be imposed and made legally binding by the NIRC. The CIR was empowered to recommend which union or unions should have bargaining rights and these recommendations could also be imposed and made binding by the courts. A Code of Industrial Relations practice was prepared, incorporating guidance on many aspects of industrial relations including disclosure of information by employers and communications between managers and employees. It was hoped that the Code would not be directly enforceable but would be taken into account by the NIRC and Industrial Tribunals. As Mr Heath had promised, the Government was fulfilling 'the mandate we had from the people of this country at the election'[24]. Such an interpretation may have been exaggerated – all governments claim a 'mandate' for passing legislation, based on election manifesto pledges – but evidence of public support for the Government was the result of accumulative unpopularity of trade unions during the 1960s[25].

Mrs Barbara Castle, ironically leading the Opposition's attack on the Bill, which was similar to her own 'In Place of Strife' proposals, vowed to 'fight tooth and nail, line by line and however long it takes . . . to destroy this Bill'[26].

Although the debates in the Commons were particularly bitter the Government's majority enabled it to triumph in the lobbies with relative ease[27]. But the fierce opposition in the trade unions – above and beyond that of the TUC leaders – was a constantly-growing problem. The strike at the SU Carburettor plant has already been mentioned. Similar political strikes had already been designated for 8 December 1970 in defiance of both the Opposition leader, Harold Wilson, and the TUC Assistant General Secretary, Len Murray, when nine national newspaper proprietors were granted a High Court order on 1 December restraining the executive of the print union from 'doing any further act' to call the newspapers' employees out on a one-day strike against the Government's legislation. Sir John Pennycuick, Vice-Chancellor, declared that the strike would be unlawful because it was not a trade dispute. Referring to the planned stoppage Mr Carr exploited the tactical differences between the Bill's opponents by raising the spectre of Communist Party influence. The planned strike, he argued, was being represented as a spontaneous protest against the Bill; 'In fact it is being deliberately organized by a body called the Liaison Committee for the Defence of Trade Unions whose activities are prominently recorded in the newspaper of the Communist Party'[28]. In the House, as well as the predictable reactions to the Bill, the Government made it clear that it would not be slow to bring in a time-table motion should the Opposition use deliberately obstructive tactics to jeopardize the Bill and the rest of the session's legislative programme.

Leading the TUC's attack on the Bill, Vic Feather repeatedly stressed that where good industrial relations existed this was not the result of the law that could not on its own '. . . compel a good relationship between a group of workers and an employer'[29]. In February 1971 the TUC's demonstration against the Bill brought a seven-mile procession to London and Mr Feather estimated that 140 000 people joined the march. Despite the intensity of the debate in the Commons the Government was having no difficulty in obtaining comfortable majorities of about 30 in the crucial divisions and on 5 August 1971 the Industrial Relations Bill received Royal Assent. The Government had thus overcome parliamentary opposition and had faced up to the unions' hostility with the hope that once on the statute book the Bill would so improve industrial relations that credible opposition to it would fade. The actual operation of the Act soon showed that such a hope was misplaced. The Act's critics had pointed out that refusal to co-operate with the Act and active determination to resist it, could render it unworkable in defiance of the will of Parliament. The TUC's and Labour's opposition to the legislative reform of industrial relations had centred as much on the principles involved as on the details of the Bill. Following the traumas between Harold Wilson's Government and the TUC over 'In Place of Strife', the joint opposition to the Act served to re-unite the Labour Party and the TUC to a single purpose. At the 1971 Labour Party conference, Jack Jones warned the Government that the unions and the Labour Party were intent on the repeal of the Act at the first opportunity. He added that:

> The time is ripe and the trade unions and the Party leadership are closer together and will remain firm and united. It is possible for the Party and the TUC to work together because every union in the TUC, whether political or not, is united in wanting this Act repealed. There is no reason why a joint policy cannot be worked out. Let us have the closest possible liaison. We have struggled over the years to establish the right of representation at work. The Industrial Relations Act will be used to try to hold back our advances and threaten the existence of free trade unionism in the one country where it is essentially and fundamentally democratic[30].

Thus despite the genuine intentions of modernizing industrial relations law and reforming abuses of trade union power the Government, by passing such comprehensive legislation, was actually likely to arouse a counter-productive reaction.

It was not surprising, therefore, that the Act's provisions for the registration of trade unions (and employers' associations) was the first target in the unions' campaign of active resistance. The Government placed the onus on the unions to register by insisting that unions on the 'provisional' register, i.e., those unions registered under previous laws, would be assumed to have automatically transferred themselves on to the new, permanent register unless they explicitly removed themselves. Thus, depending on the situation of each union, opposition to the Act began with either non-registration or de-registration. In March 1971 at a Special Congress in Croydon unions were strongly advised not to register under the Act, the General Council being reluctant to instruct members not to register before the Bill had finally passed into law. By the time of the Blackpool TUC conference the mood had hardened with the Act already being on the statute book. Despite the advice of the General Council, conference voted by over 1 million to support an AUEW motion instructing unions not to register.

Hugh Scanlon, moving the resolution, argued that, 'One step towards registration will inexorably lead towards the co-operation with the Act as a whole'[31]. Between 19 October and 5 November, 23 unions de-registered but only five registered[32]. By January 1972, 82 unions had complied with the Blackpool decision with 32 unions still intent on registration. These 32 were suspended for a year at the 1972 September TUC conference and one year later 20 of the 32 who had still not de-registered were expelled from the TUC; The National Graphical Association, rather than face expulsion, resigned from the TUC over the registration question. The seriousness of the internal TUC wrangles that led to the expulsions should not be taken too literally. As Hunter and Robertson noted '. . . if a union had already quarrelled with the TUC it may find that it is as well out of it. The sanction of expulsion is not . . . of final and devastating importance to the union'[33]. Although it can be argued that by failing to register many unions deprived themselves of some of the beneficial provisions of the Act, the 'widespread immediate and thoroughgoing'[34] opposition to the Act would have been substantially toned down had unions registered. Mr Carr was thus forced to admit that the Act 'might not work effectively – least of all to the best advantage of ten million trade union members'[35] as a result of de-registration.

Moran rightly notes that '. . . the Government believed that after initial opposition the union movement would quickly register and co-operate. Neither the Conservatives nor the civil servants foresaw that non-registration would be so widespread or so long-lasting'[36]. Brendon Sewill has confirmed this view[37]. One industrial relations expert has even ventured that it is '. . . open to question whether, even if the unions had [registered] the Act could have accomplished the reform of industrial relations which its authors had intended'[38]. This may have been the case given the level of concerted opposition to the Act. However, in defence of the Act's intentions, it must be stated that there existed a problem of industrial relations practice that had been widely regarded, throughout the 1960s, as being in need of reform.

## 2.3    The docks and railways disputes

The de-registration setback was soon to be followed by a major confrontation between the Act and the transport workers union, the T&GWU, who had failed to register. On 29 March 1972 the T&GWU was fined £55 000 for contempt of the National Industrial Relations Court, set up under the Act. The fine, imposed by the President of the NIRC, Sir John Donaldson, was suspended for 14 days to enable the union, Britain's largest with 1.25 million members, to attend the court and explain why its members failed to observe an order banning 'the blacking' of container lorries seeking to enter Mersey Docks. Sir John said that if representatives of the union appeared it would be open to the court to reconsider the matter. The NIRC also made an order for the issue of a writ of sequestration, amounting to seizure, of the union's assets three weeks after the expiry of the 14-day suspension period if the fine had not been paid. Sir John pointed out that in cases of contempt all the union's assets, which amounted to £22m in funds alone, were liable to sequestration. The T&GWU had put itself forward, in effect, as the test case to the wisdom of the TUC's boycott of the Act, and in keeping with this policy its General Secretary, Jack Jones, made it clear that his union had no intention of paying the fine. Mr Feather observed that it was a 'great pity that the law is being called upon to carry out this unworkable legislation'[39].

From the beginning the effectiveness of the NIRC was open to question while it was being boycotted. The issue of contempt of court therefore tended to become the central offence rather than the specific issue of industrial relations involved in the first place. The immense difficulty of fitting all matters of industrial relations into a legal context thus became even more obscure. As one legal expert has since put it:

> Many people doubted whether the issues before the Court were justifiable. What the NIRC was required to do was to make binding decisions and to see that they were enforced, in the context of a dispute between trade unions, individual workmen, employers' federations. This, as many said at the time, was not a function which judges and courts could perform successfully[40].

At the same time, in April 1972, use of the Act was being considered by the Government in relation to the impending railways strike following the Union's rejection of the British Railways Board's 11% pay offer. But, before the rail crisis reached the stage that the Government felt compelled to intervene, Mr Carr, who had pioneered the Act through the Commons, was promoted to Leader of the House and Maurice Macmillan was made Employment Secretary, in Mr Heath's long-expected, first major Cabinet re-shuffle.

It was Mr Barber, however, not Mr Macmillan who criticized the railwaymen in a speech on 13 April 1972. He said that it was intolerable that the public were being subjected to so much hardship, suffering and inconvenience by the nationwide go-slow by the unions[41]. 'The offer of the British Railways Board is above the recent trend of settlements in both private and public sectors. I believe that most people will consider it to be, by any standard, a fair and, indeed, generous offer'[42]. Neither were the three rail unions, whose official work-to-rule had stirred the feelings of irate commuters, impressed by Mr Macmillan's appeal that their pay claim should be taken to arbitration. But they did agree to Alex Jarrett, the Managing Director of IPC, acting as 'referee' to solve the dispute, though not to his recommendation of a 12.5% compromise award. Only at this point of impasse did the Government decide to invoke the Industrial Relations Act. On 19 April a 14-day 'cooling-off' period from the moment when normal service was resumed was ordered by the Industrial Relations Court whose President, Sir John Donaldson, ruled that the railwaymen were in breach of their contract of employment. On 20 April the three rail unions agreed to accept the Court's decision rather than run the risk of a fine for contempt of court. Ironically, on the same day the T&GWU were fined a further £50000 as Merseyside dockers continued their blacking of container lorries.

The dockers were adamant that the 'blacking' would continue, despite an appeal to stop by Jack Jones, and many railwaymen also ignored their Union's call for normal working. Indeed, the worst chaos on Southern Region occurred several days after the NIRC's decision. Only on 25 April could Mr Macmillan certify to the NIRC that the 14-day cooling-off period could begin, normal working having been resumed. So controversial had the NIRC become that at a meeting at 10 Downing Street between Mr Heath, senior Ministers and TUC leaders there was open talk of the possibility of establishing a national, independent conciliation service to settle disputes before they reached the NIRC. Although Mr Macmillan stated that both the NIRC and the Industrial Relations Act were there to stay, Mr Feather ventured that: 'It would be the aim of the TUC to bring about a conciliation procedure in industry generally which would in effect make the National Industrial Relations Court redundant'[43]. Such conciliatory talk at the top level did not prevent the grass roots escalation of the docks dispute as dockers at London, then Preston, Tilbury and Hull joined their Merseyside colleagues in the blacking of containers, in defiance of T&GWU instructions. In his capacity as President of the NIRC, Sir John Donaldson reiterated that:

> . . . no union is responsible for the actions of individuals merely because they are members . . . . A trade union can only act through its officials and it is responsible for their actions, so long as they are acting within the apparent scope of their authority. Unions can and do delegate authority to subordinate officials and give them the widest discretion to act as they think best in the interests of the section of members which they represent and in the wide interests of the union as a whole . . . . But if a union knows that its officials are acting contrary to the law, it has a duty to assert its authority and require them to comply with the law. Advising them to comply is not enough. If the official disobeys the union's orders, the union must exercise such disciplinary powers as it has and, if necessary, deprive him of his position as an official[44].

But as Crouch noted: 'The NIRC was caught between an attempt at imposing a legal code on industrial relations, and an existing balance of forces within industry which constantly forced a return to compromise'[45].

However despised the Act appeared the T&GWU changed its policy of boycotting the NIRC on 3 May 1972, and for the first time defended itself against the charges of continued contempt. The £55000 fine was also paid. Despite this change of tactics by the T&GWU, the rail and docks disputes were pushing the Industrial Relations Act to the peak of its controversy. The war of nerves in both disputes – especially in the rail crisis as the

14-day cooling-off period was ending – was anything but conducive to settlement and the CBI, pragmatically, told Mr Heath on 8 May that they were giving favourable consideration to the setting up of an independent conciliation agency, prior to the use of the Act. It was the Government's intention while such ideas were current, more to be seen to be sticking by the Act than actually sticking by it, though as yet the question of effectively putting the Act 'on ice' was never seriously considered by the Cabinet. In the railways dispute the Act's meanderings were clearly prolonging the dispute and hardening, rather than softening, attitudes. Following failure to reach an agreement at the end of the 14-days cooling-off period, the railwaymen's work-to-rule recommenced and, following the Government's application to the NIRC, a compulsory ballot of Britain's 280000 railwaymen was ordered. The result produced a total of 129441 to 23181, a ratio of 6:1 in favour of further industrial action, an outcome that one Senior Minister 'fully expected'[46]. This served to strengthen the union's hand in further negotiations with the British Railways Board, the very outcome that the Act was formulated to avoid. As Sir Sidney Greene, the NUR General Secretary, put it, 'There was no chance the ballot wouldn't be in our favour, we had the feel of the rank and file. The ballot strengthened our chances'[47]. A disappointed Mr Macmillan was still adamant that the Act, which had prolonged the dispute thus far, had not failed. The truth, however, was that the Act was falling rapidly into disrepute. The settlement of the railways dispute following the union's acceptance of a 13–13.5% wage deal happened only 6 hours before final industrial action was planned. Ministers considered the settlement to be a major political defeat as it was thought to be particularly inflationary. But the settlement was not in itself the defeat; that lay in the extension of the dispute and its escalation to a degree that would have been highly unlikely in the Act's absence. The Act, by hardening the attitudes of the railwaymen, had directly contributed to what Ministers regarded as a political defeat. The Act had not worked and had been seen not to work. Crouch has argued that the Conservatives were disregarding one of the central tenets of post-war government commitments; that strikes soured industrial relations and should be avoided at almost all costs. Such a criticism is ambiguous. On the one hand the problem of strikes had been growing during the 1960s and abuses of trade union power had become unpopular not only with the Conservatives but also with the general public[48]. The intentions of the Act were to reduce the number of strikes. On the other hand the Act had served to exacerbate the problem, firstly by being operationally unworkable and secondly by politicizing industrial disputes so that the normal tendency to compromise was overridden. The position of the NIRC is important to the argument. The fact that its judgements were seen to be political and added to political controversy was part of the problem of whether the issues before it were actually amenable to judicial interpretation. Even though it was not the Government's intention, too often the impression was that the NIRC was '. . . an arm of Government, not part of the independent arm of the judiciary'[49].

It certainly seemed clear that the prolongation of the railways dispute, as a result of rulings by the NIRC, had led not to a 'cooling-off' as the Act intended but to a hardening of bargaining attitudes on all sides.

Following the Act's failure with regard to the railways dispute, the government was dealt another blow on 13 June when the Appeal Court quashed the £55 000 fine imposed by the NIRC on the T&GWU declaring that the union was not accountable for its shop stewards. Introducing the law, or rather, more of the law, into industrial relations was proving to be much more difficult than the Government had hoped. The Appeal Court's decision further undermined respect for the NIRC, whose legal competence was now called into question. Coming on top of the other disappointments with the Act's operation this setback appeared to be more than the occupational hazard it really was. After all, the Appeal Court often overrules a High Court; but the NIRC was the only High Court whose judgements, if not political, could affect a political situation. The docks blacking dispute illustrated this perfectly. Following the continuation of the blacking in defiance both of the NIRC and the official T&GWU line, Sir John Donaldson, on 14 June, warned three leading members of the unofficial National Ports Shop Stewards Committee, Messrs Steer, Turner and Williams, that they faced arrest and imprisonment if they persisted in disregarding the Court's order to stop blacking the Midland Cold Storage depot at Hackney. The ruling of the Court, the first in which it had 'shown its teeth' against the dockers' shop stewards' leaders in the containers dispute, came only 24 hours after Lord Denning and his two colleagues in the Appeal Court overruled the Industrial Relations Court's decision that the transport union was responsible for the actions of its shop stewards. Giving judgement, in the light of the Appeal Court's decision, Sir John Donaldson said of the shop stewards' leaders: 'By their conduct these men are saying that they are above the rule of the law. No court could ignore such a challenge. To do so would imperil all law and order'[50]. Commenting on the court warning, Mr Steer said, 'Let them come and arrest me. I am perfectly happy to be arrested and go to jail. We don't take orders from judges, we carry out resolutions from the men who have mandated us. We have always said we don't recognize the authority of this Court'[51]. But warrants for the arrest of the three men were stopped by an Appeal Court only after an application on their behalf by the Official Solicitor. However, Moran rightly notes that '. . . though this saved the day in this particular case it did nothing to alter the basic fact that the Appeal Court had forced the NIRC into a direct conflict with individual stewards. It simply delayed a clash until a new case appeared'[52].

Before the Appeal Court made its ruling at least 35 000 dockers in ports throughout Britain had stopped work in protest against the threatened arrests. Ports hit included London, Liverpool, Manchester, Preston and Southampton. A month later the issue was to flare up again, the whole process of NIRC procedure and subsequent applications to the Court of Appeal having served only to prolong and intensify the dispute. But Mr Heath, addressing the Society of Conservative Lawyers on 20 June 1972, argued that:

. . . it is the first duty of any Government to uphold the law . . . . It was a serious defect in our law that industrial relations in this country should have been left in a disorderly and unreformed condition for half a century and more . . . . That is why we placed the Industrial Relations

Act on the Statute Book . . . . What the courts have made plain – and this is not in dispute – is that the trade unions do have a responsibility for actions which are carried out with their authority, and which are unfair practices as the Act defines them. Just how far this responsibility goes in any particular case, in any particular action caused by any particular individual, is of course a matter that has to be decided by the courts. But here again the courts have made plain that it is unfortunate that some union members and shop stewards should not be represented when these matters are heard by them. The application of every law benefits from being argued in the courts, and new laws especially. What is important now is that the unions should play their part in this process[53].

But both the TUC and CBI realized that the application of the law to industrial relations was proving to be more controversial than conciliatory and on the day after Mr Heath's speech, agreement was reached between the Confederation of British Industry and the Trades Union Congress to draft proposals for a new independent, non-Government conciliation body as a matter of urgency. A statement afterwards said that after the talks on conciliation and arbitration in industrial disputes, they recognized the 'vital importance of voluntary collective bargaining as the effective basis for good industrial relations'[54]. Implicit in the statement was the desire of each side to avoid both Government conciliation, which unions regarded as discredited, and recourse to the Industrial Relations Act procedures. One former Minister conceded that the Government had discovered that 'you cannot legislate against a substantial section of the population'[55]. It was also the case that the Government was 'very surprised at the degree of opposition once the Act had become law'[56]. However, the Government 'had never formulated an answer beyond believing the unions would obey the law'[57]. The difficulties the Act would have to face had not been sufficiently thought through and the Government had no effective escape route from the legal complications that made the industrial, and hence political, situation more difficult. It is not difficult to surmise that because the operation of the Industrial Relations Act had been so unacceptable to all parties involved, the CBI and TUC had given greater priority than would usually have been expected to the idea of an independent conciliation body.

As expected, Mr Heath was publicly opposed to the suspension of the Industrial Relations Act although Ministers' public and private views on the Act had already begun to differ. However, not all trade unionists favoured the limited dialogue that had developed. Mick McGahey, President of the Scottish Mineworkers, said that 'there should be no joint committee with the Tories; the Industrial Relations Act must be withdrawn from the Statute Book, not just put "on ice". The only reason trade union leaders should go to 10 Downing Street is with an eviction order'[58]. A meeting on 18 July under the aegis of the National Economic Development Council (NEDC) was concerned more with a 'tabling of problems' than with negotiations as to their solution. But Mr Feather stated afterwards that although the TUC would continue to express the strongest criticism of the Industrial Relations Act, which had 'soured the atmosphere' between the unions and Government, its withdrawal was not a pre-condition of discussing anti-inflation measures, adding that 'Inflation affects our members just as much as the Industrial Relations Act'[59]. As one NEDC official put it, 'Having the Act on ice was good enough for Feather'[60].

However, that stage had not yet developed when five London dockers ordered to be jailed for contempt of the NIRC were arrested and taken to Pentonville prison. Sir John Donaldson, President of the Industrial Relations Court, ordered the arrest of the five men because they had refused to stop 'blacking' lorries that were crossing picket lines at the Midland Cold Storage container depot at Hackney. One trade union leader recalled that 'some of the lads were determined to get into prison – Dick Turner was so anxious to be arrested'[61].

Lorry drivers who had blockaded the London docks in retaliation for the dockers' picketing campaign ended their action immediately the arrests were known. Their leader, Erik Rechnitz, said that the situation had changed so that, 'We stand now with our fellow trade unionists to fight the Industrial Relations Act and the Court's decision. It is an unwarranted interference in the trade union movement'[62]. The Industrial Relations Court gave the Official Solicitor an hour to decide whether to appeal against the jail orders on behalf of the five dockers. But when the hour was up, counsel for the Official Solicitor said there was 'no point' in taking such a step. The imprisonment of the dockers immediately politicized the issue and confirmed the Government's worst fears. In the Commons the bitterness of the debate was typified by one Labour MP who shouted 'Heil Hitler' at Mr Heath[63]. Vic Feather, the TUC General Secretary, said that they had warned 18 months ago that this situation would arise and that Ministers had then pooh-poohed the warning as an exaggeration:

> The damage that the Industrial Relations Act is doing to industrial relations and to the nation is now clear to everybody. Putting people in prison in cases like this solves nothing. It makes already difficult problems much worse and much harder to resolve. The Act must be suspended[64].

Unlike many Opposition MPs, Labour's employment spokesman, Reg Prentice, was less than sympathetic to the jailed dockers who were often referred to as the 'Pentonville five':

> They were wrong to organize picketing and blacking against the policy of their union. They were even more wrong to defy the court. The Industrial Relations Act is a bad law, but it is the law – and nobody can claim to be above it. Trade Unionists should not rally round these men as though they are latter-day Tolpuddle Martyrs'[65].

Similarly, Mr Heath told the House that the five dockers were '. . . exploiting trade union solidarity for ends which have nothing to do with genuine trade union aims'[66]. The men were freed, amid a national dock strike and demonstrations at the prison, only when Sir John Donaldson said that the situation had been changed by a House of Lords ruling on another case implying that the T&GWU was thus responsible for the action of its shop stewards. The Law Lords, on 26 July, delivered a judgement upholding Donaldson's original decisions, and they held the Court of Appeal to be wrong in requiring express delegation of authority in a rule book before a union could be held responsible for the actions of its shop stewards. The Court's original view that something more was required of the T&GWU than advice and requests to its members to cease blacking was also supported. The dockers were consequently released, thereby breaking short their martyrdom, and the political crisis caused by their imprisonment was de-fused. The legal system appeared to have 'bent itself to the needs of the politicians'[67], with the principle of the rule of law jettisoned in favour of de-escalating the political situation.

## 2.4    Putting the Act 'on ice'

It was appropriate that in the midst of the dispute, and with the Government's enthusiasm for the Act considerably in decline, an agreement setting up a joint 'trouble-shooting' conciliation and arbitration service was signed by leaders of the TUC and the Confederation of British Industry. Vic Feather said that the unions saw the agreement 'as a means of bringing about settlements without anybody having recourse to the Industrial Relations Act'[68] and Campbell Adamson, Director General of the CBI, commented that 'We at the CBI have always made it clear that the Act should only be used as a last resort. If agreements and reasonable setlements can be reached without recourse to the Act then that suits us very well'[69]. But the emotive issues of the five jailed dockers, the House of Lords' re-imposition of £55000 fines for contempt of the Industrial Relations Court on Mr Jack Jones' transport union, and general bitterness about the Industrial Relations Act did not prevent a meeting between the Prime Minister, the CBI and TUC on 1 August.

Ultimately, as the talks concerning a voluntary incomes policy continued, the Act was 'put on ice', not only because the unions desired it as a pre-condition for more specific talks on the economy, but also because both sides of industry, and the Government, realized that, in its present form, it had proved to be unworkable. Cardinal Richelieu once said that to pass a law and not to carry it out is to authorize what you have prohibited. In the case of the Industrial Relations Act, there was insurmountable difficulty in carrying out the law and the end-result of prolonged industrial, and political, conflict was the opposite of the orderly framework for industrial relations that the Conservatives had hoped to create. Although one back bench Conservative MP declared during the 1972 miners' strike that 'unless the Government act within the framework of the Act to secure a settlement, I am afraid that the Act will be stigmatized as . . . expensive and irrelevant'[70], the Government's change of attitude, as one study of the Act notes, was based on wider political considerations. Thus, '. . . when Ministers began moving towards a formal incomes policy, if possible operating with the consent of management and labour, the Act became an embarrassment'[71]. Similarly, Anderson has claimed that the Government '. . . abandoned [the Act] as a concession to the TUC in order to get a co-operative incomes policy . . .'[72]. Whilst the 'putting on ice' of the Act was undoubtedly a concessionary move by the Government, it was by August 1972 not a reluctant move. The Act had hardly worked to the Government's political advantage – indeed the opposite was the case – nor had it tackled the underlying industrial relations problems of the British economy despite its comprehensive nature.

Another study has noted the irony of the Act's failure in view of the concerted opposition it aroused as 'class legislation', '. . . if the Act had been class legislation in the narrow sense of its being in tune with the interest of business it would nave stood a far better chance of success since one of the reasons for its eventual failure was the reluctance of employers to operate its provisions'[73]. This reluctance is testimony to the Act's failure, especially when the CBI's attitude had been 'originally very pro'[74] in 1970.

The Act's effective suspension stopped just one step short of a complete U-turn. In view of the other U-turns of the Heath administration this point is often overlooked. Although abandoned by the Government as a panacea for Britain's industrial relations troubles and also as a political weapon against trade union abuses, the Act remained on the statute book until its repeal by the Labour Government in 1974. In its last year and a half some of the cases that were trundled through the NIRC were bizarre, and even tragi-comic, if less politically controversial. Nevertheless, despite its 'suspension' the unions were clearly far from totally satisfied with any solution short of outright repeal, while boycotting the NIRC led to heavy fines. This was particularly the case with Hugh Scanlon's Amalgamated Union of Engineering Workers (AUEW), whose boycott of the NIRC over the Goad affair led to fines totalling £55 000 for contempt in December 1972[75]. The course of the Goad dispute was 'acutely embarrassing to the Government[76]. In October 1973 the AUEW again refused to pay a £100 000 fine for contempt of court and in April 1974, when a national engineering strike was threatened, a group of anonymous donors paid into the court the sum awarded to the employer in question. As Moran notes the '. . . spectacular case involving the AUEW served not to cause the Act's failure – that was already assured – but to remind the Government of the legislative millstone which hung round its neck'[77].

As well as the usual trade union calls for reform or abolition of the Act, other voices urging changes became louder. In March 1973 *The Times* advocated that 'reform . . . awaits an appropriate moment and mood . . . amendment will be better soon than late. It is bound to come eventually'[78]. Mr Heath, now seeking union co-operation over Stage II of the incomes policy, offered the unions a standing invitation to discuss possible reform of the Act. The annual report of the Commission on Industrial Relations was unenthusiastic about the first year of the Act's operation. Mr Leonard Neal, Chairman of the Commission, said that the new legislation 'could not escape scrutiny' and indicated that the Commission was aware of the possibility of amendments.

In May, following the CIR report, the Engineering Employers' Federation proposed changes in the Act and expressed doubts as to the wisdom of holding ballots or using a cooling-off period, both of which had failed in the railways dispute. Both ballots and cooling-off periods had, of course, been regarded with considerable enthusiasm in the late 1960s and at the time of the Act's introduction, as methods of de-escalating industrial disputes. The course of the railways dispute showed that faith in both had been considerably misplaced. The closed shop provisions were also viewed with suspicion, opinion being that employers generally preferred to suspend non-union men rather than seek recourse to law. The Institute of Personnel Management also told the Government that the Act should be altered to remove the emergency powers, the statutory right to opt out of trade union membership, the Registrar's power to amend union rules and the presumption that wage agreements were legally enforceable. The CBI was also realistic about the Act's failure. As Moran notes:

> In the Autumn of 1973 an internal CBI working party on the legislation recommended substantial changes and during the February 1974 election campaign Campbell Adamson, Director General of the Confederation, remarked that the Act had sullied industrial relations and should be repealed[79].

Following the election of a Labour Government repeal[80] was a matter of months away.

Why, then, was the Industrial Relations Act an unmitigated failure? How did its good intentions of modernizing industrial relations in accordance with the 'Quiet Revolution' philosophy, and in accordance with Mr Heath's personal desire to modernize British industry within a European context, result in unnecessary industrial strife and political embarrassment[81]? Why was it that the Act '. . . was more trouble than it was worth [and] even the Government made little use of it'[82]?

The answer lies partly in the total opposition to the Act by the trade unions and partly in the practical failure of the NIRC to impose order in place of chaos in industrial relations. The failure of the cooling-off period and the compulsory ballot to de-escalate the railwaymen's dispute struck at the heart of the thinking behind the Act, and the 'Pentonville five' saga proved to be a political embarrassment[83] the Government could have done without. The Act was repeatedly shown to have become a legal muddle, a 'dog's breakfast of complications'[84] remote and irrelevant to the real problems of industry and its workforce. Sir Harold Wilson has written that the '. . . most arid of lawyers drafted the Act . . . which reflected all the finer points of obsessive legalism'[85]. However, opposition to the Act was still effective within the limits of the law. The non-registration tactic was perfectly legal within the Act's requirements. Thus, as Moran has noted, 'since registration was voluntary, opposition to it was consistent with the claim that the unions were not challenging the legal authority of either courts or governments'[86]. One Minister commented that the Act 'became too legalistic – much more than Robert Carr had hoped'[87]. Another Minister recalled that 'at the first weekend conference with the Department of Employment officials we went through the legal aspects and there were large chunks I didn't understand'[88].

Apart from the over-reliance on legal reform, the Act was too often presented as a panacea, on occasions within the context of wider economic policies, rather than as a starting point for a gradual change in industrial attitudes. In this sense the Act was far too comprehensive, 'attempting too much, too quickly'[89], thus giving it the inflated aura of a panacea that the Labour Party and the unions could tactically exploit. Too much thinking behind the Act was an over-reaction to the failure of 'In Place of Strife', and an over-reaction to strike statistics as an index of bad industrial relations. One study of the Act concludes that '. . . outside the area of discipline and dismissal the Act had little effect on industrial relations in highly organized companies and work places'[90]. It is open to question whether legislation in the field of industrial relations can lead to better industrial relations *per se*. There may be a more convincing case that specific legislation can remove a specific abuse of industrial power. Mr Heath's Government did not choose this latter option, though not through any desire to 'confront' organized labour. The simple and undeniable fact remains that the Industrial Relations Act, by attempting to do everything at once, from removing abuses to establishing a legal framework for solving disputes, actually made worse the problems it was intended to solve, or at least prevent. However, in defence of the Act it might be noted that it '. . . destroyed the sacred cow of industrial relations, although legislation would have been preferable ten years earlier'[91]. Even when the Act was 'put on ice' and Mr Heath was ready to consider amendments, the TUC preferred to play for time mindful of Labour's promise of total repeal. Finally, although the Act was part of the total 'Quiet Revolution' package it was contrary to the disengagement spirit of the 'Quiet Revolution'. The Act brought more government into industrial relations when the express notion of the 'Quiet Revolution', 'Selsdon', policies was to eliminate unnecessary state interference. Moran has argued that the Act reflected the '. . . wider resurgence of liberalism, especially market liberalism, in the [Conservative] Party'[92]. In the sense that the Act sought to weaken the unions' power, based on their monopoly position as suppliers of labour, as well as making provisions for the individual to seek redress against unfair trade union practices, this may indeed be true. But in general terms Moran's argument is unconvincing. The problem of the industrial relations structure recognized in the 1960s firstly by Donovan and secondly by the Labour Government's *'In Place of Strife'* proposals, were not problems easily amenable to the Left–Right or Liberal–Collectivist labelling. If Moran is right in regarding the Act as representing economic liberalism then surely *'In Place of Strife'* would have reflected a move to economic liberalism in the Labour Party. The analogy clearly falls down. Both the Labour Government, 1964–1970, and Mr Heath's Government essentially came to the view that only by legislative reform could the underlying weaknesses of Britain's industrial relations structure, which had been exploited to an intolerable degree by trade union militancy, be adequately reformed[93]. That the Labour Government was committed to industrial interventionism at the time of *'In Place of Strife'* and Mr Heath's Government committed to the 'Quiet Revolution' policies of disengagement at the time of the introduction of the Act shows that the party consensus on industrial relations reform, resulting from the abuses of trade union power, existed away from the party dispute on the, broadly, collectivist–non-interventionist axis. In this sense, because the Industrial Relations Act involved a large measure of state intervention in industrial relations practices, it was contrary to the economic liberalism of the 'Quiet Revolution', which Moran claims as the inspiring force behind the Act. In the sense that it criminalized too much the Act was contrary to what Conservatives saw as the true liberating philosophy of the 'Quiet Revolution'. The Industrial Relations Act was thus an example of the State interference that the Heath Government had set out to restrain. Indeed it can be argued further that the Act was another case of state interference that failed to the point of being counter-productive. As a result of the Act's failure in political terms and subsequent abandonment by the Heath Government as a political weapon, the trade unions were able to postpone the reforms that had been envisaged in the 1960s and to extend their power in a way that would have been unlikely had the Act not reached the statute book. It could thus be claimed that:

> The sense of confidence created in the trade union movement by the defeat of the Industrial Relations Act . . . means that unions are now more determined than ever to take a central part in the industrial life of the nation. One symptom of this is the rapid extension of trade union membership in general – which the Act facilitated – and of the closed shop in particular[94].

Ironically, as the interventionism of the Industrial Relations Act was being 'put on ice' and its political importance dropped, the Government was then reversing the economic liberalism of the 'Quiet Revolution' approach to industry. To this more direct policy U-turn we now turn.

### References

1. It is not the purpose of this account to give a detailed blow-by-blow description of the legal aspects of the Industrial Relations Act. Instead, the Act is assessed within the framework of the Heath Government's policy priorities and their subsequent abandonment.
2. Cmnd 3888, 'In Place of Strife', HMSO, 1969.
3. Interview, Michael Moran.
4. Interview, Professor Hugh Clegg. The tremendous increase in the incidence of unofficial strikes indicated that trade union militancy had mushroomed in the 1960s to have an economically and socially harmful effect. This process is described, particularly at the shop floor level, by PAUL FERRIS in The New Militants: Crisis in the Trade Unions, Penguin Books, 1972.
5. A policy document of that name was presented by Mr Carr to the 1968 Conservative Party Conference. Ten years previously a Conservative lawyers' document, A Giant's Strength, argued that trade union power was already excessive.
6. Conservative Party Manifesto, 1970.
7. See J. E. ALT, The Politics of Economic Decline: Economic Management and Political Behaviour in Britain since 1964, Cambridge University Press, 1979, pp. 260–2 for a statistical breakdown of the trend of public opinion towards strikes in the 1960s, which shows clear evidence that, especially among more affluent Labour voters, there developed a lack of sympathy to strike action.
8. Granada Television transcript of a programme on the Industrial Relations Act, broadcast 26 May 1976.
9. Interview, Cabinet Minister.
10. M. MORAN, The Politics of Industrial Relations, Macmillan, 1977, p. 48.
11. Interview, Professor Hugh Clegg.
12. Interview, Lord Scanlon.
13. The public as a whole shared the Government's sentiments. A Gallup Poll in September 1970 showed 69% in favour of a cooling-off period and only 9% against. Gallup International Public Opinion Polls (GB), 1937–75, p. 1106.
14. This solution to the problem of union militancy was very similar to that advanced by Mrs Barbara Castle's 'In Place of Strife' proposals.
15. Sunday Telegraph, 14 May 1972.

16. A Gallup Poll in September 1970 found that 71% were in favour of Government intervention to prevent harmful strikes with only 13% opposed, op. cit. (Ref. 13), p. 1106.
17. *The Times*, 12 August 1970.
18. R. HARRIS and B. SEWILL, *British Economic Policy 1970–74: Two Views*, IEA Hobart Paperback No. 7, 1975, p. 33.
19. Interview, Sir Denis Barnes.
20. Granada Television transcript, op. cit. (Ref. 8). This refusal to negotiate by the trade unions was symptomatic of the extensive nature of trade union militancy in this period.
21. Granada Television transcript, op. cit. (Ref. 8).
22. Interview, Junior Minister.
23. *Industrial Relations and the Limits of Law: Effects of the Industrial Relations Act 1971*, Warwick Study on Industrial Relations, Blackwell, 1975. (Ed. by Brian Weekes, Michael Mellish, Linda Dickens and John Lloyd), p. 9.
24. *The Times*, 25 September 1970.
25. A Gallup Poll in October 1970 found that 42% approved of the Government's proposals and only 22% were opposed, op. cit. (Ref. 13), pp. 1111–12.
26. *Hansard*, 26 November 1970, Vol. 807, Cols. 603–4.
27. The Government had a comfortable majority of 44 to give the Bill a Second Reading.
28. *The Times*, 4 December 1970.
29. *The Times*, 13 January 1971.
30. *The Times*, 6 October 1971. It is worth noting that Jack Jones, as one of the newer generation of militant union leaders, had been as opposed to '*In Place of Strife*' as he was to the Industrial Relations Act. In *The Castle Diaries, 1974–76*, Weidenfeld and Nicolson, 1980, (p. 283), Barbara Castle recalls that her officials at the Department of Employment and Productivity had regarded Jack Jones '. . . as the archetypal trade union villain and who had in fact been arid and negative then'.
31. *The Times*, 8 September 1971.
32. For Employers' Associations the question of registration caused no ideological or tactical problems.
33. L. C. HUNTER and D. J. ROBERTSON, *Economics of Wages and Labour*, Macmillan, 1969, p. 40.
34. Warwick Study on Industrial Relations, op. cit. (Ref. 23), p. 224.
35. *The Times*, 28 October 1971.
36. M. MORAN, op. cit. (Ref. 10), p. 122.
37. R. HARRIS and B. SEWILL, op. cit. (Ref. 18), pp. 33–34.
38. HUGH CLEGG, *Trade Unions Under Collective Bargaining*, Blackwell, 1976, p. 112.
39. *The Times*, 2 April 1972.
40. J. A. G. GRIFFITH, *The Politics of the Judiciary*, Fontana, 1977, p. 45.
41. See P. FERRIS, *The New Militants: Crisis in the Trade Unions*, Penguin Books, 1972, Ch. 7 for the background to the dispute in terms of inter-union militancy.
42. *The Times*, 14 April 1972.
43. *The Times*, 27 May 1972.
44. *The Times*, 29 April 1972.
45. COLIN CROUCH, *Class Conflict and the Industrial Relations Crisis*, Heinemann Educational Books, 1977.
46. Interview, Cabinet Minister.
47. Interview, Lord Greene.
48. The public, despite the difficulties the Act had faced, remained convinced of the Act's relevance. A Gallup Poll in June 1972 found that 42% approved of the Act, 22% disapproved and 36% were undecided, op. cit. (Ref. 13), p. 1187.
49. AUBREY JONES, *The New Inflation: The Politics of Prices and Incomes*, Penguin Books, 1973, p. 141.
50. *Daily Telegraph*, 15 June 1972.
51. Ibid.
52. M. MORAN, op. cit. (Ref. 10), p. 141.
53. *The Times*, 21 June 1972.
54. *The Times*, 22 June 1972.
55. Interview, Junior Minister.
56. Interview, Senior Civil Servant.

57. Interview, Michael Moran.
58. *The Times*, 6 July 1972.
59. *The Times*, 19 July 1972.
60. Interview, D. K. Stout.
61. Interview, Trade Union Leader.
62. *The Times*, 22 July 1972.
63. *Hansard*, 25 July 1972, Vol. 741, Col. 1563.
64. *The Times*, 22 July 1972.
65. Ibid.
66. *Hansard*, 25 July 1972, Vol. 841, Col. 1560.
67. J. A. G. GRIFFITH, op. cit. (Ref. 40), p. 73.
68. *The Times*, 3 August 1972.
69. *The Times*, 3 August 1972.
70. *Hansard*, 18 January 1972, Vol. 829, Col. 289.
71. Warwick Study on Industrial Relations, op. cit. (Ref. 23), p. 218.
72. MALCOLM ANDERSON in *The Political Economy of Inflation*, (Ed. by F. Hirsch and J. H. Goldthorpe), Martin Robertson, 1978, p. 258.
73. M. MORAN, op. cit. (Ref. 10), p. 61.
74. Interview, Senior CBI Official.
75. James Goad, a quality control inspector at the Car Components factory at Sudbury, Suffolk, had initiated proceedings under the Act against the AUEW to prevent him from being refused admission to union meetings. This bizarre case led not only to the fines on the AUEW but also to a series of strikes against the Act.
76. Interview, David Knox.
77. M. MORAN, op. cit. (Ref. 10), p. 61.
78. *The Times*, 30 March 1973.
79. M. MORAN, op. cit. (Ref. 10), p. 146.
80. Significantly, the Government did not use the Act during the dispute with the miners that precipitated the February 1974 General Election.
81. The number of working days lost, according to the *Department of Employment Gazette* rose from 6 846 000 in 1969 to 23 904 000 in 1972.
82. COLIN CROUCH, op. cit. (Ref. 45), p. 181.
83. A Senior Civil Servant told me that the Government 'went to great lengths to get the dockers sprung from jail'. Interview, Lord Armstrong.
84. Interview, Cabinet Minister.
85. SIR HAROLD WILSON, *Final Term: The Labour Government 1974–76*, Weidenfeld & Nicolson and Michael Joseph, 1979, p. 3.
86. M. MORAN, op. cit. (Ref. 10), p. 128.
87. Interview, Cabinet Minister.
88. Interview, Junior Minister.
89. Interview, Senior Civil Servant.
90. Warwick Study on Industrial Relations, op. cit. (Ref. 23), p. 184.
91. Interview, Cabinet Minister.
92. M. MORAN, op. cit. (Ref. 10), p. 62.
93. For the problems of trade union militancy that faced the Labour Government, 1964–1970, see E. WIGHAM, *Strikes and the Government, 1893–1974*, Macmillan, 1976, Ch. 8.
94. M. MORAN, op. cit. (Ref. 10), p. 147.

Chapter 3

# The U-Turn over industry policy

*'Finally once a decision is made, once a policy is established, the Prime Minister and his colleagues should have the courage to stick to it. Nothing has done Britain more harm than the endless backing and filling which we have seen in recent years . . . . Courage and intellectual honesty are essential qualities in politics, and in the interest of our country it is high time that we saw them again.*

*So it will not be enough for a Conservative Government to make a fresh start with new policies. We must create a new way of running our national affairs. This means sweeping away the trivialities and the gimmicks which now dominate the political scene. It means dealing honestly and openly with the House of Commons, with the press and with the public.'*

Edward Heath in the foreword to the
1970 Conservative Party Manifesto

## 3.1 Disengagement

One of the tenets of Conservative philosophy on returning to power in 1970 was that less government interference with market forces would help to restore competition and profitability to British industry after the years of inefficient socialist planning and indiscriminately wasteful subsidies. The 1970 manifesto stated that:

> Competitive free enterprise ensures choice for the consumer. Profitable free enterprise provides the resources for both capital investment and higher wages. We will pursue a vigorous competition policy. We will check any abuse of dominant power or monopoly, strengthening and reforming the machinery which exists.
>
> We reject the detailed intervention of Socialism which usurps the functions of management and seeks to dictate prices and earnings in industry. We much prefer a system of general pressures, creating an economic climate which favours, and rewards, enterprise and efficiency. Our aim is to identify and remove obstacles that prevent effective competition and restrict initiative.
>
> We are totally opposed to further nationalization of British industry. We will repeal the so-called Industrial Expansion Act which gives the Government power to use taxpayers' money to buy its way into private industry. Specific projects approved by Parliament will continue to be given Government support. We will drastically modify the Industrial Reorganization Corporation Act[1].

Similarly, as Terence Higgins, the Minister of State at the Treasury, told the Commons, 'We fully recognize the need for the Government to intervene in the overall management of the economy. The crucial thing is that we should set a framework within which private enterprise can operate and contribute to the growth of the economy'[2].

Although the strategy of disengagement from intervention marked a radical departure from the politics of the Wilson administration, it would be incorrect to describe the 'Quiet Revolution' policy as '*laissez-faire*' in the nineteenth century liberal definition of the term. The Government was committed to the mixed economy and the Welfare State as much as any Government since 1945 and the measures taken to curb the public sector were distinctly modest. The issue was more a matter of degree than the Government's critics imagined. Questions as to the role of the individual in relation to the State, the extent of governmental regulation of the economy and the importance of free enterprise initiative have always played a central part in the debates in the Conservative Party. Although there is a paternalist social tradition in Conservative philosophy, the individualist tradition has played a more inspirational role in the twentieth century, particularly since the Labour Party replaced the Liberal Party as the Conservatives' main electoral rival. It was only to be expected that the socialist ideals of Labour would rekindle the individualist beliefs of Conservatives who feared the encroachment of the powers of the state, couched in the phraseology of 'equality' and 'social engineering'. The rediscovery of individualism within Conservative philosophy was more a reaction to the political effects of socialism than to any ideological re-awakening. In the sense that the 1970 'Quiet Revolution' was committed to the mixed economy, the individualist approach was thus non-ideological. The emphasis on individualism no more implied a retreat from the mixed economy 'consensus' than did Mr Wilson's interventionism in the other direction. But in the opinion of one Conservative back bench MP, 'Heath's non-interventionism was reluctant'[3]. In effect the Government had embarked on a policy for the mixed economy that would enable it to function better, based on the creation of the greater wealth on which the giants of the Welfare State rely. Industrial disengagement thus represented to Conservative thinking a more realistic approach than had been previously forthcoming. Not surprisingly, 'some senior CBI members – but very few – resented the 'Selsdon' period but most rejoiced at the early period of disengagement'[4]. The world of business generally welcomed the return of the Conservatives with the considerable enthusiasm of self-interest, believing that Conservative policy was to be profoundly different from Labour's.

But although the 'Selsdon' or 'Quiet Revolution' approach to industry did not last long its advocates have pointed to considerable achievements. The Industrial Reorganization Corporation and the Prices and Incomes Board were abolished and having promised not to bolster up or bale out lame ducks, John Davies, the Secretary of State for Industry, preferred not to inject public money into the Mersey Docks and Harbour Board, which went into liquidation at the end of November 1970. The Government had made it clear that public money was not to be used to rescue companies from the consequences of their own errors. Similarly, tax concessions were regarded as more beneficial to industry than direct grants and selective regional asistance, and Mr Barber, in his October 1970 package, started to put this theory into practice. The control of public expenditure was vital to tax reductions, as well as to the control of inflation, and was, indeed, central to the industrial disengagement strategy. As Mr Davies told the

Commons debate on the abolition of the Industrial Reorganization Corporation, 'We put a great deal of emphasis on the need to contain the
ever-increasing scale of public expenditure'[5]. Thus, a heavily subsidized
regional policy was regarded as being wasteful and inefficient. Geoffrey
Rippon told the Commons debate on Regional Planning that '. . . regional
problems cannot be solved simply by increasing expenditure . . . nothing
could be further from the truth'[6] and Nicholas Ridley, a Junior Industry
Minister, stated that 'The Government prefer to leave the restructuring of
industry to market forces'[7]. Interventionist institutions inherited from
Labour were early targets for the 'Quiet Revolution' policy and the
abolition was announced of the Consumer Council, Investment Grants, the
Betterment Levy and the Levy Commission; the sale of council houses to
sitting tenants was encouraged, controls on local authority rents were
lifted, museum charges were introduced and, as already mentioned, in
October 1970 free school milk for children was discontinued.

Denationalization plans were modest and hardly the doctrinaire return
to nineteenth century *laissez-faire* that the Labour opposition made out.
Gamble has noted that the Government made no moves to end the state
funding of major technological projects in aerospace and heavy engineering, like Concorde '. . . nor did it try to sell off or break up those industries
already publicly owned apart from hiving-off profitable subsidiaries which
made little difference to the monopoly status of these industries or the
constraint they placed on Government policy in the fields of pay and
finance'[8]. The travel firm Thomas Cook was denationalized from British
Rail and in July 1971 the Licensing (Abolition of State Management) Act
was passed denationalizing the 200 state-owned public houses in Carlisle
and Scotland.

Denationalization itself, however, had not featured prominently in the
Government's policy priorities within the context of its industrial strategy
largely because the accepted framework of the mixed economy was based
on the public ownership of such specific industries as the railways, gas,
electricity supply and coal, and partly because the revitalization of private
industry was clearly a more urgent task.

Ironically, the Government's first controversial decision with regard to
the nationalized sector was not in pushing denationalization too hard but in
the refusal to raise nationalized industry prices to levels nearer the market
price. The origin of this policy was the fear that such price rises would
prove to be inflationary and would contradict the statements during the
1970 election campaign that the Government would act to keep down
nationalized industry prices. This argument was used by Mr Heath on
many occasions when questioned by Labour MPs about the continued rise
in prices[9]. Some Conservative back-benchers also considered that restructuring public sector prices was *per se* urgent for the Government '. . . to
take a firm and decisive stand on the question of public sector prices before
confidence in the new administration is disastrously undermined'[10]. Iain
Macleod, speaking in the Commons for the last time, had stated on 7 July
1970 that the Government regarded '. . . a searching investigation of
proposed price increases in the public sector as an essential complement to
the thorough examination of Government expenditure in which we are
engaged'[11]. Thus a 5% increase in postal charges was approved only after it

was discovered that the Post Office had already printed the stamps, and the Coal Board and the British Steel Corporation were induced to limit the price increases they preferred. Similarly the CEGB restricted its price rise to 12% in the Spring of 1971 following governmental pressure. However, it may be argued that the false economy of artificially rigging nationalized industry prices not only made the financial situation of the nationalized industries worse but also stored up the inevitable increases for politically more hazardous times, particularly during the talks on a voluntary incomes policy in 1972. Thus the nationalized industry financial targets that had been introduced in 1961 were abandoned and Government subsidies duly rose from £176m in 1971 to a massive £1308m in 1974. Such subsidization was more inflationary than the original price rises would have been and in terms of electoral popularity the strategy was of dubious value. The Government would have been better advised, as one Minister suggested, to raise prices in July 1970 immediately after taking office[12].

## 3.2   Rolls-Royce

However, the first major step away from the 'Quiet Revolution' policy of disengagement concerned Rolls-Royce. The problem stemmed from the contract concluded in 1968 between Rolls-Royce and the Lockheed Aircraft Corporation for the supply of Rolls-Royce RB-211 engines for the Lockheed airbus. At the time the contract had been regarded as a major breakthrough especially by the then Minister of Technology, Anthony Wedgwood Benn. But the fixed price contract of £150m took no account of technical delays, rising inflation and labour costs. By February 1970 Mr Wedgwood Benn supplied a £20m loan to Rolls-Royce, a cosmetic gesture of interventionism that merely postponed the final reckoning. However, by November 1970 the Conservative Aviation Minister, Fred Corfield, felt obliged to announce a further £42m of state aid that postponed the bankruptcy of Rolls-Royce for only 3 months until February 1971. The Government, however, was not prepared to put its faith in the proclaimed policy of refusing to rescue bankrupt companies and those parts of the firm considered to be essential for defence purposes were promptly nationalized. Furthermore, following protracted negotiations the British taxpayer was left with the bill for the completion of a revised RB-211 contract.

In the Commons Mr Corfield explained the Government's decision to raucous derision from the Labour benches:

> . . . the Government has decided to acquire such assets of the aero-engine and marine and industrial gas turbine engine divisions of the company as may be essential . . . . The necessary legislation will be introduced early next week . . . . The Department of Employment will provide the maximum help in finding alternative employment in all the areas affected. Interviewing teams will be sent to the factories and redundancy payments to employees are guaranteed under the redundancy fund arrangements[13].

Not surprisingly, Enoch Powell, a long-time champion of free enterprise, criticized the decision and on 8 February 1971 abstained in the division lobby, having argued that the Government had 'cast doubt and discredit in the belief in capitalism and free enterprise for which this Party stands'[14]. Mr Heath used the occasion to tell Young Conservatives at Eastbourne that the lesson to be learned from the Rolls-Royce collapse was '. . . that for too long much of our apparent prosperity has been based on illusions'. The collapse had been a 'bitter shock' he continued[15]. Similarly, Mr Heath told the Commons that 'I did not expect when we came to power to find the tragic condition which we did find in Rolls-Royce'[16]. However, one Conservative Minister recalled that:

> I knew Rolls-Royce were in a poor condition and customers were getting worried. There was gross overmanning especially in Scotland and management was so inefficient as it was an engineering dominated board. I told Heath this in January 1970 but I got no reaction[17].

The rescue of Rolls-Royce was never justified on economic grounds either at the time or by supporters of the rescue since. Certainly, there was the question of seriously damaging Anglo-American relations and the possibility of political repercussions from President Nixon. More important was the defence argument that was apposite only to the extent that the Conservative Government's defence commitment was acceptable. It was argued that the RAF and an enormous number of air forces and civil airlines depended on Rolls-Royce engines so that 'it was the only thing we could do in the circumstances'[18]. According to the Defence Secretary, Lord Carrington, 'The Armed Forces would not have survived the bankruptcy of Rolls-Royce'[19] and another Minister has argued that 'The Government didn't intervene early enough – the rescue was defensible on defence grounds'[20]. The issue of British prestige was also present at the time, with hindsight an understandable and misguided reaction. One Cabinet Minister felt that:

> No Cabinet would just have allowed Rolls-Royce to collapse. We felt in our guts that we could not allow that. The awful thing was that we just didn't know Rolls-Royce was in such a critical position[21].

The prestige argument for rescuing Rolls-Royce was widespread through Whitehall. One Minister recalled that:

> The Foreign Office had a lot to say. Alec Home was worried about the loss of prestige. I sat on the Cabinet committee while the decision was being made. We just couldn't imagine Rolls-Royce going – the name had prestige, like the BBC[22].

However, allowing for such factors as prestige, defence requirements and political repercussions, the irony remained that a Government committed to free enterprise and to prevent the waste of taxpayers' money by unnecessary intervention in private industry, had nationalized parts of a private company in contradiction to its stated policy. However, the rescue of Rolls-Royce was the first step away from the Government's industrial policy and was to prove not to be the exception to the rule.

## 3.3   The Upper Clyde Shipbuilders' crisis

This was soon to be demonstrated by the crisis centred upon Upper Clyde Shipbuilders. The Clydeside shipyards, according to many Conservatives, has a sorry history of wasteful intervention. The UCS consortium was put together from four Upper Clyde yards in February 1968 with a £5.5 m loan from the Shipbuilding Industry Board and further supplies of public funds had been made available to prevent a politically embarrassing collapse. Then, in only the week following the Rolls-Royce rescue, Mr Davies announced on 11 February 1971, a £4.5 m loan to Yarrow Shipbuilders of the Upper Clyde. Mr Davies argued that the Yarrow Consortium was breaking away from Upper Clyde Shipbuilders, with the new Yarrow Consortium having a 51% holding in the Yard. For this reason the loan was not against Government policy. The fact that the Navy might have to go elsewhere for its warships if the loan was not forthcoming also carried political weight with the Government. But as Norton comments:

> These actions, though, may be viewed as having been partly offset by the Government's promised repeal of the 1968 Industrial Expansion Act as well as other measures designed to reduce Government interference in industry and the economy[23].

A further embarrassment for the Government's policy was the leaking of a document (actually drawn up in December 1969 while the Conservatives were still in Opposition) suggesting a 'butchery' of UCS by liquidation and the sale of the Government holdings in the Yards. The author of the document was by now the Junior Minister responsible for shipbuilding at the Department of Trade and Industry, Mr Nicholas Ridley, whose political future in the Department – and indeed in the Heath administration – was thus marked for an early demise. It was not surprising, therefore, that Opposition cries of 'butchery' greeted the Government's decision in June 1971 that the £28 m debts of UCS necessitated an end to state aid. Mr Davies faced the difficult task of informing the House that 'The Government has decided that nobody's interest would be served by making the injection of funds into the company as it now stands'[24], thus causing a major polarization between the parties. Speaking in a censure debate on 15 June, Mr Davies explained that '. . . the whole effort of the Government will now be directed solely to trying to secure from this unhappy circumstance the best possible result'[25].

On 16 June as 400 UCS workers marched through London chanting 'Heath out', the Prime Minister refused to give their leaders an undertaking that all the jobs in the bankrupt shipyard would be saved. Amid the bitterness of the UCS controversy Mr Heath celebrated the anniversary of his election victory on 18 June 1971. In an interview on BBC radio he presented an optimistic front when questioned on a whole range of topics including UCS, which he described as 'heartbreaking', adding that 'We have to be realistic about it. You cannot create a healthy and prosperous economy just by going on pouring money into firms which can't make ends meet'[26].

As the Government was negotiating the restructuring rather than the closure of the Clyde yards, 20000 people marched in protest through

Glasgow, and 80000 others stopped work. Much of informed opinion was behind the Government, as it had been over Rolls-Royce.

Eventually, when Mr Davies, by now a particular ogre among Opposition MPs, announced that two of the three Upper Clyde shipyards were to be closed and sold, and 1400 of the 8500 labour force immediately made redundant, workers began occupying the shipyards. Jimmy Reid, the shop stewards' leader (and at the time a Communist Party member), proclaimed the formation of a group of UCS workers to run the three yards in the bankrupt group, deciding that:

> Nothing and nobody will come in or go out of the yards without our permission. The world is witnessing a new tactic on behalf of the workers . . . . We are not going on strike – not even a sit-in strike. We are taking over the yards because we refuse to accept that faceless men can make these decisions[27].

In the Commons on 2 August the Government's decision not to come to the rescue of UCS in its present form, described by Mr Benn as a 'major human tragedy', was upheld by a majority of 33 amid scenes of tumult[28]. At the end of July 1971 Lord Robens reported, as requested by the Government, on the position of UCS and strongly supported the decision not to provide further state aid. Nor was Mr Heath, yet, prepared to reverse his policy. In a letter to Labour MP Richard Buchanan he wrote that:

> I do not seek to minimize the consequences of any increase in unemployment in West Central Scotland at a time when the rate of unemployment there is already much too high.
>     But it would not contribute to a lasting solution of these problems for the Government to pour public money into shoring up a concern which has no prospect of viability.

As some middle and senior management joined the 'work-in', Mr Davies visited Glasgow with Scottish Secretary Gordon Campbell and met the eight shop stewards for a five-hour meeting that ended in acrimony, Jimmy Reid declaring that 'Mr Davies is here on an exercise in public relations, just to waffle, and we are not having any of it'[29]. Mr Davies decided that he would not be visiting the occupied yards. The industrial angle to the dispute was clearly passing out of the Government's control. One Industry Minister noted that one of the major problems 'was the weakness and lack of authority of the Scottish trade unions which were weak and badly led. The Communist shop stewards (led by Mr Reid) could run rings round them. We had no authoritative voice on the unions' side to organize a national debate. The "work-in" highlighted the nature of the dispute'[30]. Taylor has also noted the role played by Communist shop stewards in organizing the 'work-in'[31]. Taylor observes that 'Communists claim – with some justice – that it was their members who forced the Heath Government drastically to reverse its lame-duck policy . . . .'[32], which, while a clear exaggeration with the benefit of hindsight, did not always seem so at the time. The 'work-in' thus proved to be politically, if not economically, effective and although Mr Reid and his men were not alone in forcing the Government to reverse its UCS policy their efforts certainly contributed to the weakening of the Government's political will. Not surprisingly, their efforts were regarded by some on the Left as an heroic defence of the working class. Thompson and Hart proclaimed that 'UCS will doubtless take its place along with such events as the Tolpuddle Martyrs and the great dock strikes of 1889 among the classic episodes of labour history in Britain'[33].

Two other factors are most important in analysing why in February 1972, only nine months after announcing the liquidation of UCS, Mr Davies was injecting a further £35m of state aid. Firstly, the Chief Constable of Glasgow feared for civil order if the yards were allowed to close and requested 5000 extra men to guarantee law and order. That number of men was just not available. Although one back bench Conservative MP has argued that 'McNee's [The Chief Constable] warning was crucial . . . he wasn't a man given to making hysterical statements'[34], the crisis atmosphere surrounding the UCS controversy led the Cabinet to overestimate the threat to civil peace. Fears of an outbreak of violence on the scale of Northern Ireland suddenly seemed to be a reality and McNee's disaster scenario no doubt aroused considerable and genuine, if misplaced, anguish. Thus a Junior Industry Minister recalled that 'I can confirm there was a panic over the Chief Constable's report. This was politically engendered rather than soundly based'[35]. One Cabinet Minister summed up the mood somewhat differently:

> Of all the places where death was in the air it was Glasgow. It was the worst area to allow the death of a lame duck. Then came the report from the Chief Constable of Glasgow[36].

But if the Chief Constable's warning had greater effect on the Government than the actual UCS 'work-in', the rising unemployment figures had greater effect than all other influences put together. One Minister noted that 'we were worried the closure would mean 12 000 men unemployed on the next Monday morning. It would have been inhuman'[37]. The Secretary of State for Scotland, Gordon Campbell, told the Commons that '. . . it is an additional misfortune that this liquidation should have happened at a time when unemployment rates are so high in the Glasgow area'[38]. Indeed it was the issue of unemployment, typified by the UCS troubles, that was emerging as what the Government regarded as its most politically sensitive problem. McGill comments that 'the Government realized the seriousness of the collapse in view of the already high unemployment on the Clyde'[39]. Following from the commitment to reduce unemployment explicit in Mr Barber's July 1971 mini-budget, it was evident that saving UCS suited the Government's change of policy.

## 3.4   The political pressure of rising unemployment

The issue of rising unemployment dealt the killer blow to the 'Quiet Revolution' policy of disengagement from industry. It was the most important single factor in the rescue of UCS although only a marginal factor in the rescue of Rolls-Royce. One Cabinet Minister has noted that 'UCS was very different from Rolls-Royce. With hindsight the UCS rescue was the wrong decision'[40]. Another Minister 'opposed the UCS rescue in Cabinet – but we would have had resignations if we hadn't done it'[41]. The extent of the difference between Rolls-Royce and Upper Clyde Shipbuilders lay in the political sensitivity of the unemployment issue at the time. One Senior Cabinet Minister recalled that 'unemployment was the vital issue in the UCS rescue'[42]. Similarly, another Minister who was critical of the over-reaction to rising unemployment, recalled that:

> Heath thought that unemployment in the 1970s was the same as in the 1930s. But colleagues from high unemployment areas like the North East or Northern Ireland didn't get the impression of fear from their constituents that existed in the 30s. There was no Welfare State in the 30s. The situation had changed[43].

Thus, in announcing the £35m of aid in February 1972, only a month after the gross unemployment total topped 1 million, Mr Davies emphasized that 4300 jobs would be saved at the Govan, Scotstoun and Linthouse yards, a consideration that had not prevailed when liquidation had been regarded as UCS's fate, and when in June 1971 Mr Heath had warned that prosperity could not be created by pouring public money into loss-making private firms. Rising unemployment, the major factor in the UCS rescue, had in scarcely eight months broken the Government's political will. The 'Quiet Revolution' policy of industrial disengagement – irrespective of its industrial merits or demerits – was thus officially abandoned. As Mr Davies told the Commons debate on the unemployment situation, the UCS rescue meant that:

> . . . employment should be provided for some 4300 in the Govan complex and this might well rise if, as is expected, the capacity of the yards is increased and the order book in due course expanded. To these would be added whatever proportion of Clydebank's present 2500 can be brought in to one or other of the American projects. The total compares with 8500 previously employed by UCS at the time of liquidation. It contrasts, too, with a possible loss of jobs in total, both in the yards and with suppliers, of the order of 15000 or more which would have been the case if UCS had been allowed to totter on to its almost inevitable and final dissolution[44].

A more sceptical view was forthcoming from the *Economist*, which less enthusiastically stated that '. . . if the Government is going to spend £35m on modernizing any industry one of the worst possible economic choices is shipbuilding, whose future probably lies in low wage countries and certainly does not lie so many miles up the Clyde'[45]. Such practical economic effects, however, had now been overtaken by the political considerations of reducing unemployment from what the Government misguidedly perceived to be a politically intolerable level.

However, the reason why the Government reacted to rising unemployment as it did deserves further explanation in the context of the return to direct interventionism[46]. At the outset it must be stated that the rising trend of unemployment had been inherited from the Wilson Government partly as a result of the deflationary policies of Roy Jenkins, the Chancellor of the Exchequer. It was thus ironic that Mr Wilson should make political capital out of the unemployment figures by referring to Mr Heath's Government '. . . whose most notable achievement is the creation of the highest unemployment since the Thirties'[47]. Whatever the faults of Mr Heath's Government in relation to rising unemployment, the deliberate 'creation' of unemployment was not among them. Similarly, it could be argued that the Rolls-Royce and UCS problems had their origins in the mistakes of the Wilson administration. However, the unemployment figures proceeded steadily upwards during the first year and a half of the Heath administration, rising from 600000 when the Conservatives took office to over one million in January 1972, without seasonal adjustments and including school leavers and adult students. Although the seasonally adjusted 'economic' figures are the most reliable, the gross total is the 'politically' important total and the breaching of the one million mark in 1972 was regarded as a politically intolerable level[48]. Given the Government's total commitment to reduce the unemployment level the rescue of UCS in February 1972 was predictable. In short, the Government seriously panicked as the unemployment figures continued to rise, especially as earlier measures had proved to be inadequate, or in effect, less immediately adequate.

Although Britain's post-war Keynesian orthodoxy had seemingly maintained 'full employment' levels the upward trend towards the one million mark evoked fears of a return to the mass unemployment and social hardship of the 1930s, fears that Mr Heath and his Ministers regarded as justified. Evidence with hindsight shows such fears to have been greatly exaggerated, but evidence at the time was much less optimistic. According to one close adviser, Mr Heath was 'emotionally concerned with unemployment – he was constantly talking about the wasteland of . . . unemployment'[49], while a Senior Treasury Official noted that 'during 1971 the Government became increasingly worried about unemployment, especially in Scotland'[50], the very place where the UCS crisis dragged on. To another Senior Civil Servant Mr Heath's worry about unemployment soon became an 'excessive concern'[51], so that the ever-increasing figures led to the conclusion that 'the only experience to go on was pre-war'[52].

It can be argued that although the gross unemployment figure in January 1972 of over one million was a politically sensitive statistic, considerable doubt has been expressed as to whether it was an economically accurate statistic. John Wood has pointed out that the 'crude' total, as he puts it, covers a multitude of different types of unemployment, which is a misleading guide to the Government in devising economic policy[53]. It is significant that even Mr Wood's critics, for example Kevin Hawkins[54], present their arguments within the detailed frame of reference that Mr Wood emphasizes, and which was conspicuously lacking among policy makers in 1971/72. Certainly, the emotive response from the Opposition when the one million mark was passed was testimony to the fear that 'mass' unemployment was returning.

Indeed, the very word 'unemployment' conjured up visions of starving workers marching from Jarrow to seek economic and social justice. It is true that the unemployment of the 1930s was a social blight, bringing unnecessary misery to thousands of people. It is also true that unemployment 40 years hence presented a degree of social hardship that is incomparable to the 1930s. This is chiefly because the general standard of living (including that of the unemployed) is vastly higher than in the 1930s. During the 'Thirties' unemployment was punitive, physically hard, and sometimes humiliating.

Such conditions had disappeared by the 1970s. In 1971 alone, over £500m was paid out in benefits to the unemployed – a figure higher than the total paid out during the whole of the 1950s – and individual payments of benefit enabled a reasonable standard of living to be maintained. In fact, as long as PAYE is calculated on accumulative and not on current receipts, then a surprisingly large number of people are actually better off financially when unemployed and, even when tax refunds are not payable, the various benefits available provide an income not far short of the normal wage for many people.

Because of this, unemployment is not the destroyer of human dignity and self-respect that it once was, and during periods when there is competition for work many men choose unemployment rather than a job, in cases where little or no monetary gain would be forthcoming by returning to work. Furthermore, the greater number of vacancies and more extensive range of available jobs that existed in the 1970s was in marked contrast to the 1930s.

The one million total, therefore, was considerably misleading. On the one hand the figures underestimated the unemployment total by failing to quantify those seeking work while not actually registered as unemployed. But the major failure of the figures was in over-exaggerating the total by failing to distinguish between those changing jobs in the short term and the long-term unemployed; between those genuinely seeking work and those who could be classified as unemployable for a variety of reasons; between the students and young people temporarily registered; between men and women; between those of vastly different skills; and between those genuinely seeking work and those 'moonlighting'. In short, the one million figure was neither a political nor an economically reliable statistic. The evidence suggested, when viewed more closely, that as the economic nature of unemployment in the 1970s was radically changed from that of the 1930s, so the political connotations were far less pronounced.

However, while this may seem clear with hindsight it was not so clear in the political climate of both the early 1970s and the post-war 'consensus' period as a whole. Thus the Government's reaction was in many ways a Pavlovian one of taking whatever measure Keynesian orthodoxy suggested to remedy a problem – and this is the key point – with which the Conservatives did not want to be associated. Given that post-war levels of unemployment had been low and given the novelty of the one million milestone the Government's panic can be seen to be far from irrational. Mr Heath and his generation of Conservatives had always strove to bury the 1930s accusation that the Conservative Party was the party of unemployment, a factor that had led to Labour's landslide success in 1945. Indeed, this factor was central to the Government's reaction in strictly political terms, as was the factor of trade union militancy on an even more intense scale, should the Government be seen to be condoning the rising unemployment total. Public opinion poll findings also lent weight to Conservative fears that reducing unemployment ought to be a priority over reducing inflation. In March 1972 a Gallup poll found that 28% as opposed to 25% regarded unemployment as the more urgent problem than inflation[55].

Nevertheless, the reaction of the Government, and in particular the Prime Minister, was a political panic that involved the complete reversal of the 'Quiet Revolution' industrial strategy of disengagement. It is widely believed that one particular visit of Mr Heath's to the Midlands acted as a catalyst in the process. One Minister recalled that:

> The day we switched to intervention in industry was when Ted Heath did a tour of the Midlands. He came back immensely depressed at the unemployment. He had thought the Midlands would take on Europe and was more depressed than he ought to have been – he couldn't spot a run-down factory if he saw one[56].

Similarly, a Treasury adviser confirmed that '. . . what shocked Heath was his famous visit, which included the Midlands – a supposedly prosperous area'[57]. Even if Rolls-Royce, because of the defence arguments, could be classified as an exception the Upper Clyde rescue could not and the way was then open for the completion of the U-turn by the adoption of directly interventionist policies accompanied by massive increases in Government spending.

## 3.5    The Industry Act and the return to interventionism

To this purpose and following the March 1972 budget when new proposals for regional aid had been announced, Mr Davies stipulated, in a White Paper, 'Industrial and Regional Development'[58], the establishment of an Industrial Development Executive, to promote industrial expansion and stimulate centres of growth.

The Executive was made unanswerable to Ministers, but with a Minister of Industrial Development, under the direction of Mr Davies, empowered to advance money to industrial firms. The scarcely-concealed origins of the package lay in the unemployment figures, which to the Government's dismay showed no signs of a spring decline, levelling off at just over one million, with the publication of the March total. Funding of the proposals required legislation and in May 1972 Mr Davies introduced the Industry Act. It was a 'combination of Ted Heath's worry about unemployment and changing the face of British industry to be able to compete within the EEC'[59].

For Mr Davies, who personally seemed to take more than his fair share of the Government's collective embarrassment over the U-turns, the Industry Act was not intended to prop up inefficient management or work forces. He stressed that it was certainly no part of government, 'in normal circumstances to intervene in the ebb and flow process, save only where quite exceptional circumstances demand some temporary action to allay the harshest social impact of failure'[60].

But the Industry Act was proposing a massive leap in the direction of state intervention[61] because the Government had found the 'normal circumstances' that Mr Davies referred to as politically embarrassing.

Supporters of the Industry Act tended to argue that the 'Industrial Reorganization Corporation (IRC) should never have been abolished'[62], and that 'the first two years were the worst part of the Heath Government'[63], assessments that were anathema to a large section of the Conservative Party. Some Conservative back-benchers found the Government's U-turn unacceptable and a betrayal of the 1970 Election Manifesto. One back-bencher commented that 'We are on the slippery slope once we start providing individual industries with inflation subsidies'[64].

Certainly the all-embracing interventionist nature of the Industry Act was in sharp contrast to the principles of the 'Quiet Revolution' philosophy. One critic argued that:

> The worst fault of the Industry Act is that special assistance is to be provided on no known principles, but simply according to the discretion of Ministers and officials. This misinterprets the role of Government intervention: it ought not to be to usurp entrepreneurial functions, but rather to adjust the structure of rewards and penalties so that it pays businessmen to act in a socially desirable way'[65].

Similarly, the Industry Act enshrined post-war regional policy '. . . based almost exclusively on the principle of bringing work to the workers'[66]. Apart from the obvious criticism that such a policy must prove to be wasteful, the effect was to further discourage labour mobility, or inadequacy, which is an established underlying weakness of Britain's industrial structure.

The Industry Act certainly split the Conservative Party on the familiar lines of Left and Right or Paternalists and Individualists. One former Junior Minister has rightly described it as the 'most interventionist piece of legislation passed by Parliament up to that time'[67]. It represented a considerable move to the Left away from the 'middle way' Conservatism of the post-1945 era. No post-war Conservative Government, however deeply committed to the consensus of Keynesian measures to keep down unemployment, had resorted to such undisguised direct interventionism. The passing of the Industry Act would have been a radical measure for the Labour Party let alone a Conservative Party that had come to power vowing to reverse the trend of state regulation. However, considering that Mr Heath had judged the 'Quiet Revolution' policies to have failed to revive Britain's industrial fortunes, the Industry Act, and the policy of state intervention, was the rational alternative given that reducing unemployment had become the Government's political priority. However, it was not surprising, therefore, that the leftwards direction of policy which the Industry Act represented confused many Conservative supporters. To some it was the 'start of the great schism in the Party'[68], to be justified or condemned on ideological grounds. Thus one Minister commented that 'The Industry Act was right on principle. I've never been a Manchester School Liberal'[69]. To a senior CBI official 'UCS in itself was not that important – the Industry Act was the shock'[70]. While one critic of the industry U-turn observed that 'Heath was caught on an intellectual tide, Selsdon man was the victim not the villain'[71]; a less charitable critic described Mr Heath as having 'little understanding of the mechanism of private industry'[72], and as being 'economically illiterate'[73]. Mr Heath's critics from the Left, not affected by the state of confusion among many Conservatives, could simply exploit the political embarrassment and inconsistency that the U-turn represented. Andrew Roth commented that Mr Heath '. . . even began donning, slightly dyed, the industrial aid garments of the hated Harold Wilson'[74].

The strategy of the U-turn on industrial policy, although embarrassing for the Government, had been carried through the Conservative Party with no little skill and represents a dress-rehearsal, in a more specific way than was the abandonment of the Industrial Relations Act, for the major political U-turn of the Heath administration, the introduction of a statutory prices and incomes policy. But arguments that the U-turns were reversals of the means, rather than the ends, by which the Government was able to lose face in return for the, albeit temporary, settling of 'practical' difficulties, are far from convincing. The nationalization of Rolls-Royce, the ultimate rescue of UCS and the introduction of an interventionist Industry Act were prime examples, not of pragmatic policy reversals, but of the failure of Government's *political* will. There were other examples, too, of the Government's new approach. The Consumer Council, scrapped in the 1970 'Quiet Revolution' phase, was revived under the aegis of the Office of Fair Trading and a Consumer Protection Advisory Committee was established. The run down of the coal industry was put into reverse with a £175m per annum subsidy in December 1972 and the writing-off of the National Coal Board's £475m deficit. Derek Ezra, the NCB Chairman, commented that the Government's change of policy 'would lift the clouds of uncertainty that for many years have overshadowed the industry'[75]. As well as the State aid to the coal industry, Peter Walker, the Secretary of State for Trade and Industry, also announced a massive modernization and expansion programme in the British steel industry involving the investment of £3000 million over a decade. In January 1973, Christopher Chataway, the Minister for Industrial Development, announced that the Government intended to spend £6.5m on new factory building in a move to ease regional job loss.

Two months later Mr Chataway announced that £5m of taxpayers' money was being used to relaunch the British motor cycle industry, a decision leading to the further intervention in that industry that has been critically chronicled by Jock Bruce-Gardyne[76]. In June 1973 it was further announced that, to encourage the movement of service industries to assisted areas, help under the Industry Act was to be made available in two ways. First, a grant to the employer of £800 for each employee moved with his work, up to a limit of 50% of the number of additional jobs created in the assisted area. Second, a grant would be paid towards the rent of premises for up to 3 years in the intermediate areas and 5 years in the development and special areas. As a result of such measures and in the context of the reflationary 'dash for growth' programme, unemployment had fallen to below 600000 in May 1973, a lower level than that which the Government had inherited from Labour. However, as opponents of the U-turn on industry policy point out, the Government ultimately left office with state expenditure – and inflation – at unprecedented levels. Nor, as many critics have argued, has the policy of massive government intervention in industry proved to be successful on either a short-term or a long-term basis. A Report by the House of Commons Expenditure Committee on the effectiveness of regional policy noted that 'Regional Policy has been empiricism gone mad, a game of hit and miss, played with more enthusiasm than success'[77]. Ironically, the dispute with the miners that ended with the Conservatives' demise occurred in an industry that the Government had generously subsidized.

In just short of two years the Government had come to reverse its 'Quiet Revolution' policy, replacing it with a policy almost completely its opposite. The Conservative Government's hopes of 1970 – that the waste and inefficiency of government interference in industry, with the consequent wastage of taxpayers' money, had come to an end – were to have proved illusory. Furthermore, according to the Conservative Right the retreat to blanket interventionism led to the worsening of one of Britain's most chronic structural problems – the lack of adequate labour mobility resulting from large council house subsidies and the fossilization of certain industries through wasteful subsidies. The crucial issue in this reversal was the Government's over-reaction to the rising level of unemployment without which the UCS rescue and the Industry Act would have been avoided, which is a judgement made easier with hindsight.

It is not surprising that Mr Heath, who personally directed the U-turn, brought relations between the Conservative Party and its natural ally, industry, to a low point. One Cabinet Minister commented that whenever Heath met industrialists 'he could not resist attacking them for their failure to invest'[78]. Other senior advisers noted that the Prime Minister 'often complained about industry's failure to invest'[79]; 'was over-affected by the poor performance of industry'[80], and 'was often rude to the CBI – he thought they talked rubbish'[81]. A close policy adviser recalled that 'I've been to a number of dinners between Heath and industrialists and Heath always abused them – he never got on with them'[82] and a strong back bench critic observed that 'Heath was fond of saying that no-one more than he had told the CBI and industry to invest – but they wouldn't invest despite what he kept telling them'[83].

One observer argued that Mr Heath's antipathy to business led to an intensification of the Government's interventionist policies as if no other course of action was practicable:

Mr Heath took it hard that the massive reductions in taxation rates had not produced an upturn in orders for plant and machinery. There was a growing feeling that the boardrooms were letting the Government down. It was argued that if the City was going to abdicate from what was seen to be its responsibility to spur on the manufacturers to place their orders when there was plenty of spare capacity to fulfil them, then the Government had no choice but to step in and do it instead[84].

According to one CBI official, 'In 1972/73 Heath became very anti-industry. He moved his love from industry to the City. At Chequers, Jim Slater was held out to us industrialists as the kind of man who does what you industrialists can't do'[85]. But Mr Heath's admiration for the City was only temporary.

Ironically, in May 1973 as the Central Statistical Office published figures showing the strength of the industrial boom, with exports soaring to a record £954m to record the first trade surplus since October 1972, and with a slight indication of a slowdown in the inflation rate, Mr Heath chose to attack the international trading group Lonrho as the 'unpleasant and unacceptable face of capitalism'[86], adding that his comments on Lonrho did not apply to the rest of British industry. Mr Heath returned to the same theme at the Conservative Women's Annual Conference on 23 May by stating that condoning the abuses of capitalism was not part of Conservative philosophy. But one critical Conservative has since noted that 'It was symbolic that the only memorable phrase that Heath coined was "the unacceptable face of capitalism" – gratuitously kicking into his own goal'[87].

The Government's industrial policy and Mr Heath's personal approach to industry thus varied during the period 1970–1974. Mr Heath's lack of sympathy for industry based on a belief that industry was not performing adequately was certainly a contributory factor in the U-turn and in the leftward move of policy direction. But the main reason for the abandonment of the 'Quiet Revolution' policy of reversing the trend of state intervention lay in the political over-reaction, albeit understandable in the historical context of the modern Conservative Party, to the rising unemployment figures. That single factor led the Government to sacrifice the industrial policy on which it had been elected more than the individual industrial rescues of Rolls-Royce and Upper Clyde Shipbuilders. Mr Heath personally led those who regarded rising unemployment as politically unacceptable and who considered unemployment in the 1970s as similar to the 'mass' unemployment of the 1930s, with similar political and electoral connotations, views that are easier to dismiss with the benefit of hindsight than they were at the time[88]. When Mr Heath's mind was made up that unemployment had to be reduced at all costs the 'Quiet Revolution' policy of disengagement from industry was over and the subsequent U-turn offers a perfect example of Mr Heath's total control over policy making in Whitehall, and his total control over the Conservative Party, by virtue of his Prime Ministerial power.

## References

1. Conservative Party Manifesto, 1970.
2. *Hansard*, 7 July 1970, Vol. 803, Col. 623.
3. Interview, Conservative MP.
4. Interview, Senior CBI Official.
5. *Hansard*, 26 January 1971, Vol. 810, Col. 350.
6. *Hansard*, 9 July 1970, Vol. 803, Col. 884.
7. *Hansard*, 30 October 1970, Vol. 805, Col. 6311.
8. ANDREW GAMBLE in *Conservative Party Politics* (Ed. by Z. Layton-Henry), Macmillan, 1980, p. 39.
9. E.g., *Hansard*, 19 November 1970, Vol. 806, Col. 1424.
10. *Daily Telegraph*, 11 August 1970.
11. *Hansard*, 7 July 1970, Vol. 803, Col. 511.
12. Interview, Cabinet Minister who recommended the price increase.
13. *Hansard*, 4 February 1971, Vol. 810, Cols. 1922–23.
14. *Hansard*, 8 February 1971, Vol. 811, Cols. 80–83.

15. *The Times*, 8 February 1971.
16. *Hansard*, 11 March 1971, Vol. 813, Col. 587.
17. Interview, Junior Minister.
18. Interview, Junior Minister.
19. Interview, Lord Carrington.
20. Interview, Cabinet Minister.
21. Interview, Cabinet Minister.
22. Interview, Junior Minister.
23. PHILIP NORTON, *Conservative Dissidents: Dissent within the Parliamentary Conservative Party 1970–74*, Macmillan, 1978, p. 90.
24. *Hansard*, 15 June 1971, Vol. 819, Col. 233.
25. *Hansard*, 15 June 1971, Vol. 819, Col. 241.
26. *Daily Telegraph*, 19 June 1971.
27. *The Times*, 31 August 1971.
28. *Hansard*, 2 August 1971, Vol. 822, Col. 1084.
29. *The Times*, 4 August 1971.
30. Interview, Junior Minister.
31. See also P. FERRIS, *The New Militants: Crisis in the Trade Unions*, Penguin Books, 1972, p. 777 on the extent of Communist participation.
32. ROBERT TAYLOR, *The Fifth Estate: Britain's Unions in the Modern World*, Pan Books, 1980, p. 123.
33. WILLIE THOMPSON and FINLAY HART, *The UCS Work-in*, Lawrence and Wishart, 1972, pp. 94–95.
34. Interview, David Knox.
35. Interview, Junior Minister.
36. Interview, Cabinet Minister.
37. Interview, Junior Minister.
38. *Hansard*, 2 August 1971, Vol. 822, Col. 1140.
39. J. McGILL, *Crisis on the Clyde*, Davis Poynter, 1973, p. 87.
40. Interview, Cabinet Minister.
41. Interview, Cabinet Minister.
42. Interview, Cabinet Minister.
43. Interview, Junior Minister.
44. *Hansard*, 28 February 1972, Vol. 832, Cols. 52–53.
45. The *Economist*, 4 April 1972.
46. A more detailed analysis is to be found in the next chapter.
47. *The Times*, 26 September 1971.
48. The seasonally adjusted figure was below one million.
49. Interview, Senior Civil Servant.
50. Interview, Senior Treasury Official.
51. Interview, Senior Civil Servant.
52. Interview, Senior Trade Union Leader.
53. JOHN B. WOOD, *How Little Unemployment*, IEA Hobart Paperback No. 65, 1975.
54. KEVIN HAWKINS, *Unemployment*, Penguin Books, 1979, pp. 25–27.
55. *Gallup International Public Opinion Polls (GB), 1937–75*, p. 1171. Alt, however, has argued, by analysing opinion poll data over a number of years, that '. . . a preference for reduced unemployment as a policy goal [is] altruistic; that is, as reflecting a preference for alleviating someone else's suffering. This interpretation arose because the number of people who preferred reduced unemployment [to reduced inflation] was far greater than the proportions who were worried about becoming unemployed or who had never had any experience of unemployment. This altruistic preference could also be called *generous* [emphasis in original]; it is held by those who feel they can best afford it, whether through ignorance of or insulation from the inflationary costs of such a preference . . . . The central argument [is] that preferring reduced unemployment is a generous altruistic policy choice and is far less likely to occur when the costs of such a choice are higher and when they are clearly perceived', J. E. ALT, *The Politics of Economic Decline*, Cambridge University Press, 1979, pp. 195–99.
56. Interview, Junior Minister. This comment was typical of many in that Mr Heath saw Britain's economic problems within the wider European economic unit of the EEC.
57. Interview, Treasury Adviser.

58. Cmnd 4942, *Industrial and Regional Development*, HMSO, 1972.
59. Interview, Cabinet Minister.
60. *Hansard*, 22 May 1972, Vol. 837, Cols. 1009–10.
61. Mr Heath was forced to reshuffle the DTI Ministers to carry the U-turn to its logical conclusion. In April 1972 Messrs Ridley and Corfield were dismissed to the back benches and Sir John Eden was moved to Posts and Telecommunications. Christopher Chataway was appointed to take charge of the new industrial development machinery. Tom Boardman, a back-bencher with wide managerial experience, was brought in to take over from Sir John Eden. In November 1972 Peter Walker was appointed Secretary of State for Trade and Industry.
62. Interview, Cabinet Minister.
63. Interview, David Knox.
64. *Hansard*, 22 May 1972, Vol. 837, Col. 1090.
65. S. BRITTAN, *The Economic Consequences of Democracy*, Temple Smith, 1977, pp. 147–48.
66. P. J. CURWEN and A. H. FOWLER, *Economic Policy*, Macmillan, 1976, p. 169.
67. LORD GOWRIE in *The Conservative Opportunity* (Ed. by Lord Blake and John Patten), Macmillan, 1976, p. 141.
68. Interview, Cabinet Minister.
69. Interview, Cabinet Minister.
70. Interview, Senior CBI Official.
71. Interview, John B. Wood.
72. Interview, Conservative MP.
73. Ibid.
74. A. ROTH, *Heath and the Heathmen*, Routledge and Kegan Paul, 1972, p. xv.
75. *The Times*, 2 December 1972.
76. JOCK BRUCE-GARDYNE, *Meriden: Odyssey of a Lame Duck*, Centre for Policy Studies, 1978.
77. Second Report from the Expenditure Committee, Session 1973–74, on Regional Development Incentives, HMSO, 1974.
78. Interview, Cabinet Minister.
79. Interview, Senior Civil Servant.
80. Interview, Senior Policy Adviser.
81. Interview, Lord Armstrong.
82. Interview, Senior Policy Adviser.
83. Interview, Conservative MP.
84. J. BRUCE-GARDYNE, op. cit. (Ref. 76), p. 80.
85. Interview, Senior CBI Official.
86. *Hansard*, 15 May 1973, Vol. 856, Col. 1243.
87. LUCILLE IREMONGER, *British Prime Ministers of the 20th Century* (Ed. by John P. Mackintosh), Weidenfeld & Nicolson, 1978.
88. It may be possible to draw a parallel between Mr Heath's reaction to unemployment in 1972 and Sir Anthony Eden's reaction to Colonel Nasser's policies in 1956. In both cases the British Prime Minister ascribed the conditions, and lessons, of the 1930s to situations that were superficially similar but in fact essentially different.

Chapter 4

# The 'N minus 1' experiment and the reaction to rising unemployment

*'The fact is that restraint in incomes is our only guarantee against unemployment
. . . . We must get the level of settlements down further, if we are to put an end to the
spiral of rising prices and get back as quickly as possible to higher levels of
employment. This should be one of the nation's top priorities in the coming year.'*

Anthony Barber, 9 November 1971
*Hansard*, Vol. 825, Col. 856

## 4.1   The background to 'N minus 1'

The issue of inflation, or 'rising prices' to the majority of the electorate,
played a crucial part in the Conservatives' electoral victory in June 1970. It
seemed to have caught the mood of voters, especially women, in a way that
it had not previously done and the Conservative Party Manifesto had
stated that controlling inflation was to be the first priority for a Conservative Government. As Douglas Hurd put it, 'We knew that rising prices,
and in particular food prices, were the main issue which worried the
electorate in 1970. Repeated research proved this beyond reasonable
doubt'[1]. In the Queen's speech in July 1970 inflation control was, not
surprisingly therefore, reiterated as the policy priority[2].

Although it can be plausibly argued that both the 1970 Manifesto and the
Queen's speech were not necessarily the most accurate guides to actual
policy priorities[3], the emphasis on curbing inflation *per se* was new to
British politics in policy terms. The whole post-war Keynesian orthodoxy
had been aimed at preventing the unemployment levels of the 30s from
reappearing and a moderate rate of inflation had been regarded as
acceptable, indeed inevitable, for full employment to be realized. The
Conservative Governments 1951–64, particularly under Harold
Macmillan's Premiership, had regarded the maintenance of 'full
employment' as their main policy objective and, with public expenditure
largely under control, the problems associated with 'creeping' inflation
were considered to be of lesser importance. Apart from the overall
consensus on unemployment, the balance of payments problem had been
an alternative source of policy initiatives and the Wilson administration
1964–70 had indeed treated both inflation and unemployment as functions
of the desire to get the balance of payments 'right'. Labour's 1970
Manifesto and Mr Wilson's election campaign strategy are testimony to
this. In broader historical terms it would be fair to say that inflation control
had not featured as a major economic problem since the Tudor inflation,
fuelled by the influx of gold and other precious materials from the
Americas to England, of the sixteenth century.

It is ironic, however, that, given the extent of the Conservatives' policy planning in Opposition, no specific anti-inflation programme had been worked out. The approach to inflation was not a long-term approach, as was the reform of industrial relations law, but a series of *ad hoc* statements, made during the 1970 Election campaign, about the problem of 'rising prices'. The identification of 'rising prices' as synonymous with inflation is a crude and vulgar simplification but a tempting one for any Opposition politician to make during an election campaign. During the 1970 campaign Mr Heath and other Conservatives often referred to 'rising prices' as this was the electorate's own definition of the problem. One such statement was soon to cause Mr Heath considerable political embarrassment. In the Commons on 3 November 1970, Mr Wilson brought up the question of Mr Heath's use of the phrase to reduce prices 'at a stroke' during the 1970 election campaign. Mr Heath replied that 'I never used the words "at a stroke"'[4]. Mr Heath protested, rightly, that the phrase had originated in a press release at his press conference on 16 June, issued on his authority as Party Leader. But politically the damage was done. 'At a stroke' became the favourite phrase of Labour MPs, in a similar way that 'pound in your pocket' had been Conservative MP's rallying cry in the previous Parliament.

But the 'at a stroke' controversy, though politically embarrassing, was not an issue of policy towards inflation. Actual policy consisted of abolishing Labour's Prices and Incomes Board, as promised in the manifesto. The philosophy of compulsory wage control was also rejected in keeping with the 'Quiet Revolution' policies of reducing government intervention. However, one critic has argued that 'Heath only knew what was wrong with prices and incomes policy because Wilson had come unstuck with one'[5], rather than because of any deeply held philosophical opposition to State determination of wages and prices. At first glance such criticism seems harsh when judged by the standards of the 1970 Election Manifesto. But in fact the Heath Government, immediately it took office, regarded inflation as a problem caused almost exclusively by wage settlements that were too high and sought to curb wage increases in order to curb inflation, a view that cannot be squared with a free-market or monetarist approach, which regards the government's control over the money supply as the crucial factor in reducing inflation. However, it must be stated that the free-market or monetarist approach was, with the exception of a few academic economists, largely unknown to either the politicians or the electorate[6]. Monetarist doctrine itself had not yet been comprehensively formulated in the early 1970s and consequently monetarist remedies had not yet come into political usage. As well as the politicians the Treasury, not surprisingly after 25 years of Keynesian consensus orthodoxy, took the same line. Harris has observed with reference to the Heath Government's inflation policies, that:

. . . Treasury orthodoxy does not appear to have given high priority to the money supply as an influence on the rate of inflation. Furthermore, if the budget deficit were to be financed by government borrowing rather than by monetary expansion there would follow a rise in rates of interest which were being deliberately held down in the hope of stimulating investment and economic growth[7].

Thus in the autumn of 1970 the 'N minus 1' policy emerged. Its aim was to de-escalate pay settlements, if necessary by standing firm and risking industrial action. This policy was based on the cost-push theory of inflation that gave prominence to institutional factors, such as trade unions, in the initiation of inflation and played down the role of public expenditure and the money supply. In the context of intensifying trade union militancy in the 1960s and early 1970s this approach was widely accepted, especially in the absence, as already mentioned, of a theoretical monetarist critique. In the words of Brendon Sewill, Tony Barber's Chief Adviser at the Treasury:

> In the autumn of 1970 we in the Treasury had to cobble together a makeshift policy. This emerged as the 'N minus 1' policy, so nicknamed since the rough rule of thumb was that each pay settlement should be slightly less than the one before[8].

The 'N minus 1' policy thus sought to influence pay claims in the same way that a prices and incomes policy would, that is by dealing with each wage claim in percentage terms, not in absolute terms, with the hope of reducing the percentage increase irrespective of other factors, for example, specific labour markets. The 'N minus 1' policy thus regarded individual prices and incomes as the key to inflation control and as such was closer to the Wilson prices and incomes policy than the economic liberalism of the 'Quiet Revolution'. Whether this represents a U-turn or not is difficult to surmise. Certainly the 'N minus 1' policy was indirectly interventionist and not intellectually far removed from the direct interventionism that was to reappear in November 1972.

However, at its outset 'N minus 1' was not a statutory policy and it was operating with the background of disengagement associated with the 'Quiet Revolution'. Indeed, statutory intervention was expressly ruled out. Sir Alec Douglas Home told his constituents that:

> A number of people tell us that the only answer is to go back to Labour's wage and price controls. But it is precisely these controls that ended in the explosion of wage and price increases that started a year ago. Controls attack the symptoms of inflation, not the cause[9].

The absence of statutory controls did not mean that the Government was standing back from wage negotiations. 'N minus 1' was a policy of partial intervention concluded in the language of freedom from controls. To Mr Heath the question was one of reconciling responsibilities to the requirements of a free society:

> . . . people must face up to their own responsibilities, recognizing what the change of course is and how they can benefit from it. When I say 'people' I mean all of us. The Government has certain responsibilities to change policies, as we are doing. The employers have responsibilities. So do trade union leaders and trade unionists. Local councils have responsibilities to their ratepayers. The alternative to accepting responsibilities is for the Government to compel people. What I am trying to do, what this Government is trying to do, is to solve the country's problems in a free society[10].

In the public sector, therefore, where the Government held the ultimate responsibility, the 'N minus 1' policy had to work and to be seen to work. Thus Mr Carr's meeting with nationalized industry chairmen, to whom the importance of the 'national interest' in dealing with pay claims was stressed, received wide publicity. In the private sector the Government hoped that its lead would be followed as settlements were gradually reduced and the Department of Employment was reluctant to allow its conciliation process to be used if the claim was considered to be inflationary.

However, following an outcome to the dustmen's strike in November 1970 that the Government reluctantly decided to validate, the first major test of 'N minus 1' occurred before 1970 was out, when the power station workers began to 'work to rule' in support of their pay claim of 25%, a dispute that typified the militancy of trade unions in terms of inconveniencing the public – and hence other trade unionists – in the pursuit of a pay claim. On 7 December one-fifth of England and Wales was blacked out as the 5–7 p.m. peak began to get under way and the following day there were no national newspapers. The dispute dragged on with the electricians' leader, Frank Chapple, rejecting Mr Carr's appeal to go to arbitration, and Sir John Eden, the Minister for Industry, accused the power workers of endangering lives: 'Nothing, absolutely nothing, can justify the widespread disruption which this has caused and I cannot believe that the men themselves intended to carry this so far as to endanger human life'[11]. As the novelty of a semi-candlelit society wore off, the dispute became increasingly bitter and by the time a State of Emergency was declared on 12 December a war of attrition between Government and power workers was not an impossibility. With shop display lights and Christmas illuminations banned and with some curbs on non-vital industry, the strength of public opinion finally forced the four unions involved, on 14 December, to call off their work-to-rule in return for the reference of the problem to a Court of Enquiry headed by Lord Wilberforce. Even so the Wilberforce Enquiry's award 'was considerably higher than the Government had hoped'[12]. Brendon Sewill has noted that:

> The first challenge to this policy came in December with the go-slow by electricity power workers. The Chancellor made a forthright speech in which he suggested that the Government had a responsibility to show that industrial blackmail does not succeed. This somewhat perturbed the more cautious colleagues but nevertheless caught the public mood. Within a few days the go-slow was called off but the final Wilberforce settlement conceded more than was necessary[13].

The Government was much happier with the next test of 'N minus 1'. At the end of January 1971 the Post Office workers went on strike for a 15% increase in pay or a minimum all-round increase of £3, a claim that was in keeping with the general trend of trade union militancy although out of keeping with the traditional image of postmen and their union. The postal workers' leader Mr Tom Jackson said that his members hoped for a 'short, sharp, strike'[14], but with the Government prepared to stand firm the dispute was to prove to be lengthy. The Opposition Employment spokesman Mrs Barbara Castle argued, as the strike entered its second month, that the Government had 'deliberately chosen this union and this strike to make an example of, because they thought the union was weak, and they have done so with a completely irresponsible disregard for the consequences in this industry'[15]. Such criticism missed the point of the 'N minus 1' policy, which was not to treat union claims on their merit but to attempt a de-escalation whether the union was strong or weak. The Postal Workers' Union proved to be weak and after seven weeks returned to work, having accepted a face-saving formula. The strike had cost the Post Office more than £24m in lost revenue and the postmen more than £26m in lost earnings.

But in terms of 'N minus 1' the Government had recorded a success and indeed the trend in pay settlements was lower than in 1970. For example, during 1971 the nurses and ancillary workers in the Health Service negotiated 8–9% increases, which were below their previous settlement. Ministerial optimism was considerable not only in terms of specific cases but because 'N minus 1' was aimed at the overall reduction in inflationary expectations. James Prior, the Minister for Agriculture, told the Commons debate on food prices that 'We shall get price increases down by reducing labour costs. This is why the Government have taken action wherever possible to bring down the overall level of wage settlements . . . there are encouraging signs that the upward trend in pay settlements has been checked'[16]. Similarly, Robert Carr, expressing the Government's mood of optimism, repeated the determination not to introduce a statutory incomes policy:

> There is concrete and encouraging evidence that the rising tide of the general level of settlements in both public and private sectors has been checked and is beginning to recede. The Government will intensify and press home its incomes policy. But we will not once again lead the country up the blind alley of a statutory incomes policy of the kind practised by the Labour Government[17].

The Chancellor, Mr Barber, had also spoken out on the inadvisability of introducing any statutory policy, arguing that:

> We do not believe that a freeze on prices and pay is the answer. Sooner or later the dam would burst again. Nor do we believe the answer lies in the detailed statutory control of pay settlements, with all the vast administrative paraphernalia which would be necessary. It would be crude, unworkable and unfair[18].

One Cabinet Minister has argued that 'N minus 1' was 'quite a successful policy. It was always alleged that the private sector led the public sector but in fact the private sector led a de-escalation of settlements'[19]. In April 1971, Mr Heath was able to refer to 'success in the public sector' when outlining his policy of resisting inflationary wage demands, a success that should not be underestimated given the degree of union militancy over wages that had built up since the middle of the 1960s. His comments on the private sector's role in a 'free society' are particularly revealing:

> In a free society the Government cannot dictate to the private sector of industry but it can, and should, point out to them the consequences of the decisions taken in that sector. These consequences are plain enough

for everyone to see. Inflationary wage settlements have two effects. They give an upward twist to prices: they create a further threat to the jobs of all those who work in industry. I have often summed up our policy as one of freedom with responsibility. By responsibility I mean quite simply this: we do not ask managements or unions to act against their own interests. But what we do ask is that they should take a long-term view of those interests[20].

The rejection of statutory controls by Messrs Heath, Prior, Barber and Carr, as quoted above, and the emphasis on the limitations of the role of government in a 'free society' was to prove to be only temporary. Within 18 months a policy based on the opposite principles of intervention and compulsion had been adopted after the Government had over-reacted both to the increase in unemployment and the outcome of the 1972 conflict with the miners. If in July 1971 it was Mr Heath's belief that '. . . slowly perhaps, but surely, the size of wage settlements is coming closer to reality'[21] then the abandonment of such a belief by March 1972 indicates the swiftness with which 'N minus 1' was abandoned.

But, before moving on to the crucial questions of rising unemployment and the 1972 miners' strike, which marked the end of the 'N minus 1' experiment, it must be noted that the Government received an added bonus in the early summer of 1971 when the Confederation of British Industry announced its 5% limit 'price initiative'. From the CBI's point of view '. . . if the Government were willing to boost the economy we would help by getting a voluntary price policy'[22]. As the Government was already in the process of reflating the economy the CBI initiative was helpful in the context of the cost-push theory of inflation inherent in 'N minus 1'. Thus Mr Heath told the House that:

The CBI policy has been remarkably successful because it has been so efficiently policed by the CBI. In my view there would be no doubt about the continuance of that policy if there were an equal response in wage negotiations from the trade unions[23].

In effect, the CBI voluntary price policy that 'stuck surprisingly well'[24] was of greater political value than economic value. One Conservative MP, Jock Bruce-Gardyne, pertinently observed that '. . . if members of the CBI observe the CBI's appeal for price restraint it seems quite clear that the recovery in profit margins which has been occurring, will disappear . . .'[25]. The initiative was based on the vulgar error that inflation is synonymous with rising prices. Price restraint does not itself reduce inflation and may even make it worse. The reduction in the pressure for higher wages as a result of the CBI initiative was uncertain and at best small. As for the effect on demand inflation of artificially lowering prices, the argument is complex. The first effect of reducing prices is to increase demand inflation. But the CBI price initiative was accompanied by Government measures to reflate the economy and thus increase demand inflation still further. How far these Government measures were due to the CBI initiative is debatable, but the CBI argued that these measures would not have been adopted without their initiative. When, at the end of July 1972, the year's initiative had expired, it was further extended until the end of October 1972, in a modified form, as an act of goodwill to the tripartite talks on a voluntary incomes policy. That these talks ended without agreement at great disappointment to the CBI will be mentioned in greater depth later on. Thus the CBI's price initiative was not only misguided but was a self-inflicted handicap when viewed in the context of the statutory prices and incomes policy announced in November 1972. Such an outcome was by no means inevitable at the outset of the CBI prices initiative in August 1971. Then it seemed 'N minus 1' was succeeding; the Government's main political worry was in the rising unemployment figures.

## 4.2    The politics and economics of unemployment

Fearing a return to the 1930s, the rise in unemployment induced a political panic among many Ministers, particularly the Prime Minister, who saw the problem as more politically than economically disastrous, a reaction that was rational in the overall context of post-war Keynesian policy objectives. Although Douglas Hurd has stated that the loss of nerve over rising unemployment has been exaggerated since, his observations on the 1971/72 period are most relevant:

> It is true that Mr Heath felt strongly that the modern Conservative Party had to shake off the spectres of the past, of which mass unemployment was the most formidable. No-one of Mr Heath's background and generation could easily dismiss rising unemployment as a statistical fiction or as unimportant. Despite this, the political advisers of the Government were at all times more concerned about inflation than about unemployment. We knew how the 1970 election had been won – we knew how the next election could be lost. At meeting after meeting we concentrated on the course of prices. No other consideration had in our minds anything of the same political importance[26].

Mr Hurd makes a plausible case that the Government was not so much frightened of unemployment but desirous of growth. But the argument is not convincing. Growth has been a panacea for all governments but Mr Heath's Government pursued a policy of 'dashing' for growth, of rapid reflation on an unprecedented level. This does not suggest a long-term growth policy and a reaction to the events of the time, namely levels of unemployment, which were regarded as politically unacceptable to a Conservative government. While it may be argued that the Government's fears that the Conservative Party would once again be associated with high unemployment were considerably exaggerated, this was not immediately obvious in the political climate of the early 1970s when Keynesian orthodoxy ruled in Whitehall, in the academic world, and within both major political parties. Far nearer the mark than Mr Hurd's analysis is the observation of one Minister that 'we panicked over the one million unemployed. Growth was wrongly paced, starting too slow, and then after the one million (unemployed) we put the foot down too hard'[27]. Another Minister noted that 'we over-estimated unemployment at the expense of the money supply'[28]. Nor does the fact that, as Terence Higgins has claimed, the Government hoped for a sustainable rate of growth invalidate the proposition that the growth policy began as a 'dash for growth'. Mr Hurd's defence of the Government's policy may be plausible, if unconvincing, but Mr Higgins' assertion that the Government's policy was 'the antithesis of a "dash for growth"'[29], bore no relation to the fact that the 5% growth policy was originally an expedient to reduce what the Government regarded as a politically unacceptable level of unemployment.

The over-estimation of the political problems of unemployment increased with the official figures throughout 1970 and 1971 until the dreaded one million threshold was crossed, though only in the crude total, in January 1972. However, the causes of rising unemployment were not the effects of the Heath Government's policies and certainly there was no deliberate plan to 'create' high unemployment, which the Labour Opposition often claimed. Similarly, Blackaby is wrong to claim that the Government '. . . intended simply to hold the level of unemployment at around half a million until the rise in wage rates moderated . . .'[30]. Government did not welcome rising unemployment nor was the rising unemployment part of the overall strategy. Indeed, the reverse was the case. As the *Economist* noted, Roy Jenkins' stewardship of the economy was partly to blame, for '. . . Since unemployment tends to lag about twelve months behind economic actions, the story of [1971] dole queues starts with Mr Roy Jenkins' refusal to introduce a give-away pre-election budget in 1970'[31].

A fuller explanation also reveals the Wilson Government, not the Heath Government, as more culpable for some of the causes of rising unemployment. During the late 1960s there was a series of increases in the size of social security benefits relative to take-home pay. In addition, the introduction of statutory redundancy benefits increased the cost of unemployment to the employer. It gradually became apparent to many in lower paid jobs that they were earning little more than they could get without working. For such employees the incentive to remain in work was being destroyed and indeed some duly gave up work. Similarly, as Brittan and Lilley have argued, the large increase in benefits

> . . . made a period of sustained job searching [or leisure] more attractive than employment to many lower paid workers. This created demand pressures at the lower end of the wage spectrum reinforced by bargaining pressure from workers who resented receiving little more than dole money for their efforts[32].

Those in work were emboldened to demand higher pay by the knowledge that loss of work meant little decline in income. Hence, there was a wave of 'dirty-job' pay claims among the low paid that sparked off the 1969/70 wage explosion. The net effect was higher wages all round with a compression of differential as the low paid won disproportionate rises. This led to labour shedding, especially among the least well paid. As a result, many of the newly unemployed preferred to stay on the dole unless they could obtain jobs earning significantly more.

It follows that the rise in unemployment did not signify a commensurately increased pool of potentially employable labour. Thus, as the unemployment total surged forward there was very little resemblance to the situation of unused capacity which existed in the 1930s and which Mr Heath and his Ministers feared. One former Minister, correctly assessing the political repercussions, pointed out that 'unemployment in the 1970s isn't the vote loser it was in the 1930s'[33]. Another Minister recalled that:

> We were wedded to the belief that we could not have high unemployment without major industrial troubles on our hands. This was a crucial mistake. The Government was mesmerized by unemployment and insufficiently prepared to accept the need for a labour shakeout[34].

It was the political not the economic effects of unemployment that were crucial to some Conservatives. One back bench Conservative MP, in recalling the effects of rising unemployment, thought the problem a 'psychological issue, especially to a first generation Conservative like myself. We were determined not to associate the Conservative Party with high unemployment'[35]. As the *Economist* put it 'Mr Heath's Government . . . is experiencing the dilemma that what is good for the economy may be bad politically and socially'[36]. Keegan and Pennant-Rea argue – and this is a crucial point – that '. . . in the unemployment panic of winter/spring 1972, [the Conservatives] were still, despite some doctrinal differences, essentially influenced by the post-war bias in favour of employment rather than disinflation'[37]. The clear evidence is that the Government's decision was based on political attitudes associated originally with the slump of the 1930s.

Ralph Harris notes that the Government might have resisted the calls to spend its way out of unemployment by 'pondering the reassuring press report of the latter-day Jarrow "marchers" who joined a demonstration [against unemployment] in London after travelling down comfortably by Pullman train'[38]. The serious point to be made was that the official statistics were a deceptive measure of not only the absolute level of unemployment but also the social distress in an age of wage-related benefits and prompt tax repayments.

The upward movement of the unemployment figures was steady throughout 1971. Despite a mild winter the total was 721 000 in February 1971, 754 000 in March and 774 000 in April[39]. At this stage the public statements of Ministers still conveyed an air of reality, with the Government refusing to take the blame for workers who priced themselves out of jobs. Mr Barber told the Commons in February 1971 that:

> It is a sad spectacle to see some trade union militant leaders almost forcing their members to price themselves out of jobs. It is time that this House and all those who are directly involved in negotiation of wages settlements realized that the more excessive the claim the more likely it is that it will lead to redundancy and unemployment[40].

Mr Heath, in March 1971, said that:

> . . . we are much closer to reality and recognize cost inflation for what it brings – even higher prices in the shops and a threat to the jobs of thousands. In the redundancies we are now seeing, cost inflation has led to the loss of many people's jobs[41].

Similarly, the Prime Minister told the Commons that:

> You know quite clearly what the cause of the present unemployment is. Members will not avoid the facts by trying to shout me down. The facts are these: that over the last 12-month period for which full information is available import prices rose by only 4%, company profits fell by 2½%, indirect tax rates remained the same, but labour costs per unit of output rose by 12%. That is the cause of men becoming redundant today[42].

With particular reference to Mr Wilson's inconsistent approach, Mr Heath commented that the increased unemployment figures 'are pointing out the lesson which [Mr Wilson] himself, when he was in office, was always prepared to tell us: that if wages rose beyond productivity there would be high inflation'[43].

However, later in March 1971 Mr Barber's reflationary budget betrayed the Government's worry that unemployment was too high and that government action, rather than allowing people to price themselves back into jobs, was required. Taxation was reduced by £546m, Selective Employment Tax and Purchase Tax abolished from April 1972 and replaced by VAT. Pensions were increased, all income tax allowances in respect of children were increased by 2½%. Ironically, Mr Barber concluded that, 'It is right that I should end with the warning. All our hopes for the future will be dust in our mouths if we do not repel the assault upon the value of our money. This must remain our first priority'[44].

At the time it was not yet clear that Mr Barber would be reluctant to heed his own concluding warning and many Conservative MPs regarded the budget as fulfilling many of the 1970 election manifesto pledges, particularly the promise to cut taxation that had become an article of faith to many of those back-benchers who expressed their considerable support.

But away from the euphoria on the Conservative benches, and the indignation of the Opposition, there were those who regarded the budget as contradictory. One commentator noted that:

> In their political speaking ministers warn that if wage claims are pressed too far they will lead to bankruptcies, redundancies and unemployment. Although controversial this embodies one possible approach to wage inflation. It is, however, in complete contradiction to the Budget Speech, which forecast an increase in unemployment if nothing was done and then undertook to increase purchasing power to prevent this happening[45].

This contradiction marked the beginning of the loss of the Government's political will. It is not surprising, therefore, that when unemployment failed to stabilize as the Treasury had predicted[46], the Government launched into the very trap of massive reflation inherent in the contradictory March budget. On 14 July 1971, with unemployment still rising, a £100m public works programme for the development areas was announced and on 19 July Mr Barber presented another reflationary mini-budget. Purchase tax was cut by 18% – hire purchase controls were abolished, and capital allowances for industry increased.

To assist industry the first year allowance on all capital spending on plant and machinery was raised from 60% to 80% up to August 1973. Service industries in development areas were allowed free depreciation for im-mobile plant and machinery. Both these measures were intended to benefit industry by about £190m over three years. With taxation also cut to the tune of £1100m in the financial year the CBI was naturally enthusiastic, welcoming the measures as:

> . . . the kind of response to the CBI initiative that we have hoped for. It will give a further and quick stimulus to demand. It should also provide a much needed fillip to investment both through the prospect of faster growth and through the improved tax incentive[47].

Jock Bruce-Gardyne has since argued that 'the 19 July 1971 measures marked a turning point in the sense that the curbing of unemployment had overtaken the curbing of inflation as the primary objective of economic policy'[48]. Although this is true it was a year later that the Government's political panic led to the massive increase in the money supply, to expressly reduce unemployment[49]. The July 1971 budget was a considerable step in a reflationary direction, which indicated the sort of change in priorities that Mr Barber's later budgets were to confirm. One economic commentator shrewdly pointed out that 'the Treasury's main arguments against mone-tary and fiscal stimuli 1970/71 were couched in balance of payments terms; and when sterling turned out for a time to be embarrassingly strong the Treasury became discredited. The way was then open for the so-called "Barber Boom"'[50]. Similarly the Treasury forecasts for unemployment throughout 1971 were, according to one special adviser, 'unduly optimistic'[51].

However, following the July measures the unemployment figures con-tinued to increase, reaching 900 000 in October 1971, and over one million by January 1972. It is worth mentioning that at the 1971 Conservative Party Conference Mr Heath warned trade unionists that:

> If you continue to demand wage increases in money wages far in excess of anything that can be earned from production you will continue to price yourselves and others out of a job[52].

In the context of the Government's policy such a comment was at least paradoxical, in the sense that even if declaring itself not guilty of increasing unemployment the Government was still pursuing policies to bring the level down. Thus, by November 1971, the Government in the Queen's Speech pledged that its 'first care will be to increase employment by strengthening the economy . . . '[53]. The emphasis on reducing unemploy-ment was in contrast to the 1970 Queen's Speech and the 1970 Conserva-tive Party election manifesto, which had stressed the control of inflation as the Government's policy priority. However, the change of priorities had not led to any noticeable political advantages; instead Mr Heath had played into Labour's hands because the Conservatives had bitterly criti-cized the 1964–70 Labour Government, which had permitted unemploy-ment to rise for the sake of its balance of payments strategy. As one Conservative MP of the time has noted:

> In Opposition, Conservative leaders – Mr Iain Macleod first among them – had consistently denounced the rising levels of unemployment

under Labour from the middle of 1966 onwards . . . . They were therefore immediately vulnerable if the figures continued to rise as indeed they did[54].

Mr Wilson was thus able to exploit the Government's situation, ironically in view of the reflationary measures taken, to full political advantage. Mr Wilson told the House that:

> From this bench and in the country he [Mr Heath] repeatedly forecast for the winters of 1968/69 and 1969/70, a figure of 750 000 unemployed. We did not come anywhere near it. It required his stewardship to reach it, to surpass it, and now to be set to exceed that figure, which we never reached by one third[55].

The subject of unemployment dominated the Conservatives' party political broadcast on 17 November 1971 on BBC radio. 'This Government is committed completely and absolutely to expanding the economy and to bringing unemployment down', Mr Heath commented[56]. Mr Barber, while denying that Conservative policies had caused unemployment, cited the Government's intentions to bring figures down: 'The truth is that no British Government has ever before taken so much action with the direct purpose of creating more employment'[57].

Within days, however, the published figures showed a sharp monthly rise of more than 40 000 to a total of 970 022, a figure which, despite their protestations of innocence, was deeply embarrassing to the Government, given the extent of reflation already undertaken. Considerable back bench criticism of Mr Chataway's reprieve for the £6m per annum loss-making Post Office Giro Scheme, thus saving 3500 jobs in the Bootle area, seemed trivial in comparison to the alleged political sensitivity of the unemployment situation. As Mr Barber told Patrick Hutber of the *Sunday Telegraph*:

> With the present level of unemployment I have certainly been prepared to increase public expenditure to help bring it down. I have generally had two particular considerations in mind. The first is to try to ensure that the expenditure takes place in the areas of high unemployment. For instance, the spending on naval shipbuilding. But also one should aim at selecting forms of public expenditure which will take place over the next couple of years or so and then tail off, so that one does not pre-empt the situation beyond that period . . . . Of course, our main aims here were to reduce taxation and to achieve better priorities in public spending – and these we certainly have achieved. But with unemployment as high as it has been we have not hesitated to expand public spending on those places and on these things where it could help most[58].

Nor did Mr Barber hesitate to take further action, announcing on 23 November a boost of £160m in public investment over the next two years with the declared aim of creating and maintaining jobs.

Labour MPs were critical that the package was 'too little, too late' but although most Conservative MPs supported the measures politically, others suspected that fate had been handed an inflationary hostage[59], notably Mr Powell who scorned the idea that reflationary measures could, *per se*, cure unemployment:

The giant lobby at Westminster against unemployment is a sad anachronism. It is one thing to lobby MPs when the object is to persuade them to do what they did not want to do. It is another thing when the object is to persuade them to wave a wand which they have perceived is no longer magic, and perhaps never was[60].

In January 1972 the Speaker had to suspend the sitting in the Commons following the commotion caused by the figures reaching the 1 000 000 mark, a total further artifically raised by the side-effects of the miners' strike. Two Labour back-benchers crossed the floor to confront the Prime Minister. Dennis Skinner shook his fist and jeered at the Prime Minister, seated a foot or two away. Tom Swain, a few minutes later, strode to the Despatch Box where Mr Heath was standing, and contemptuously threw down on it an evening newspaper carrying the unemployment figures.

Such histrionics were ironic given the Government's political determination to reduce an unemployment level which it neither caused nor welcomed, although, to the ever-present background of trade union militancy, the Government was stimulating demand with greater enthusiasm than at any time during the previous Labour administration, 1964–70. Thus as the *Economist* noted '. . . the dreaded figure [of one million] came in a week that left no doubt that a consumer boom was in full swing[61]. A week later the same journal observed that 'The million is being impressed on the public consciousness in rather the same way as the £800 m balance of payments deficit of 1964 was impressed on the public consciousness by Labour Government propaganda'[62]. Not only was the one million impressed on the public consciousness[63] but on ministers' consciousness and it is at this point that political panic set in, even though the objective of lowering unemployment had become more of a policy priority with every reflationary measure. As one Senior Economic Adviser to the Treasury put it, 'Heath never wanted unemployment to rise – the panic over it proves that'[64].

Thus, Mr Barber presented his fourth budget on 21 March 1972 expecting, and hoping, that further reflationary measures would reduce the unemployment total, as well as assisting the decline in the level of pay settlements[65]. Taxation was cut by £1200 m, pensions increased and, as already mentioned, a new system of regional development grants was introduced. Conservative MPs seemed to be generally satisfied with the Budget, particularly David Knox who welcomed the reflationary measures 'in the same way that I welcomed the measures last July'[66].

For the Opposition, Mr Jenkins expressed the fear that the Budget '. . . will in due course lead to the need either for swinging the unacceptable public expenditure cuts or for substantial taxation increases'[67] on the grounds that Mr Barber's deficit financing to the tune of £2441 million was excessive. In effect, a Labour Shadow Chancellor was criticizing a Conservative Chancellor for moving too far leftwards from the consensus centre, by expanding public expenditure too excessively. Mr Jenkins' criticism of the Government's deficit financing was pertinent, however, despite his earlier disapproval of Mr Barber's 'Quiet Revolution' public expenditure package in October 1970.

Whether the drop in the April unemployment figures, by 12 419 to 1 005 144, was the result of Mr Barber's March Budget or the lagged effect of his July 1971 mini-budget, many Conservatives believed that they had inherited, not created, the rising trend of unemployment. As an IEA publication has put it, 'If the economy had not been squeezed so hard by Labour in the first place, unemployment would have stabilized at a lower level and the *political* pressure [my emphasis] for rapid reflation would not have been so strong'[68]. To the few monetarist critics that there were at the time, such an expansion was fuel on the inflationary fire. Ralph Harris points out that:

> So it came about that the Chancellor launched into a massive monetary expansion towards the end of 1971 – just when the rising trends of both prices and unemployment were on the turn as a result of previous monetary policies. In the Budget of 1972, when the improvement was still plainer to see, the Government decided to 'go for growth' by budgeting for a deficit of £3000 million . . . . By the end of 1972 the rate of increase in M3 approached an unprecedented 30%[69].

## 4.3    The 1972 miners' strike

Thus coupled with the measures initiated by the interventionist Industry Act, the Government had sacrificed not only the 'Quiet Revolution' policy of disengagement but also control over public spending by massive deficit financing, a sure recipe for inflation although the Government and its Treasury advisers, following traditional Keynesian post-war policies, did not fully appreciate this at the time. At this point it is worth noting that the 'N minus 1' policy, which seemed to be succeeding within its own limits in mid-1971, had been abandoned.

The superficial reason for the demise of 'N minus 1' lay in the Government's conflict with the miners over their pay claim. The dispute deserves some attention, given the widely-held view that its outcome was crucial. In September 1971 the National Union of Mineworkers put in a 47% pay claim. Lawrence Daly made his union's position clear by stating that 'If we get an unsatisfactory response we are bound to consider, in consultation with the membership, various forms of industrial action'[70]. By December 1971, having rejected the NCB's offer of 7.1%, the 280000 members of the NUM voted by a 55.8% majority for a national strike in support of their claim pending further talks between the NUM and NCB.

Expressing the general mood of the Government and the press, the *Economist* commented that 'The miners do not look in a particularly strong position. No worker wants to hear strike talk so close to Xmas and there is plenty of coal stock to ride out a lengthy strike after all'[71]. One Conservative back-bencher adopted a much more conciliatory tone stating that '. . . no-one can benefit from a long, drawn-out confrontation . . . . The industry would suffer a mortal blow. I therefore make an earnest plea to all involved – the sooner we can get back to talking, working and earning, the better for everyone'[72]. Liberal MP Emlyn Hooson commented that 'Anyone who knows the nature of the miner's work and the circumstances in which he performs it can have no doubt that he is grossly underpaid'[73].

Originally the Government did not plan to intervene in the hope that the NUM and NCB could reach a face-saving compromise. On 4 January, at the eleventh hour, a meeting in London between Derek Ezra, Chairman of the NCB, and Messrs Gormley and Daly, did not reach agreement and the following day the NUM executive voted by 23:2 to reject the Coal Board's slightly improved offer of another 10p per week for 86000 day wage men, making a total of 121000 who would receive £2 a week more in keeping with the 'N minus 1' policy. Thus on 9 January 1972, Britain's 280000 coal miners came out on strike. Mr Derek Ezra, successor to Lord Robens as Chairman of the Coal Board, thought that the strike was avoidable though he declined to mention that the NCB's hands were tied by the Government:

> We have made every possible effort to avoid the strike happening. If our last offer had been put to the miners in a ballot, it would have secured acceptance by the necessary majority – or the union could have made use of the arbitration machinery. But it did neither, so we are faced with the strike[74].

Largely because of the hazardous nature of the miners' work, public opinion, which usually supported the Government in the face of disruption caused by strikers, favoured the miners[75]. This public sympathy was because of the miners' '. . . harsh working conditions and the fact that they had gradually been falling down the wages league'[76]. Furthermore, the miners' last strike was in 1926 so that they were not associated in the public mind with the unpopular, unofficial action that had increased in the 1960s. Even some Conservative back-benchers reflected the national mood in saying that the miners were underpaid. Geoffrey Stewart-Smith stated that, 'The minimum wage before the strike was not a living wage. In that I support the miners entirely and I believe too that the increased offer made by the Board is still not a living wage'[77]. David Crouch told the House that:

> This is not a time for economists to pontificate on what we can or cannot afford. Let us for once forget percentages and consider people instead. I believe it is time for management to decide what is a just payment for men doing an essential and dangerous job in an industry providing an essential fuel in our economy[78].

But more important than the support for the miners, from whatever quarter, was the question of picketing and particularly the success of the 'flying pickets'. Shortly after the start of the strike Mr Gormley stressed the need to stop the movement of coal:

> We shall put picket lines wherever necessary to make sure the strike is a success, providing it is within the law. We have assurances from other unions that they will not cross picket lines and we shall make sure that pickets are in the right place[79].

Such picketing proved to be effective, especially at the Saltley coke depot where 6000 trade unionists prevented supplies from being delivered and railwaymen refused to move coal trains[80]. One Cabinet Minister recalled that 'the flying pickets at Saltley were crucial. At all costs the order was that the depot must be kept open. Then came the message that the police couldn't cope and that brute force had overruled the functioning of the law'[81]. At the end of January 1972 the CEGB warned of the likelihood of blackouts when the Chairman, Arthur Hawkins, criticized the miners' pickets who had put power stations under siege: 'We are not of course in any way parties to this dispute, but have been forced into a state of siege by the action of the miners' pickets who have deliberately set out to strangle the nation's power supply'[82]. Reports of clashes between 'flying pickets' at power stations and the police had now become less isolated and increasingly unpopular with the public. The effectiveness of the picketing was now all too evident.

By 10 February power blackouts had hit all parts of Britain, and following the breakdown of renewed talks, the Government announced a State of Emergency and sweeping measures to save power[83].

On 15 February ten power stations had to close because railway workers refused to move coal supplies. Power cuts led to over one million workers being laid off and as Lawrence Daly commented, 'If this isn't a confrontation with the Government, I don't know what is'[84].

Douglas Hurd has written that the 'weeks of the 1972 miners' dispute were the worst of all'[85] and noted in his diary on 11 February that 'the Government are now wandering vainly over a battlefield looking for someone to surrender to – and being massacred all the time'[86]. Finally, Lord Wilberforce was appointed as Chairman of a Court of Inquiry into the miners' pay dispute[87].

On 18 February the Wilberforce inquiry effectively surrendered on the Government's behalf to the miners' demands. The Court's main recommendation that gave the miners 21% were: £5 a week more, making a minimum of £23 for 85 000 surface workers; £6 a week more, an increase of £1 in the underground differential, giving a £25 minimum for 125 000 underground workers; £4.50 giving a minimum of £34.50 for 70 000 face workers. The Court also recommended that all increases should be backdated to 1 November 1971, and should run for 16 months until 28 February 1973. It made no recommendation on union claims for payment of the adult rate for all at the age of 18, affecting 17 000 people, and an extra week's holiday, but urged both sides to complete negotiations on them by 1 May. The Court also found that the miners were a 'just case for special treatment' through a 'general and exceptional increase'[88]. It accepted that they had fallen badly behind in relative earnings and often in actual pay and had set a model to industry as a whole by cooperating in greater efficiency and productivity.

The Inquiry also believed that inequities in pay through introduction of a new wages structure had been a 'special and powerful factor'[89] in present unrest and required adjustment. It said that survival of a viable coal industry with contented workers was in the national interest and that the Government must provide necessary finance if the industry was not to contract. Briefly, the miners showed signs of rejecting the Report but following a final meeting at Downing Street, Mr Heath convinced the NUM leaders that they had secured an acceptable amount. The NUM ballot on the settlement accepted the terms by 210 059 votes to 7581, a majority in the ratio of 27:1[90]. But one study of the miners' strike concluded, prophetically, that the miners '. . . have not yet been taken off the horns of [a] declining industry dilemma. The pay settlement is clear. The future context of economic and financial management for coal is not'[91].

The Government had certainly suffered a political defeat. In a broadcast to the nation Mr Heath argued that it was not the Government, but all the people, who had lost:

> . . . We can put right the damage to industry. The strike has not helped the economy and it will not help create new jobs. But things can be put right. It will take a little bit longer and it will mean that little bit more effort all round. But it can be done. There is no doubt about that. When people said, 'the miners won a great victory' or 'the Government lost that one', what did they mean? In the kind of country we live in, there could not be any 'we' or 'they'. There was only 'us' – all of us. If the Government is defeated then the country is defeated[92].

But Mr Heath's argument was not convincing. In political terms, having staked the Government's authority on enduring the strike, the Government had lost the battle and was politically defeated. Lindsay and Harrington noted that 'The score of 1926 had undoubtedly been evened. It was a shattering experience for the Tory Government'[93]. However, the implications for the 'N minus 1' policy have been largely exaggerated. At the time Ministers regarded it as the end of 'N minus 1', which had helped to reduce the annual rate of increase in earnings from 14% in November 1970 to just under 9% in January 1972. It was widely held that the attempt to cut wage rises without the aid of a formal incomes policy had foundered on the miners' militancy in 1972. In the following months apologists for incomes policy repeatedly quoted the miners' victory as breaking the wages dam thus necessitating statutory action. One Treasury official argued that 'the miners' strike effectively broke "N minus 1" in the public sector'[94]. Another similar view was that 'N minus 1' depended on the Government winning the battles, for example with the postmen, and the '1972 miners' strike was a first class political defeat; political defeat meant a different strategy'[95].

Even with hindsight, there are many adherents to the view that the 1972 miners' strike meant the end of 'N minus 1' as an effective policy. No-one believed that the miners were to be a genuine exception. Although one Minister who dissented from the accepted view argued that '. . . Wilberforce didn't mean the end to "N minus 1"; as there are circumstances when a pacemaker need not be followed, we should have gone on treating things individually'[96], the comment that 'N minus 1' was 'successful up to Wilberforce'[97] is still a typical reaction among many of Mr Heath's former Ministers. However, the evidence points the other way. Brittan and Lilley have argued that:

> Strangely enough there was no published evidence at the time or since that settlements after the miners' strike were higher than before it – though further deceleration was not obvious . . . .
> Yet almost everyone from the Government downwards at the time believed that escalation had begun anew. The conventional wisdom was that wage settlements, particularly in the public sector where market

forces were least effective, were making good the ground they lost during the Labour incomes policy. An answer to a Parliamentary Question given in July 1972 nonetheless revealed that of the 33 public sector settlements reached between March and June 1972 none allowed increases above 11% and the average was 9% – half of what the miners had obtained.

Even though wage pressures were not visibly growing in the wake of the miners' strike (any more than they had after the inflationary Wilberforce power workers' settlement in February 1971), political pressures for an incomes policy were rising . . . .

Moreover, the civil service had throughout been sceptical of the possibility of defeating wage inflation without an incomes policy, the need for which has been an article of faith in Whitehall since the war[98].

Mr Heath himself told the House in June that the average rate of settlements since the Wilberforce inquiry was only 9%[99]. The conventional view that the miners' settlement began an upward trend is simply incorrect. Wage settlements were declining and continued to decline after the miners' settlement in February 1972. This is now known to have been true even in the public sector where all the settlements were below 11%. It is therefore difficult, if not impossible, to agree with Brendon Sewill that '. . . by the Spring of 1972 there was no evidence that inflation was being brought under control: on the contrary *with the success of the miners' strike* [my emphasis] it looked like getting out of hand'[100].

Wages only accelerated, and then very sharply, in July 1972. Brittan and Lilley argued convincingly that this was the month that the unions were called in for tripartite talks on incomes policy and that a large number of pre-emptive settlements were made[101]. The rate of increase jumped to 17% in the six months after that decision compared with under 12% in the six-month period between the miners' strike and the decision to go for an incomes policy. The moot point remains, how far was it the decision to seek to control incomes by administrative means that sparked off a wage explosion and not *vice versa*. Even if the acceleration of wage levels after July 1972 is regarded as coincidental this still does not indicate that it was the outcome of the Wilberforce Inquiry, five months previously, that was responsible. But the argument itself that each wage settlement is crucial to all those that follow – the theory behind 'N minus 1' – is far from convincing. The 'going rate' of settlements does play a part in the trade unions' assessment of pay claims. But then so do other factors such as the supply and demand for labour in particular industries, the overall level of union militancy, and the industrial 'muscle' of the union involved. Nor are percentage terms particularly helpful to policy makers. People earn, and consume, in absolute not percentage terms. Percentage increases are an approximate shorthand way, an imprecise way, of measuring the move- ment of wages. 'N minus 1', by relying too much on the percentage shorthand, overlooked the simple fact that similar percentage increases, when translated into absolute terms in pounds sterling, can reveal dissimi- lar increases in real terms. Brittan and Lilley point out that a great deal of the apparent changes in militancy of union wage demands can be explained '. . . by economic forces such as price expectations, the effects of rising tax-take on take-home pay and of a deterioration in the terms of trade on real wages'[102]. According to the precise definition of 'N minus 1' the 38% pay rise for MPs and 105% rise in the Queen's Civil List in December 1971 were public breaches of the Government's policy. Indeed, one Conservative back-bencher, J. R. Kinsey, pointed out the inconsistency of the Government's approach:

> I rather doubt the wisdom of introducing rises of this scale for Members of this House. I question the . . . strategy of the Government in introducing increases of this amount while asking the rest of the country to take less pay rises in their own pockets. We should set an example[103].

Both the MPs' 28% and the miners' 21% were 'settlements' above the national average in excess of 'N minus 1'. But in the miners' case the Government suffered a political defeat whereas the MPs' award was not regarded as politically contentious even though it was a public sector breach of 'N minus 1'. This leads directly to the main fault of 'N minus 1', that being the inherent idea that everyone should receive the same pay increases in accordance with a 'going rate' or 'norm'. There is no economic (or moral) reason why everyone should ideally receive identical increases, either in real or percentage terms; indeed, there are powerful arguments, based on rewards for effort or skill and on the beneficial effect of market forces, for quite the reverse. Nor is there any social merit in identical increases – as the miners implied by asking to be treated as a 'special case'. Nor can it be argued that the demise of 'N minus 1' following the miners' settlement led to a pay explosion for the reasons already given.

It is no coincidence that the abandonment of 'N minus 1' occurred after the Government had given priority to reducing unemployment rather than to lowering inflation. For, as far as inflation was concerned, the measures taken to reduce the one million unemployed were directly inflationary in a way that individual wage settlements were not. Wage increases, including those in the public sector, are not, in themselves, inflationary unless there is a corresponding increase in the money supply. Monetary policy, however, was not regarded as crucial, for as already mentioned, monetarism as a political creed had not yet arrived upon the British political, and hence policy making, scene. One senior Treasury knight conceded that 'the money supply as such was only just beginning to be watched – the Government's advisers were Keynesians'[104]. Similarly, as one critic observed, Mr Heath 'had no interest in monetary policy'[105], which is a fair criticism in so far as virtually everyone concerned with policy making also had little interest in monetary policy. The mistake of the Heath Government was to panic over high levels of unemployment and consequently to lose control of the money supply thus accelerating inflation, an analysis that was not readily acceptable or available at the time. Once this had happened 'N minus 1' was effectively doomed. Thus the over-reaction to unemployment, not the miners' strike, brought the end of 'N minus 1' policy. Shortly after Mr Heath's Government had left office Sir Keith Joseph, the former Social Service Secretary, analysed this major failing with particular clarity:

. . . Why then did we try incomes policy again? I suppose that we desperately wanted to believe in it because we were so apprehensive about the alternative – sound money policies. To us, as to all post-war Governments, sound money may have seemed out of date: we are dominated by the fear of unemployment. It was this which made us turn back against our own better judgement and try to spend our way out of unemployment[106].

This over-reaction to unemployment which Sir Keith Joseph criticized was not surprising when put into the context of Mr Heath, and indeed the Conservative Party, since the end of the Second World War '. . . being brought up in the Keynesian tradition'[107]. When a Government claims responsibility for managing the economy to ensure full employment it deprives individuals and unions of the normal responsibility of pricing themselves into jobs. In effect, the Government promises to provide the money to purchase everyone's labour services at whatever price these services are offered. This is an invitation to 'irresponsible' wage claims. The promise to finance such claims leads inevitably to accelerating expansion of the money supply. The resultant 'race between the printing press and the business agents of the trade unions'[108] cannot long be tolerated by Government. The inevitable cries for an 'effective' prices and incomes policy became louder throughout 1972. Following the reflationary action taken to reduce unemployment the Heath Government, in the summer of 1972, thus sought out the solution of a prices and incomes policy.

## References

1. D. HURD, *An End to Promises: Sketch of a Government 1970–74*, Collins, 1979, p. 20.
2. *Hansard*, 2 July 1970, Vol. 803, Col. 88.
3. Such as tax reform, EEC entry and Industrial Relations Law reform.
4. *Hansard*, 3 November 1970, Vol. 805, Col. 847.
5. Interview, Conservative MP.
6. Thus as a Gallup Poll showed in September 1970, 36% favoured a compulsory incomes policy and 41% favoured voluntary restraint. The question of monetary control was not regarded as relevant. *Gallup International Public Opinion Polls (GB) 1937–75*, p. 1107.
7. R. HARRIS and B. SEWILL, *British Economic Policy 1970–74: Two Views*, IEA Hobart Paperback No. 7, 1975, p. 16.
8. R. HARRIS and B. SEWILL, op. cit. (Ref. 7), p. 48.
9. *The Times*, 21 November 1970.
10. *The Times*, 10 November 1970.
11. *The Times*, 10 December 1970.
12. D. HURD, op. cit. (Ref. 1), p. 102.
13. R. HARRIS and B. SEWILL, op. cit. (Ref. 7), p. 48.
14. *The Times*, 18 January 1971.
15. *Hansard*, 22 February 1971, Vol. 812, Col. 32.
16. *Hansard*, 10 May 1971, Vol. 817, Cols. 96–97.
17. *The Times*, 26 April 1971.
18. *The Times*, 2 February 1971.
19. Interview, Cabinet Minister.
20. *The Times*, 20 April 1971.
21. *Sunday Telegraph*, 25 July 1971.
22. Interview, Senior CBI Official.
23. *Hansard*, 2 May 1972, Vol. 836, Col. 138.

24. Interview, Senior CBI Official.
25. *Hansard*, 20 July 1971, Vol. 821, Col. 1307.
26. D.HURD, op. cit. (Ref. 1), p. 89.
27. Interview, Cabinet Minister.
28. Interview, Cabinet Minister.
29. TERENCE HIGGINS, *Sunday Times*, 10 July 1977.
30. F. T. BLACKABY (Ed.), *British Economic Policy 1960–74: Demand Management*, Cambridge University Press, 1979, p. 62.
31. The *Economist*, 7 November 1971.
32. SAMUEL BRITTAN and PETER LILLEY, *The Delusion of Incomes Policy*, Temple Smith, 1977, p. 159.
33. Interview, Junior Minister.
34. Interview, Junior Minister.
35. Interview, Conservative MP.
36. The *Economist*, 23 October 1971.
37. W. KEEGAN and R. PENNANT-REA, *Who Runs the Economy? Control and Influence in British Economic Policy*, Temple Smith, 1977, p. 182.
38. R. HARRIS and B. SEWILL, op. cit. (Ref. 7), p. 14.
39. The figure was over 800 000 if Northern Ireland was included.
40. *Hansard*, 18 February 1971, Vol. 811, Col. 2157.
41. *Daily Telegraph*, 14 March 1971.
42. *Hansard*, 18 March 1971, Vol. 813, Col. 1645.
43. *Hansard*, 18 March 1971, Vol. 813, Col. 1642.
44. *Hansard*, 30 March 1971, Vol. 814, Col. 1397.
45. S. BRITTAN, *The Economic Consequences of Democracy*, Temple Smith, 1977, p. 35.
46. *Hansard*, 28 June 1971, Vol. 820, Col. 58.
47. *The Times*, 20 July 1971.
48. J. BRUCE-GARDYNE, *Whatever Happened to the Quiet Revolution?*, Charles Knight, 1974, p. 76.
49. The expansion of the money supply was made worse as a result of the Bank of England's new 'Competition and Credit Control' regulations introduced in September 1971. The commercial banks were allowed to raise their deposits from about four to nearly seven times their liquid assets. Money was consequently easier to borrow and portfolio holders had much higher ratios of money to real assets than they considered ideal. Their surplus money tended to go into real estate and buildings, which they considered more likely to keep pace with inflation, than shares.
50. S. BRITTAN, op. cit. (Ref. 45), p. 9.
51. Interview, Treasury Official.
52. *Sunday Telegraph*, 17 October 1971.
53. *The Times*, 4 November 1971.
54. J. BRUCE-GARDYNE, op. cit. (Ref. 48), p. 151.
55. *Hansard*, 2 November 1971, Vol. 825, Col. 28.
56. *The Times*, 18 November 1971.
57. Ibid.
58. *Sunday Telegraph*, 21 November 1971.
59. *Hansard*, 8 December 1971, Vol. 827, Col. 1399.
60. *The Times*, 27 November 1971.
61. The *Economist*, 22 January 1972.
62. The *Economist*, 29 January 1972.
63. Thus a Gallup Poll in February 1972 found that 70% of those questioned thought that the Government was not doing enough about unemployment, compared with 18% who took the opposite view.
64. Interview, Treasury Adviser.
65. *Hansard*, 21 March 1972, Vol. 833, Cols. 1345–46.
66. *Hansard*, 21 March 1972, Vol. 833, Col. 1595.
67. *Hansard*, 22 March 1972, Vol. 833, Col. 1528.
68. G. T. PEPPER and G. E. WARD, *Too Much Money?*, IEA Publication, 1976, p. 14.
69. R. HARRIS and B. SEWILL, op. cit. (Ref. 7), p. 13.
70. *The Times*, 15 September 1971.
71. The *Economist*, 11 December 1971.

72. *Hansard*, 18 January 1972, Vol. 829, Col. 264.
73. *Hansard*, 18 January 1972, Vol. 829, Col. 282.
74. *Sunday Telegraph*, 9 January 1972.
75. A Gallup Poll in January 1972 found that 55% were sympathetic to the miners and only 16% to the employers. op. cit. (Ref. 6), p. 1165.
76. T. F. LINDSAY and M. HARRINGTON, *The Conservative Party 1918–79*, Macmillan, 1979, pp. 271–72.
77. *Hansard*, 18 January 1972, Vol. 829, Col. 274.
78. Ibid., Col. 300.
79. *The Times*, 11 January 1972.
80. See RICHARD CLUTTERBUCK, *Britain in Agony: The Growth of Political Violence*, Penguin Books, 1980, pp. 65–74, for a detailed description of the background planning that made the picketing so effective.
81. Interview, Cabinet Minister.
82. *Daily Telegraph*, 31 January 1972.
83. *Hansard*, 14 February 1972, Vol. 831, Cols. 33–43.
84. *The Times*, 15 February 1972.
85. D. HURD, op. cit. (Ref. 1), p. 102.
86. Ibid.
87. It was expected from past experience of the power workers' dispute that Lord Wilberforce would err on the side of the miners rather than the NCB. This offered the Government an escape route from the dispute.
88. Cmnd. 4903, *Industrial Courts Act 1919. Report of a Court of Inquiry*, HMSO, 1972.
89. Ibid.
90. The general public, polled by Gallup in March 1972, thought that the Wilberforce award was fair by a majority of 81% to 9%. op. cit. (Ref. 6), p. 1171.
91. *A Special Case? Social Justice and the Miners* (Ed. by J. Hughes and R. Moore), Penguin Books, 1972, p. 155.
92. *The Times*, 28 February 1972.
93. T. F. LINDSAY and M. HARRINGTON, op. cit. (Ref. 76), p. 272.
94. Interview, Senior Treasury Official.
95. Interview, Professor Hugh Clegg.
96. Interview, Junior Minister.
97. Interview, Junior Minister.
98. S. BRITTAN and P. LILLEY, op. cit. (Ref. 32), pp. 164–65.
99. *Hansard*, 15 June 1972, Vol. 838, Col. 1725.
100. R. HARRIS and B. SEWILL, op. cit. (Ref. 7), p. 66.
101. S. BRITTAN and P. LILLEY, op. cit. (Ref. 32), pp. 165–68.
102. S. BRITTAN and P. LILLEY, op. cit. (Ref. 32), p. 66.
103. *Hansard*, 16 December 1971, Vol. 827, Col. 355.
104. Interview, Senior Treasury Official.
105. Interview, Ralph Harris.
106. Quoted in TREVOR RUSSELL, *The Tory Party: Its Policies, Divisions and Future*, Penguin Books, 1978, p. 41. It may, of course, be noted that Sir Keith's own analysis occurred fully two years after the panic over the unemployment figures and that at the time Sir Keith either supported the Government, or chose to remain silent.
107. Interview, Treasury Adviser.
108. This race was predicted with amazing prescience as the inevitable consequence of Keynesian policies by Jacob Viner in a review of Keynes' 'General Theory' soon after its publication. 'In a world organized in accordance with Keynes' specification there would be a constant race between the printing press and the business agents of the trade unions, with the problem of unemployment largely solved if the printing press could maintain a constant lead . . . '. *Quarterly Journal of Economics*, Vol. 51, 1936, pp. 147–67.

Chapter 5

# The 'Heath Dilemma' and the drift to incomes policy

*'It is recognized now that without a corresponding expansion of the money supply inflation cannot continue. Since indisputably money supply is more or less in the control of Government, the means of controlling and, if desired, of ending inflation, exist. If the supply of money is largely and rapidly increasing, prices and incomes are bound to rise, and no amount of prices and incomes policy, voluntary or compulsory, can prevent it . . . . If the money supply were under control prices and wages would not rise because they could not.'*

Enoch Powell, reported in the
*Sunday Telegraph*, 18 June 1972

## 5.1 The 'Heath dilemma' strategy

So far we have seen how the Heath Government, launched on the optimism of the 'Quiet Revolution', was deflected from its course by overestimating the seriousness, both economically and politically, of comparatively high unemployment. This led to the down-grading of inflation as a policy priority and to the U-turn over industry policy and culminated in a policy of vast public expenditure and direct government intervention in industry. Moreover, following the debacle over the railwaymen's ballot in May 1972, the inadequacies of the Industrial Relations Act were all too self-evident, and its political usage was 'put on ice'.

The Government's overall policy now lay in a 'dash for growth' – a reflationary package accompanied by a prices and incomes policy, preferably voluntary, but statutory if need be. Lord Gowrie has noted that the reaction to the rising unemployment rate that was central to the U-turn on industry policy was 'the spur'[1] to Mr Heath's attempts to achieve an incomes policy, based on the assumption that this would be more conducive to the growth policy. Similarly, Gamble has argued that '. . . in 1972/73 the Heath Government showed it was prepared to risk inflation in order to achieve growth, but it believed in any case that the . . . increase in demand would not prove inflationary in the long run'[2]. This policy, like previous policies, and the decisions regarding policy changes was directly supervised by the Prime Minister who, despite having 'no coherent body of economic thought'[3], did want Britain's economy 'to be strong enough to face the competition within the EEC'[4]. An added problem was that, as one senior Treasury official put it, 'Heath distrusted the Treasury partly because of our scepticism over the economic benefits of the Common Market'[5]. The direction of policy, therefore, as it became more interventionist became more Prime Ministerial.

As the Government perceived the situation, a high-growth economy with the support of both sides of industry would create a better climate for consultation on inflation control, which was viewed, at that time, to the exclusion of other factors, as the result of high wage settlements. But, as one commentator noted, the policy of expansion was also designed 'to give British industry the confidence to invest ahead of EEC membership and remove the fear that any growth would soon come to an end as a result of another economic "stop"'[6]. The 'European' dimension to the Government's policy reversals was indeed crucial, particularly to Mr Heath whose whole political career had been associated with moves towards greater European co-operation. Mr Heath had embarked on the modernization of British industry originally in terms of the 'Quiet Revolution' and when he perceived that such policies were not going to work the search for an alternative approach assumed a far greater urgency because of the imminence of European entry and the competition this would bring about.

Mr Heath's abandonment of the 'Quiet Revolution' approach and the adoption of a high growth/incomes policy package may be regarded as the 'Heath dilemma'. In short, given that the chill winds of European competition were soon to affect British industry, the 'Heath dilemma' was a rational approach to an immediate problem. The 'Heath dilemma' was that, as 'N minus 1' and disengagement from industry had been deemed as failures, the rational solution appeared to be direct government action to stimulate the necessary investment – i.e., the Industry Act – and to find an alternative to the wages/prices spiral that Mr Heath, and virtually the whole of the economic establishment, believed to be the root problem of inflation. Thus, a high growth policy was a logical way out of the 'Heath dilemma' provided that an incomes policy, voluntary or statutory, could be made to stick. The 'Heath dilemma' was the dilemma of a Prime Minister who was running out of time, as the inefficiency of the economy he was seeking to transform needed urgent attention.

Thus, with the aim of sustained growth and the prevention of another economic 'stop' caused by balance of payments constraints, the Government made a fundamental U-turn on the floating of the pound on 23 June, as a 'temporary measure'[7]. The float, in response to a heavy speculative assault on sterling, was designed to remove the balance of payments constraint on growth that had existed during the Wilson administration 1964–70. It must not go unnoticed that, in the context of policy changes, Mr Heath 'did a U-turn on exchange rates'[8], which was 'a great reversal of all he had stood for, having previously opposed any floating'[9]. In the 1960s Mr Heath's anathema to the idea of a floating exchange rate was well known. Similarly, in the 1960s Mr Heath had derided Harold Wilson's incomes policy. But by the summer of 1972 Mr Heath's commitment to a joint programme for curbing wage and price increases was a strong personal one. It is widely believed, with much justification, that Mr Heath had been impressed by the way that the German Chancellor, Herr Brandt, regularly consulted on a permanent basis the leading trade unionists in Germany on all matters vital to the German economy – the prosperity of which, in comparison to Britain, was, and had been for some years, plainly evident. The discovery of an equivalent group in Britain was a task that Mr Heath set himself with great dedication in the summer of 1972, a task made easier by the fact that a ready-made institution, the National Economic Development Council, existed for that very purpose. This new approach, and the urgency of its task, was a clear example of the 'Heath dilemma'.

## 5.2   The tripartite talks

Consultations were thus begun in earnest[10]. Talks with the CBI concentrated on the moderation of pay claims if price restraint was to be continued[11]. As an act of good faith in its discussions with the unions the Government gave three major councils – Birmingham, Newcastle-upon-Tyne and Hammersmith – permission to charge less than the £1-a-week increase in council house rents, which they would have been required to implement in October under the Housing Finance Act. The more conciliatory tone of ministers' speeches continued on 7 July when Mr Davies, the Industry Secretary, remarked that: 'I do sincerely hope that my friends in the unions, with many of whom I have worked for years, will give a favourable and an early response to the Prime Minister's invitation for co-operative action'[12]. Similarly, Mr Barber told an audience on 8 July that inflation alone blocked the road to greater prosperity:

> That is why we have asked both the CBI and the TUC to join us in a combined effort to curb the rising cost of living. The economy is now expanding twice as fast as during recent years. Unemployment has been coming down very fast. The rise in prices over the past year has been halved[13].

In the light of the tripartite negotiations the TUC conference's debate on wage restraint assumed a greater importance. But, not unexpectedly, a T&GWU motion opposing wage restraint was carried unanimously; speaker after speaker expressing the opinion that pay restrictions could only damage the living standards of trade unionists, a view consistent with the arguably counter-productive level of union militancy that had developed since the mid 1960s. A contrary opinion came from a Treasury report, 'The effect of wage and price movements on employment', which estimated 1.4 million unemployed if pay claims were not drastically curtailed. The Bank of England also echoed the need for wage restraint in its quarterly bulletin. Implicit behind the thinking in both the Treasury and the Bank's reports was that a statutory prices and incomes policy was desirable should the tripartite talks fail to reach agreement[14]. But Mr Heath had told the Commons in July that he would not resort to statutory controls[15].

Another voice in the incomes policy lobby was Reginald Maudling's. Mr Maudling had long supported the idea of incomes policy and had indeed disagreed with his colleagues, in Opposition during 1964–70, over its desirability. Mr Maudling was also a strong supporter of a government-inspired growth policy and as Chancellor from July 1962 until the Conservatives lost office in October 1964 had pursued a high growth, i.e., high public spending, policy. However, his voice was now outside the Cabinet; Mr Maudling resigned in July 1972 over the Poulson affair. Writing in *The Times* on 12 September 1972 he envisaged an incomes policy not as a source of, but as an alternative to, conflict, a view that at the time had a wide currency following the 1972 miners' strike:

> I do not believe that policies of conflict will or can work. We can do a few things here and there to make striking less attractive. I do not believe this reaches the fundamental problem. We have in the past to a

considerable extent succeeded in damping down individual wage settlements in the public sector, but this is a catch-as-catch-can solution dearly
bought and, as we now see, precariously balanced. It is not a permanent
answer. We must find a mixture of voluntary agreement and Government supervision which will operate to restrain the political springs of
cost inflation. I have no doubt that as much as possible should be done
by voluntary agreement . . . but the lesson of experience seems to be
that we must be vigilant to detect the practical limits of voluntary action
and ready if necessary to extend them by the use of legislation. One
thing is certain; we cannot just go on as we are[16].

Mr Maudling's remedy cannot have been far from Mr Heath's mind as
another tripartite meeting took place at Chequers on 14 September.
According to the official communiqué 'substantial progress' was made.
The parties considered a first report by the special working group of
Government, TUC, CBI and NEDC representatives of the studies that
were initiated at the previous tripartite meeting on 7 August. The aim of
those studies was to establish the facts and assess the practicability of
action by those concerned (a) to improve the relative position of the lower
paid consistent with slowing down the rate of inflation; and (b) to reduce
the rate of increase in prices during the next 12 months. The communiqué
emphasized that the report merely summarized the results of those studies,
and did not make recommendations[17].
  Discussion ranged over the whole field of issues covered by the report.
The three parties reiterated that it was their aim to find means of increasing
the real prosperity of the nation as a whole. In the discussion of ways of
contributing to the improvement of the relative positions of the lower paid
while slowing the rate of inflation, four possibilities were examined.
1. Flat-rate increases within industries, together with the possibility of
   providing for genuine incentive arrangements.
2. The devising of methods by which industries that are traditionally lower
   paid can pay higher wages while avoiding excessive price increases and
   unemployment.
3. Threshold agreements providing for flat-rate adjustments.
4. The possibility of influencing prices that do not fall within the CBI price
   initiative.
  The tripartite talks were developing into a detailed plan for the
management of large sections of the British economy along what has been
regarded as corporatist lines of close liaison between the state, official
trade union leadership and those parts of British industry represented by
the CBI[18]. At the political level the control over inflation was to depend on
wage and price controls previously agreed upon. Although such a
'voluntary' policy was never finally agreed there were those who regarded
such policies as reminiscent of that to which the term corporate state was
first applied[19]. The case is far from convincing given the differences in
political structure between Britain in 1972 and, say, Italy in 1932. But the
question of whether or not Mr Heath's policy was corporatist deserves
further attention. Firstly, the idea that Mr Heath set out to establish a
corporate state on an ideological basis is clearly at odds with Mr Heath's
well-known avoidance of ideology or theory. Rather, the moves towards

tripartite solutions were *ad hoc* decisions based on what Mr Heath believed to have failed previously in Britain, and on what he had been so impressed with on his visits to Chancellor Brandt, the core issue of the 'Heath dilemma'. Secondly, it is incorrect to make the 1972 tripartite talks a dividing line between non-corporatism and corporatism. The process of the changing relationship in Britain between the Government and interest groups was a gradual one, developing – as did the 1972 tripartite talks – in an *ad hoc* manner. To label this development, and Mr Heath's version of it, as corporatism is thus a considerable over-simplification. Grant and Marsh have thus argued that:

> The whole nature of government–industry relations undeniably under-went a major change during and after the Second World War. This period marks the final establishment of what has been variously referred to as 'collectivism', 'corporatism' or 'the new group politics'. Whatever terminology is used the basic pattern of relationships is clearly apparent. Government intervention in the economy has created a situation in which a close and continuing relationship between government departments and organizations representing industrial interests has been found to be indispensable to both sides[20].

Mr Heath's faith in a tripartite solution may be viewed as a continuation of this trend – a successor to Mr Wilson's 'beer and sandwiches' – after the abandonment of the 'Quiet Revolution'.

What makes Mr Heath's policy particularly interesting is the context of the 'Quiet Revolution's' rejection of incomes policy and the implications for the Conservative Party of the move leftwards that the 'Heath dilemma' represented. This does not imply that the tripartite talks were an alternative for tough negotiation. Indeed, this was clearly shown over Mr Heath's September 'package'. On 26 September another tripartite meeting at Chequers produced the proposal from Mr Heath of a £2 limit on all pay rises and a 5½% peg on prices to counter inflation. Mr Heath described his 'package' as:

> A clear, simple and straightforward basis for voluntary agreement between the three parties. First, we are committing ourselves once again to a 5% rate of growth for the next two years. Second, for the next 12 months we are proposing that the prices of manufactured goods be held to an increase of not more that 4% so that rises in retail prices need not exceed about 5%. Third, for the next 12 months we propose that increases in pay for a normal working week should be £2 for everybody. Threshold agreements would ensure that the low-paid maintain a substantial real increase throughout the year. Fourth, as part of the package we would ensure that pensioners also had a share in the nation's increasing prosperity[21].

On 27 September TUC leaders rejected the plan as being 'unacceptable'. Withdrawal of the Industrial Relations Act was publicly but not privately central to the unions' opposition. Jack Jones commented that 'there must be insistence on the withdrawal of the Industrial Relations Act if any satisfactory compromise is to be worked out'[22]. In a statement Mr Feather said that the TUC recognized that the proposals had been submitted as a basis for consultation and its only commitment was to discuss them before the next tripartite meeting. The economic committee would examine not only the £2 ceiling, but the advisability and practicability of such flat rate rises, particularly in the public and private sector. They would also examine the willingness and ability of the CBI and Government to control price increases sufficiently to avoid further inflation[23], with its consequences for working people and pensioners, particularly if the 1972 Housing Finance Act were enforced and Value Added Tax introduced at 10%. 'With these factors in mind, and with no suggestions from the Government for limiting the rise in income of the self-employed and shareholders, the proposals in their present form are unacceptable to the General Council'[24]. Although disappointed with the TUC's response Mr Heath was still prepared to persevere.

With the next round of talks in mind Mr Heath told the Conservative Party Conference that the talks were concerned with curbing inflation and creating a fairer society, which '. . . the people of this country want'[25]. This was not entirely party conference rhetoric. One trade union leader noted that Mr Heath 'had a considerable degree of fairness and a desire to be just'[26]. Largely because of this 'all the trade union leaders developed an enormous respect for Ted Heath'[27].

But, despite Mr Heath's sense of fairness, an agreement was not forthcoming. The tripartite talks on 16 October produced differences between the TUC and CBI over voluntary control of retail prices as well as manufacturing prices and incomes, backed by a monitoring body on which the Government, TUC and CBI would be represented, although the Government would not appoint all the members and the chairmanship would be allocated in rotation. The trade union leaders stood firmly for a statutory form of control over at least some areas of the 450 000 retail outlets, but Mr Feather insisted that the TUC was determined to make a constructive effort to reach agreement. Campbell Adamson was spurred to reveal more precisely the line the CBI had taken. 'The CBI takes two views rather strongly. First of all, that these talks were not engaged with statutory controls, they are engaged with voluntary controls. We believe that if you get people voluntarily to agree things they are much more likely to stick to them'[28]. He said the CBI had looked at statutory controls around the world and they had not been successful. 'Quite apart from the fact that we would not agree to have statutory control of prices of any kind, we also agree that retailers, many of whom we have talked to, are aware of the situation we are in and are very anxious to help in countering inflation'[29]. Mr Adamson explained that the CBI tabled a document proposing a monitoring body 'because we feel we understand fully the TUC's difficulty here – their feeling that this must be an effective voluntary agreement on prices as well as incomes'[30].

It is not surprising that the tone and content of the talks produced criticism, albeit from a small number of dissenters, that the crucial question of the money supply was being ignored. As one former CBI official correctly pointed out:

The talks were notable for the large amount of Ministerial time which they absorbed, for the wide range of the subjects they covered [some of which·are perhaps connected with inflation only because in economics everything is connected with everything else], and for their total neglect of the money supply. During days of discussion under the Chairmanship of the Prime Minister, the quantity of money was scarcely mentioned if it was mentioned at all; it was not even admitted as a determinant of inflation worthy of discussion in some other forum. The tripartite talks embodied the institutional analysis of inflation in its most uncompromising form[31].

However, at the time such monetarist analyses were so isolated and so little comprehended that they were never likely to have any effect.

In the Commons, despite the disagreements, Mr Heath reaffirmed his desire for a voluntary policy, refusing to admit that the Government would resort to a statutory policy on prices and incomes if the tripartite negotiations with the TUC and Confederation of British Industry failed to establish agreement on a voluntary arrangement to reduce inflation. But he was careful to use words that would not inhibit his freedom to fall back on a statutory policy. The question was, having sought a 'voluntary' policy, at what stage a statutory policy would be introduced should it be deemed necessary. Mr Heath, having abandoned the 'Quiet Revolution' commitment to reduce the role of the Government in the economy and having abandoned the crude semi-interventionist 'N minus 1' policy, had now opted for the prices and incomes policy alternative in one form or another. One close adviser to Mr Heath described how 'the meetings at Chequers . . . from 1971 showed that attitudes were changing towards an incomes policy. Few supported it at first but nearly everyone by the end'[32].

The tide of informed opinion in favour of an incomes policy had assisted Mr Heath's efforts[33]. But individual dissenters, taking a longer-term view, preferred a different analysis. Professor A. A. Walters of the London School of Economics argued in a letter to *The Times* on 21 October 1972 that:

> The answer to unemployment is certainly not a massive dose of Government spending financed by newly created money. And the attempt to repress the inflation through the imposition of a bureaucratically controlled and regulated rationing system will make things worse by reducing the rate of growth of output[34].

The analysis of Professor Walters and others was far from the minds of the participants in the next session of tripartite talks held on 26 October, to a background of a joint Electrical, Electronic Telecommunications and Plumbing Union/General and Municipal Workers' Union (EEPTU/GMWU) 37% pay claim. But in the final session of the Downing Street talks the TUC repeated that there could be no deal on wage restraint unless the Government took legal powers over prices and promised that there would be no parallel statutory powers over wages, not even tripartite supervision of pay movements.

The union leaders rejected a suggestion by Sir Frank Figgures, Director General of the National Economic Development Council, that the Government could declare its intentions to promote legislation allowing legal sanctions against anyone blatantly defying the voluntary limit of 5% on price rises. Mr Heath said that the Cabinet would have to study this compromise proposal, but the CBI team said that it would be unacceptable to industry unless wages were involved too, which the unions duly rejected.

As the earlier moods of optimism faded Mr Heath and his Ministers could not conceal their disappointment that Mr Feather, General Secretary of the TUC, and his colleagues should have come to the talks determined to force on to the statute book the control of prices without any suggestion as to how this could be achieved, especially when a seven-hour meeting on 30 October produced the same impasse. Thus, scarcely concealing the impending U-turn, Mr Heath told the 1922 Committee that the country 'will respond to firmness and resolution'[35], and that the Government was determined to do what the national interest required.

The question of trade union persistence on price control had finally emerged as the stumbling block. One participant recalled that:

> The union leaders, particularly Jones and Scanlon, were determined there should be no pay policy if there wasn't a freeze on prices – Jones was also very keen on extra for the pensioners. But at so many of the discussions the Government explained that it was impossible to control every price and then Jones and Scanlon would insist on every price being controlled[36].

Similarly, one Cabinet Minister argued that although the talks were genuine the conflict between the union representatives prevented agreement and led to the talks failing 'because of Jones and Scanlon'[37].

Ultimately, although 'the talks were not window dressing and many trade union leaders had a great respect for Ted Heath'[38], no agreement was reached on a 'voluntary' policy. There was also the question of how reliable a voluntary policy would prove to be. One Cabinet Minister recalled that the TUC and CBI '. . . couldn't really deliver anything – they're not responsible to the people in the way governments are'[39]. Similarly, given the Government's inflationary 'dash for growth' policy based on deficit-financed increases in public expenditure it is unlikely that a voluntary policy could have held down prices and wages, even with maximum co-operation and goodwill, for any longer than the shortest of short terms. The whole idea that the talks were actually dealing with inflation control was, to monetarist or 'right wing' critics, illusory, an interpretation that has usually been made with the benefit of hindsight.

## 5.3    The resort to statutory controls

On 2 November the talks reached their final impasse. Mr Heath immediately announced that the Cabinet would meet to consider the situation, saying that it was the TUC that had made agreement impossible, but also paying tribute expressly to Victor Feather, General Secretary of the TUC, and Sir Sidney Greene, for the spirit in which they had taken part in the long series of tripartite talks since July. Mr Heath's comments left little doubt that a statutory prices and incomes policy was inevitable:

> I am immensely sorry it has not been possible to reach agreement. On Monday afternoon I shall make a full statement to Parliament. The

Government, of course, has a unique responsibility in all these affairs for this country. The Government fully accepts its responsibility and the Cabinet tomorrow will decide the action to be taken[40].

Mr Feather blamed the breakdown of the talks on the Government's refusal to negotiate until the union side made up its mind whether it wanted a completely voluntary or a completely statutory package. The CBI was particularly disappointed that the tripartite talks had failed. The CBI President, Michael Clapham, commented that:

We are really very sad at the outcome of these negotiations because such an enormous amount had been at stake. We are faced with the problem of wild inflation and we know very well that inflation is disastrous for the country. It transfers resources from the poor and the weak to the rich and the powerful and we felt we were offered in these talks the opportunity of coming to a new sort of social contract – an understanding between government and industry and the unions about the way in which the economy should be managed and about the way in which the resources of the country should be shared out[41].

A study of the role of the CBI points out that 'the introduction of a statutory policy was far from what the CBI thought of when it launched its voluntary prices initiative in 1971'[42]. One senior CBI official thought that the Government had let them down:

A statutory policy was a real disappointment for the CBI . . . . Heath should have given us more time; he acted precipitously as far as we were concerned. The CBI members were angry at the prices freeze after sticking to the voluntary policy[43].

Keegan and Pennant-Rea have argued that the CBI was never really offered a 'share in the reins of power'[44] in the way that the TUC were and that the tripartite nature of the talks was more form than substance. Given Mr Heath's personal coolness towards the CBI, and industry generally, this seems a valid observation. Mr Heath's antipathy towards industry was based on what he regarded as industry's failure to invest. The disappointment caused to the CBI following their voluntary prices initiative was another example of Mr Heath's coolness. One trade union participant in the talks stated that 'the CBI contributions were idiotic and they were always falling out. Heath was closer to us than to the CBI'[45]. On both the personal and the policy level evidence suggests that Mr Heath had greater respect for the trade union than the employers' side. As one trade union leader commented '. . . our relations with Heath weren't bad. Vic Feather was very good with personal relationships. He could have got on with Satan'[46]. Another union leader recalled that 'I never knew a Prime Minister who listened more to us. Heath wasn't business oriented; he was a politician to his finger tips'[47].

The fact remained that despite the mutual admiration between the Prime Minister and the trade union representatives and despite the CBI's willingness to continue the talks, the Heath Government on 6 November 1972 completed its incomes policy U-turn. A 90-day standstill was imposed on price, pay, rent and dividend rises. A Counter Inflation (Temporary Provisions) Bill prescribed fines as the sanction to enforce observance of the standstill, not exceeding £400 on a summary conviction. But one senior Whitehall adviser argued that the Government '. . . only went for a statutory policy because the TUC were mad keen on statutory prices control'[48]. After describing how the tripartite talks broke down Mr Heath told the Commons:

> As the House will be aware, the representatives of the TUC stated that they did not regard the total package of proposals as a basis for negotiation. They said that, although they would take them back to the General Council, they would do so without being able to recommend their acceptance. The General Council met this morning. The statement which they have issued shows that there has been no change in the TUC's position.
>
> Although it has not been possible to reach agreement in this round of discussions, the Government is fully prepared to continue to take part in tripartite discussions with the CBI and the TUC on subjects of mutual concern to the three parties.
>
> The responsibility for action now rests with the Government. We have come to the conclusion that we have no alternative but to bring in statutory measures to secure the agreed objectives of economic management in the light of the proposals discussed in the tripartite talks[49].

In terms of the 1970 Conservative Party Manifesto pledge not to repeat Labour's statutory policy and the rejection of the philosophy of compulsory wage control the events of 6 November 1972 were indeed a U-turn. But the 'N minus 1' policy involved considerable supervision of public sector wages in that pressure was put on the nationalized industry involved to stick to the 'N minus 1' going rate. The philosophy behind 'N minus 1' and behind the tripartite talks, and behind the statutory incomes policy, was the same. In each case the Government believed inflation to be a function of wage increases almost to the exclusion of all else and certainly to the exclusion of such aspects as public expenditure and control of the money supply. The U-turn on incomes policy in November 1972 in making incomes policy statutory was thus a completion of a gradual reversal of policy.

In effect, the statutory incomes policy with its prescribed pay limits applicable to everyone was an extension of the 'N minus 1' policy of everyone receiving the 'going rate'. Mr Heath thus described his policy as applying 'right across the board to incomes, prices and dividends'[50], in the mistaken belief that such restrictions were fair because they applied to all. In effect, identical restrictions applied to dissimilar individuals or groups of individuals, are, like identical percentage wage increases, particularly unfair in that they negate the very real differences in effort, skill and creative endeavour that are reflected by the market mechanism. However, in strictly political terms the main point about the U-turn was that the Government was pursuing, directly rather than by stealth, a policy it had vowed not to pursue on taking office. Enoch Powell did not fail to remind the Prime Minister of this contradiction by asking in the Commons debate:

Does he not know it is fatal for any government, party or person to seek to govern in direct opposition to the principles on which they were entrusted with the right to govern? In introducing a compulsory control on wages and prices in contravention of the deepest commitments of this Party, has he taken leave of his senses?[51]

Mr Heath simply replied that the Government was returned to power to act in the national interest. But in strictly political terms Mr Heath had suffered a blow not from Mr Powell, who was a Conservative back-bencher despite being the Government's most effective critic, but from the Labour Opposition. The Labour Party could attack the Conservatives for being unprincipled, in that they had actually introduced a statutory policy in contradiction to the 1970 election manifesto, and for being 'unfair' in that the statutory policy did not have the blessing of the trade unions and was thus not a 'consensus' policy. Labour was able to shift the debate on to its own terms of social justice once Mr Heath had taken the ultimate step of presenting his statutory controls as the fairest possible in the circumstances. Labour was able to make maximum political capital out of the U-turn – simply because it was another U-turn – and out of the implications of the statutory approach. Thus Mr Wilson told the Commons that:

> This is not the time to remind the Government that of all the many strongly worded statements ever since Mr Heath became Leader of his Party, in every debate in the House, every proposal of the Labour Government, and in the general election, this represents even the biggest reversal of positions he has taken up on any subject since he broke his 'at a stroke' promise on coming into office.
>
> We repeatedly warned him that no agreement would be fair, just or workable which did not provide for guarantees on food prices – not just domestically created prices and a limited range of other essentials – rents, both private and public, rising mortgage interest rates, VAT and school meal prices, which he is going to increase next April, as well as dividends[52].

Mr Heath's decision to introduce a statutory incomes policy was therefore susceptible to both Mr Powell's logic and Mr Wilson's political skills. It was both a source of schism within the Conservative Party and a source of political advantage for Labour.

On 10 November the Counter Inflation (Temporary Provisions) Bill was given a second reading by 307 votes to 272, the only Conservative dissenter being Mr Powell, who voted with the Opposition, and Jock Bruce-Gardyne, Neil Marten and John Biffen who abstained.

To avoid any discontent in the Conservative Party in the country, all Conservative constituency chairmen in England and Wales, area agents, constituency agents, and members of the National Union Executive Committee received from Lord Carrington, Party Chairman, a 1000-word letter tracing the history of the Government's talks with the TUC and the Confederation of British Industry and justifying the decision to freeze prices and pay increases by law, stating that:

> . . . I know that we can count on your support in getting across to our colleagues in the Party, and to the country as a whole, what we have

attempted to do by voluntary agreement and the necessity for the firm but fair action that we have now taken . . . . I am sure you will agree that this issue is vital to us all[53].

The U-turn of incomes policy caused no resignations from the Cabinet and only limited disquiet from the back bench MPs[54], so it is fair to agree that 'the Conservative Party took the U-turn very well . . . there was no serious trouble'[55]. The swiftness and smooth execution of Mr Heath's introduction of a statutory incomes policy was testimony to the Prime Minister's total control over policy-making and his ability to carry through such a U-turn with the Conservative Party both in Parliament and in the country. This is a classic example of the use of Prime Ministerial power to direct policy and then to authorize that Cabinet, Parliament and the Party as a whole fall into line. In such an atmosphere dissension could be easily viewed as disloyalty and unity would be bought with little more than an appeal to the national interest acting in tandem with Party interest. In general, however, the view of the Conservative Party both in Parliament and in the country was that the Prime Minister had made the right decision. Only Enoch Powell in the Conservative Party was publicly prepared to denounce the Prime Minister's policy as '. . . so suddenly assembled and so ill-digested that it took his own Cabinet colleagues and Conservative Central Office by surprise . . . . There is something vertiginous about the spectacle of men solemnly recommitting themselves to a proven absurdity'[56].

On 30 November 1972 the Counter Inflation (Temporary Provisions) Bill reached Royal Assent, thus officially completing the series of policy changes that Mr Heath had made since taking office in June 1970. But the U-turn on statutory incomes policy was arguably the most politically important, although to an extent, as previously explained, it embodied a continuation of the previous policies, only now under another name. What hastened the U-turn on incomes policy was the over-reaction to rising unemployment during 1971 that led firstly to the abandonment of the 'Quiet Revolution' policies of disengagement and secondly to the inflationary growth policy. The U-turn on floating the pound was a consequence of the 'dash for growth', which made the incomes policy option more attractive to the Government. These policies formed the core of the 'Heath dilemma' by which a rational alternative to the 'Quiet Revolution' had to be found, given the urgency of EEC entry. It was these factors, not the Wilberforce settlement that concluded the 1972 miners' strike, which precipitated the incomes policy U-turn. Nor must it be overlooked that the toughness of the statutory policy occurred at the very time when the Government's growth policy, with massively increased public expenditure, was about to have its inflationary effect.

## References

1. LORD GOWRIE, *The Conservative Opportunity* (Ed. by Lord Blake and John Patten), Macmillan, 1976, p. 145.
2. A. GAMBLE, *Conservative Party Politics* (Ed. by Z. Layton-Henry), Macmillan, 1980, pp. 40–41.
3. Interview, Conservative Party Official.
4. Interview, Journalist/Author.

5. Interview, Senior Treasury Official.
6. S. BRITTAN, *The Economic Consequences of Democracy*, Temple Smith, 1977, pp. 45–46.
7. *Hansard*, 23 June 1972, Vol. 839, Col. 877.
8. Interview, Conservative Party Official.
9. Interview, Cabinet Minister.
10. The tripartite talks were not, in fact, the first step towards agreement on overall matters of economic management. From early 1971 an NEDC steering committee – the 'Group of Four' or 'Four Wise Men', Vic Feather, Campbell Adamson, Sir Douglas Allen – had met to agree on a joint approach to the problems facing the Government. In 1972 they were joined by Sir William Armstrong whose personal predilection in favour of an incomes policy was considerable. This small group of advisers prepared the way for the full-scale attempt to find a 'voluntary' policy to which the tripartite talks were dedicated.
11. The CBI's 5% price ceiling was extended at its official expiry date at the end of July 1972 in a modified form until the end of October.
12. *The Times*, 8 July 1972.
13. *Sunday Telegraph*, 9 July 1972.
14. For a number of years Treasury thinking has been susceptible to incomes policy arguments aimed at keeping wage increases down.
15. *Hansard*, 13 July 1972, Vol. 840, Col. 1845.
16. *The Times*, 12 September 1972.
17. *The Times*, 15 September 1972.
18. This argument in a general theoretical context is best represented by R. E. PAHL and J. J. WINKLER '*Corporatism in Britain*' in *The Corporate State: Myth or Reality*, Policy Studies Institute, 1976, pp. 5–24.
19. For an historical examination of the use of the term corporatism from the 1930s to the present day, see PHILIPPE C. SCHMITTER, '*Still the Century of Corporatism?*' in *Trends Towards Corporatist Intermediation* (Ed. by P. C. Schmitter and G. Lehmbruch), Sage, 1979, pp. 7–52.
20. W. GRANT and D. MARSH, *The CBI*, Hodder and Stoughton, 1977, p. 23.
21. *The Times*, 27 September 1972.
22. *The Times*, 28 September 1972.
23. Ironically the rate of inflation for the third quarter of 1972 was 6.5% compared to 10.1% for the third quarter of 1971.
24. *The Times*, 28 September 1972.
25. *The Times*, 16 October 1972.
26. Interview, Trade Union Leader.
27. Interview, Cabinet Minister.
28. *The Times*, 17 October 1972.
29. Ibid.
30. Ibid.
31. BARRY BRACEWELL-MILNES, *Pay and Price Control Guide*, Butterworths, 1973.
32. Interview, Conservative Party Adviser.
33. Two publications in particular contributed to the intellectual tide favouring an incomes policy: HUGH CLEGG, *How to Run an Incomes Policy and Why we Made Such a Mess of the Last One*, Heinemann, 1971, and AUBREY JONES, *The New Inflation: The Politics of Prices and Incomes*, André Deutsch and Penguin, 1973. With hindsight, the argument of each author has proved to be singularly unconvincing.
34. *The Times*, 21 October 1972. It is worth stressing that individual dissenters, such as Professor Walters, were not to be counted in large numbers at the time, as monetarism, as a theory of political economy, had yet to sufficiently challenge Keynesian orthodoxy. (Eight years later, when Professor Walters was made a personal economic adviser to Prime Minister Margaret Thatcher the intellectual and political climate had changed.)
35. *The Times*, 1 November 1972.
36. Interview, Senior Treasury Official.
37. Interview, Cabinet Minister.
38. Interview, Cabinet Minister.
39. Interview, Cabinet Minister.
40. *The Times*, 3 November 1972.
41. Ibid.

42. W. GRANT and D. MARSH, op. cit. (Ref. 20), p. 196.
43. Interview, Senior CBI Official.
44. W. KEEGAN and R. PENNANT-REA, *Who Runs the Economy? Control and Influence in British Economic Policy*, Temple Smith, 1979, pp. 128–29.
45. Interview, Trade Union Leader.
46. Interview, Trade Union Leader.
47. Interview, Trade Union Leader.
48. Interview, Lord Armstrong.
49. *Hansard*, 6 November 1972, Vol. 845, Cols. 625–27.
50. *The Times*, 7 November 1972.
51. *Hansard*, 6 November 1972, Vol. 845, Col. 631.
52. *Hansard*, 6 November 1972, Vol. 845, Cols. 628–29.
53. *The Times*, 10 November 1972.
54. P. NORTON, *Dissension in the House of Commons 1945–74*, Macmillan, 1975, pp. 522–23, notes that only Enoch Powell voted against the Third Reading and only two other back-benchers, Jock Bruce-Gardyne and John Biffen, abstained.
55. Interview, Conservative Party Official.
56. *The Times*, 9 October 1971.

Chapter 6

# The operation of Stages I and II

*'The first major British laws to control wages were the fourteenth century Statutes of Labourers, which vainly tried to curb the rise in wages after the Black Death of 1348. The attempt at comprehensive price control a thousand years earlier by the Roman Emperor Diocletian has now become almost an historical cliche.'*

S. Brittan and P. Lilley
*The Delusion of Incomes Policy*
Temple Smith, 1977

## 6.1   The freeze

Like Mr Wilson's freeze in 1966, Mr Heath's Stage I standstill served as a breathing space when the more detailed operation of a full incomes policy could be worked out. Partly because freezes apply to everyone and last a comparatively short period of time they are more generally regarded with hostile compliance rather than with total rejection.

As expected, trade union criticisms centred on the 'unfairness' of the freeze with Jack Jones warning that there could be no hope of further discussion between the unions and the Government on curbing inflation until the prices standstill was more effectively improved. 'We want to draw the Government's attention to the fact that the price freeze is not working'[1], Mr Jones said. The T&GWU executive called for an early end to the wage standstill and a tightening of the price freeze in the best interests of the working people. More alarming for Mr Heath than Mr Jones' plan was the massive Liberal victory, in December 1972, in the Sutton and Cheam by-election by a majority of 7417 votes, a 30% swing that resulted in the Labour candidate losing his deposit. Although the Conservative held Uxbridge, where the Liberal lost his deposit, the electoral disillusionment with the Government, among its former supporters, was already well under way – a disillusionment that was not to subside until the fall of the Heath Government[2].

## 6.2   By-election anxieties

The Government's abject by-election record deserves further comment, and requires a slight digression from the details of Stages I and II, notwithstanding the interdependence between the Government's electoral strategy and its economic strategy. Although every Government suffers by-election defeats, particularly in marginal constituencies, the Conservative Government 1970–74 faced a graver problem. Following the December 1972 loss of Sutton and Cheam to the Liberals it transpired that virtually no Conservative seat was safe from the self-styled Liberal revival.

The challenge was not from Labour, which won only one by-election, at Bromsgrove in 1971[3], during the Parliament, but from a Liberal vote comprised almost entirely of disaffected Conservatives more eager to register their protest than at any time since the loss of Orpington in 1962 to a similar Liberal swing. In July 1973 the 'impeccable majorities'[4] at Ely and Ripon were overturned and Berwick-on-Tweed fell in November, although Hove was held against the Liberal tide[5].

Douglas Hurd mentions the Liberals' exploitation of community politics and the poor state of Conservative Party organization in many previously safe constituencies as contributing to the Liberal success. These factors, along with the identification of the Liberals as a non-socialist alternative, certainly depressed the Conservative vote to the Liberals' advantage. But the chief issue that caused the disillusionment among Conservative voters was inflation. Mr Hurd reported to the Prime Minister before the loss of Ely and Ripon that Sir Richard Webster, the Director of Organization at Conservative Central Office, 'felt the atmosphere was similar to that in summer 1963, when everyone wanted to kick the Government. This time, however, there was just one issue, and that was prices'[6]. As one back-bencher correctly observed, a 'high rate of inflation is terrible for Tory voters'[7]. Similarly, a former Minister noted that 'Conservative voters were very worried about inflation and the rot was setting in. That's why they voted Liberal. The Tories must stand for sound economic management in the public's view'[8]. Because rising inflation particularly eroded savings, Conservative voters in prosperous middle class safe seats were feeling its effects proportionately to a greater extent than other social groups. To traditional Conservative supporters Mr Heath's talk of fairness and concern for the low-paid was, only just, excusable; but when this social concern was accompanied by rising inflation stoked by the Government's expansionary policies the urge to protest by voting Liberal became impossible to resist. This point applies not only to the by-election disasters but ultimately to the 1974 February Election defeat 'which came not because Labour gained votes but because we (the Conservatives) lost them'[9]. In strictly electoral terms Mr Heath's '. . . unconservative, almost radical politics'[10] were alienating the traditional Conservative voters. As Keegan and Pennant-Rea point out it was under Mr Heath's administration that the policy machine '. . . clearly lost control over inflation'[11].

This process, according to the critics on the Right, was not the result of bad luck but the result of the abandonment of the 'Quiet Revolution' policies and the consequent adoption of inflationary pump-priming aimed originally at reducing unemployment and later explained in terms of 'growth'. The Heath Government's by-election debacles, it was therefore argued, stemmed directly from the Government's policies. While it is obviously a supposition to claim that without the Heath Government's policy reversals the by-election catastrophes would not have occurred, the interpretation of the Conservative Right must be taken seriously given the scale of the defection to the Liberals in safe, supposedly impregnable, Conservative seats, from December 1972 onwards and throughout 1973. The Right argue that the by-election disasters happened after the major policy reversals, not before, and that the crucial impact on Conservative voters was the rate of inflation. The irony of the situation was that Mr

Heath and his Ministers were forever warning of the dangers of inflation and had introduced a prices and incomes policy to control inflation, while simultaneously they were stoking the inflationary fires. However, in the context of the 'Heath dilemma' this was not an irrational policy, firstly because of the absence of an accepted monetarist critique and secondly because the 'Quiet Revolution' alternative had been deemed to be a failure. The Government had simply not yet understood that if the money supply was inflated, inflation would follow and consequently Conservative voters would become increasingly restless. Thus, as unemployment was falling during 1973, a consumer 'boom' was in full swing, and the 'dash for growth' policy was at its height, the unpopularity of the Government was increasing – a contradictory trend in overall post-war terms, when expanding the economy had generally led to Government popularity.

Thus, returning to the detailed development of Stages I and II in view of the Government's actual inflationary measures it was not surprising that the Government's back bench critics regarded the counter-inflationary policy as a diversionary charade. The trade unions also attacked the incomes policy but from a different point of view, stressing the unfairness of the freeze while prices were rising[12]. On 13 December 1972, 170000 of the 250000 hospital ancillary workers took part in token strikes against the pay freeze.

Ironically, as the pay restraints were being tightened the Government's plans for massive public expenditure were outlined[13]. Thus, the Conservatives planned to spend between 2% and 6% more in 1973–74 than Labour had planned to spend in the same years according to Labour's White Paper in 1969. In particular, state industries were earmarked for £452m special aid over 3 years. Peter Jay shrewdly observed that '. . . it is a White Paper that only the boldest of Labour governments would have dared to present'[14], an indication of how far the 'Heath dilemma' had pushed Conservative policy to the Left. Despite the freeze, the 1972 Christmas consumer boom and the fall in unemployment total to 744876 raised doubts about the Government's ability to maintain its 5% growth target without overheating the economy and consequently the Bank of England's Minimum Lending Rate was raised from 8% to 9%. Following further meetings between the TUC Economic Committee and the Government, lingering doubts that a statutory Stage II would be introduced were dispelled and the Government's intention to 'go it alone', if necessary, was hardly concealed. As Mr Barber put it on 5 January, 'while we hope for maximum co-operation, we have made it clear that whatever the outcome of the talks the Government is determined to bring forward its proposals for arrangements to follow the standstill as soon as possible after next week's talks'[15].

Similarly, the TUC was unwilling to change its bargaining position significantly from that which had led to the collapse of the tripartite talks the previous November. On 19 January, as the miners submitted a £7 a week pay claim, and members of the Civil and Public Services Association stopped work to protest at the unfair application of the freeze, the TUC Economic Committee reiterated its opposition to the Government's anti-inflation measures. The following day, despite an agreement on the resumption of pay bargaining, the Downing Street talks, as so often before, ended in deadlock, with the Cabinet determined to introduce statutory pay curbs with penalties for those breaking the guidelines. Paul Johnson, in an article analysing Mr Heath's relationship with the unions, concluded that:

> In short, though Mr Heath now talks the language of compromise, he is still committed to the substance of confrontation. Nor is this surprising. Mr Heath is a man of strong and distinctive character, from which his approach to politics springs. He cannot change this character any more than he can change the colour of his skin. For all these reasons I believe the unions would be wrong to work with Mr Heath, though naturally they must listen to what he has to say[16].

This view, that Mr Heath remained committed to the substance of 'confrontation', was a common criticism from the Left of Mr Heath's Government. By itself that view was too simplistic. All Governments have to face 'confrontations' in a free society when the right to strike is guaranteed. But these confrontations are rarely one-sided; usually they result from the strike action of a trade union seeking to take the best advantage of its position as a monopoly supplier of labour. In this sense it is the Government that is confronted. In other cases a Government may prolong a confrontation by preventing a settlement between the union and the employers involved.

Mr Heath's Government has often been regarded as pursuing the politics of confrontation. As far as the Industrial Relations Act was concerned such criticism is fair in that the Act was impractical and made industrial confrontation worse. But even in this case the Act was effectively 'put on ice' by the end of 1972. The U-turn over industry policy and the panic over unemployment are testimony to the Government's desire to avoid 'confrontation' when 'confrontation', it would be argued, was a more realistic alternative to the policy changes that ensued. Mr Johnson referred to the incomes policy as 'still' a policy of confrontation, the implication being that the U-turn on incomes policy represented a move away from confrontation and towards consensus. However, as previously explained, the Government's determination to hold down wages as the cure for inflation was the panacea behind both 'N minus 1' and the 'voluntary' attempt at a prices and incomes agreement and the statutory policy. Questions of confrontation under 'N minus 1' were largely due to the unions confronting the Government – in the case of the miners, successfully. But under the statutory incomes policy 'confrontation' became more not less likely as the compromise solution of a court of inquiry, on the lines of Wilberforce, was ruled out. The Government faced the added problem of bringing the law into disrepute by bringing it into wage negotiations and thus cutting down the available options open. In this sense the Heath incomes policy was more likely to lead to a set-piece confrontation, which in fact is what happened. These observations are important in defining the political and philosophical limitations to incomes policies in general, and Mr Heath's policy in particular, which on 13 January 1973 entered Stage II[17].

## 6.3    Stage II and the dash for growth

The core of the policy was control of pay and prices by two statutory agencies, a Prices Commission and a Pay Board. The pay code was based on a limit of settlements of £1 a week plus 4%. The existing freeze was extended 60 days from the end of February to permit a Bill to be presented to Parliament setting out a statutory Pay and Prices Code. Pay rises were further restricted to £250 per year. Profits were restricted not to exceed the average level in the best two of the five previous years. Such a control of profits would normally be expected from only the boldest of Labour governments. Conservative governments had hitherto sought to encourage profitability; indeed this had been one of the aims of the 'Quiet Revolution' policy of reducing the state's role to coerce private industry. Whether or not this was wise it certainly indicated how far to the Left Conservative policy had moved. As well as the imposition of dividend control, price rises would only be permitted if manufacturers were faced with unavoidable cost increases.

Reactions were predictable. The unions expressed great disappointment but *The Times* Editorial purred that 'Mr Heath has fully discharged [his] special responsibility; and our endorsement is unqualified'[18]. The Opposition launched a strong attack on the policy especially as a further fall in unemployment served to de-fuse the political appeal of the unemployment issue.

On 19 January TUC leaders decided not to co-operate in implementing Stage II, and withdrew from consultations with the Government to draw up their own proposals. The TUC Economic Committee also rejected a proposal that union members should sit on the Price Commission and Pay Board. Mr Feather commented that 'We are not asking for any more talks. The Government has decided to go it alone'[19]. Not all union leaders agreed. Tom Jackson urged further talks and an end to the TUC's 'sulking'[20].

Apart from Mr Heath's supporters among Conservative MPs, Stage II was less than popular. The TUC published its own plans criticizing the inflexibility of the Government's policy, and the CBI, which was by now not slow to embarrass the Government, was sceptical about the beneficial effects that Stage II would have on industry. Mr Clapham, the CBI President, stated that:

> I remain seriously worried by some aspects of Stage II as set out in the recent White Paper and draft Bill. The basic problem is this: the Government is walking a tightrope at the moment in reconciling two major objectives. The first is the essentially short-term one of controlling inflation. But this has to be achieved without frustrating the longer-term objective of restoring British industry to health. Neither can be sacrificed to the other without disaster. Unfortunately, from what I have seen so far of Stage II, I am not at all sure that the Government has struck the right balance[21].

Similarly, Bacon and Eltis have criticized Mr Heath's incomes policy restraints that forced companies '. . . to cut profit margins when they wanted to increase them'[22], thus further restricting a vital source of investment.

The inevitable industrial protest over Stage II occurred in mid-February when gas workers began an overtime ban after the Industry Minister, Tom Boardman, made it clear that there could be no increase on the £2.25 a week pay offer to the 47000 gas workers. The Government was as determined to see the dispute through as it had been in its pre-incomes policy 'N minus 1' phase[23]. As gas cuts took effect Mr Heath characteristically stated that the public supported his policy while Mr Boardman, to appease the fear of Tory back-benchers that toughness was a prelude to capitulation, stated bluntly that 'There can be no purpose in a court of inquiry [in the gas dispute] as there is nothing to inquire into'[24]. On 15 February Mr Heath declared that under Stage II the option of compromise 'is no longer open'[25]. Peter Walker told the Commons that any pay exception to the gas workers would be unfair to others, therefore the Government had to stand firm. However, with talk of further industrial disruption by the miners, railway workers, and hospital workers over Stage II, Mr Powell prophetically warned that the Conservative Party could not remain the party of national unity under Mr Heath's policies:

> Anyone who supposes that national unity lies through victory in a confrontation between the Conservative Party and organized labour understands nothing of this nation. The Government cannot find a way out . . . without itself accepting and discharging the responsibility for inflation, which its present words and policies are designed to shift on to other shoulders[26].

It is worth pondering Mr Powell's criticism. The Government were no more desirous of confrontation than they had been before the statutory policy was introduced. However, the open assumption of the statutory policy was that inflation could only be controlled by wage restraint – by law not negotiation. This indeed made confrontation more likely for reasons previously explained. It was the question of 'discharging the responsibilities for inflation' that made any forthcoming confrontation so unnecessary, in that the Government's expansionary policies were putting pressure upon the very wages and prices that were being legally restrained.

In such a paradoxical situation Mr Barber presented what he himself called a 'neutral' budget on 6 March[27], concentrating concessions and benefits on supporting the counter-inflation policy, at a net cost to the Exchequer of £120m in a year. Of that total concessions on VAT cost £110m, with income tax charges costing £9m, exemption limits being raised so that married people over 65 could earn up to £1000 tax free. Pensions, sickness and unemployment benefits were also increased. As well as the fight against inflation the policy of sustained economic expansion was stressed and for this reason, despite back bench pressure, there were no public expenditure cuts. Mainly because of this, Conservative MPs gave the budget a loyal but muted welcome in marked contrast to the euphoric response to previous tax-cutting budgets.

Of all Mr Barber's budgets and mini-budgets the one in March 1973 contained the greatest paradox. While some Conservatives did not have their heart in the growth policy and high public expenditure it implied, the central tenets of the 'Heath dilemma' alternative to the 'Quiet Revolution', Party loyalty demanded the semblance of an enthusiastic acceptance[28]. For the TUC, who had most consistently over the years advocated a high-growth policy, there was the political necessity of opposing the strategy of a government that had seemingly clashed with the unions on more occasions than any other since the General Strike. The further paradox was that the Government's policy for 5% growth was coupled with the imposition of the strictest and most comprehensive prices and incomes restraint since the War, restraints that the unions found as unacceptable as they, privately, found the growth policy amenable.

As one critic of the incomes policy observed:

> Leading Ministers do not regard the present wage and price controls as emergency measures designed to produce lower and more realistic expectations about the most probable course of wages and prices. Instead, they see them as but the beginning of a permanent system of regulation. They have resurrected the medieval concept of a just price and a fair wage – concepts that are quite unworkable without the underlying theological agreement on status and hierarchy that made the medieval system possible[29].

Indeed, the very question of anomalies arising from the freeze had already provoked industrial action so it was with some relief that Mr Macmillan announced on 7 March the proposed terms of reference for the Pay Board's examination of particular anomalies. With the appointment of Derek Robinson as the Pay Board's Deputy Chairman the Board was asked:

> to report as soon as possible, and in any case by not later than 15 September, on the treatment of anomalies, particularly those that have arisen from the impact of the standstill on groups whose pay is, or has been, determined by links with the settlements of others or by formal procedures for comparing their pay with that of other groups[30].

In effect, Mr Robinson's role at the Pay Board was similar to that of Mr Aubrey Jones, the Chairman of the Wilson Government's Prices and Incomes Board.

As well as the sporadic strike action against pay restraint by the gas workers, ASLEF drivers and hospital workers, which the TUC agreed to support following a meeting of the Economic Committee on 14 March, the CBI again expressed its dissatisfaction with the Government's policy. The Director-General, Campbell Adamson, warned that Stage II gave little incentive for investment and industry could be brought to a 'grinding halt' if the Government failed to appreciate the need for adequate profits to fund investment[31]. Such criticism would have been virtually unthinkable, or at least not made public, during the Government's first year and a half.

Although unwilling to appease the CBI or to provide money to public sector workers demanding more than Stage II allowed, the Government did feel able to donate a £15m subsidy to the building societies to hold interest rates below 10%, although the true origin of the policy lay in the imminence of the local council elections rather than altruistic reasons.

If not earlier, certainly by the end of April 1973, Ministers seemed satisfied with the workings of Stage II, regarding the TUC General Council's announcement of 'resentful and reluctant acquiescence' in Stage II as an attitude less discouraging than had been feared on several occasions since the imposition of the standstill in November 1972. The *Economist* argued that 'the Government has won an historic, if temporary, victory for the country by successfully enforcing Stage II of its incomes policy'[32]. However, the TUC's official May Day demonstrations against the Government's incomes policy led to considerable industrial disruption, with an estimated 1 600 000 workers rallying to the call for a one-day strike.

Although the stoppages were far from total they were sufficient to remind Ministers [if they needed reminding] that differences between the Government and the unions had not evaporated despite the series of private tripartite talks and public dialogues that had preceded and accompanied the Government's prices and incomes policy.

But, as the Government saw it, the demonstrations were irrelevant to the overall economic strategy under which 107 settlements involving 2 900 000 workers had already been made under Stage II. Furthermore, both the NEDC and the CBI reported that the economy was growing by an annual rate possibly exceeding the 5% growth target. Mr Barber was thus able to tell the House that 'the present Government have succeeded in doubling the rate of economic growth and in trebling the rate at which the standard of living has been rising'[33]. In this context it is not unrealistic to agree that for Mr Heath 'the growth policy was the habit of a lifetime'[34]. The CBI in its quarterly report described the rate of economic recovery as one of the fastest so far, with new orders and output rising, strongly indicating an export-led boom in full swing. However, as one critic noted 'whenever governments talk of faster growth they usually mean printing more money . . .'[35].

In political terms it is worth noting that the boom associated with the 5% dash for growth[36] that was bound to temporarily raise living standards, was not accompanied by a surge of popularity in the Government as had occurred during the late 1950s when Harold Macmillan's appeal that 'You've never had it so good' caught the imagination of the electorate. Indeed, the reverse was the case as the by-election defections to the Liberals were to prove. In retrospect, it appears that even if the Government's policy was 'the apotheosis of crude Keynesianism'[37] the electoral appeal of such a policy had disappeared. Labour Party spokesmen had simply to attack Mr Heath's policy as 'unfair' to gain an important political advantage. Having presented his incomes policy legislation in the socialist language of 'fairness' Mr Heath could hardly expect the Labour Opposition not to exploit every increase in the cost of living, irrespective of its cause. Mr Wilson had an ideal platform – although completely different from that of Mr Powell and the Conservative monetarists – on which to attack the Government:

> Stage I was manifestly unfair because incomes were immediately frozen and prices soared. Stage II is unfair because the Government, while imposing a severe limit on incomes, refuses to deal with the principal items in household expenditure, particularly food and housing[38].

Thus, at the height of the boom, Labour consolidated its hold on the important metropolitan districts in England in the district council elections, controlling outright 26 out of 36 metropolitan districts compared to the Conservatives' five.

The chief reason for the Conservatives' electoral unpopularity, despite the increase in living standards, was inflation, which was now being fuelled by world commodity price increases on top of the Government's policies. Patrick Jenkin, the Chief Secretary to the Treasury, told the House in May 1973 that 'Inflation is now a world-wide phenomenon. Prices are rising at annual rates of 8% to 9% in almost all advanced industrial countries'[39]. Similarly, Mr Heath commented that '. . . as we have to import such a vast proportion of our raw materials for our industry and a good 50% of our foodstuffs this is bound to affect price levels'[40]. But as one Cabinet Minister rightly noted 'the problem with the growth policy was that it led to an import boom'[41].

Such unfortunate events might have suggested that the 5% growth policy was already unrealistic. The policy did have its critics, none more lucid than Peter Jay who wrote of the 'boom that must go bust', warning that:

We have got the most acute prospect of general overheating on the back of the weakest balance of payments in the post-war period. We have the most serious distortion of the balance of demand – as between consumption, public and private, on the one hand and exports and investments on the other – which we have experienced in the past 25 years . . . . If allowance is made for the facts that it takes up to 12 months to adjust the expansion rate of the economy and that output is now rising almost twice as fast as capacity, it is obviously dangerous to continue to fuel an expansion rate of 5% or more. The balance of demand between public and private consumption on one hand and net exports and investment on the other is almost certainly more distorted than in any post-war economic cycle. This means quite simply that when the full employment rate is reached the rate of consumption is so high that far too few resources are left over for the exports that must pay for 'full employment' levels of imports and for the rate of investment associated with full employment[42].

Bacon and Eltis have similarly observed that a high fraction of the economy's spare labour was '. . . drawn into national and local government employment, mainly the latter, so that labour became scarce in the South of England and the Midlands extraordinarily quickly with the result that the output of many producers could not meet demand'[43]. But Mr Jay's warnings were soon to have their effect. Following Peter Walker's announcement of a general butter subsidy of 2p per pound to families receiving family income supplement, pensioners receiving supplementary benefit, and other recipients of supplementary allowances, a total of about 5 million people[44], came the first sign that the great 'dash for growth', originally inspired by rising unemployment in 1971, was actually being restrained.

At the end of May 1973 the Chancellor, Mr Barber, cut public spending by £500m only 2 months after his last expansionary budget. Among the measures were cuts in expenditure on roads, local government services, public building projects and improvements, selective assistance to industry, defence, nationalized industries, agriculture and industrial training. The burden of the cuts was thus well spread, partly with Stage II negotiations in mind. Although Mr Barber was praised by *The Times* as 'willing to read the signs and modify his policies when the evidence shows this to be necessary'[45], the fact remained that only 2 months after his budget the Chancellor had been forced to concede that he was on the wrong track, or rather his Treasury advisers had miscalculated the extent of successive expansionary measures.

But it was still Mr Barber's view that '. . . the economy is continuing to grow in line with the budget forecast which was for an annual rate of 5% over the next 18 months to the first half of 1974'[46]. On this occasion the comments of the Opposition leader Mr Wilson were particularly pertinent. He noted that it was easy to achieve growth '. . . for a time and at a price if one prints money by borrowing at the rate of £4000m per year. There are distinguished Latin American precedents in support of that'[47].

To the background of what was becoming known misleadingly as the 'Barber boom'[48], falling unemployment and steadily rising inflation, the tripartite talks on Stage III of the Government's prices and incomes policy began in the summer of 1973. It is appropriate here to quote Lord Robbins that '. . . all experience hitherto suggests that in free societies [prices and incomes] controls . . . whatever their initial success, tend to crumble and eventually break down'[49]. However, as late as November 1973, Mr Heath was still optimistically declaring that '. . . the prospects and opportunities for British industry today are more exciting and more solidly based than at any time since the Second World War'[50].

## References

1. *The Times*, 8 December 1972.
2. Some Conservatives would argue that the sense of disillusionment was not to disappear until the election of Mrs Margaret Thatcher as Leader in 1975.
3. The swing to Labour at Bromsgrove was a staggering 10.1%. At the same time Labour held Southampton, Itchen with a 2.8% swing and Goole with an 8.7% swing.
4. D. HURD, *An End to Promises: Sketch of a Government 1970–74*, Collins, 1979, p. 109.
5. It should be noted, however, that as I. CREWE *et al.* have pointed out in 'Partisan Dealignment in Britain 1964–74', *British Journal of Political Science*, Vol. 7, 1977, pp. 129–90, the electorate was considerably more volatile in the 1970s than it had been at the time of Torrington in 1958, and Orpington in 1962. Thus any government faced more acute by-election losses than had previously been the case.
6. D. HURD, op. cit. (Ref. 4), p. 109.
7. Interview, Conservative MP.
8. Interview, Junior Minister,
9. D. HURD, op. cit. (Ref. 4), p. 134.
10. Interview, Conservative Party Official.
11. W. KEEGAN and R. PENNANT-REA, *Who Runs the Economy? Control and Influence in British Economic Policy*, Temple Smith, 1977, p. 181.
12. Public opinion, however, supported the Government; 41% thought the counter inflation policy to be good for the country and only 24% thought it to be bad, *Gallup International Public Opinion Polls (GB) 1937–75*, p. 1223.
13. Cmnd. 5187, *Select Committee on Expenditure*, HMSO, 1973.
14. *The Times*, 20 December 1972.
15. *The Times*, 6 January 1973.

16. *The Times*, 11 January 1973. Mr Johnson's article was written, of course, before his widely publicized change of political allegiance.
17. Cmnd. 5205. *Programme for Controlling Inflation*, HMSO, 1973. Stage II of the policy was due to begin in the Autumn.
18. *The Times*, 18 January 1973.
19. *The Times*, 20 January 1973.
20. *The Times*, 22 January 1973.
21. *The Times*, 2 February 1973.
22. R. BACON and W. ELTIS, *Britain's Economic Problems: Too Few Producers*, Macmillan, 1976, p. 22.
23. The 'N minus 1' policy is often erroneously cited as a policy of 'confrontation' when compared with the Heath Government's incomes policy.
24. *The Times*, 15 February 1973.
25. *The Times*, 16 February 1973.
26. *The Times*, 24 February 1973.
27. *Hansard*, 6 March 1973, Vol. 852, Col. 235.
28. It is worth noting that the Conservative Party had had a series of internal debates between the 'growthmen' and the 'deflationists', particularly following the resignation of Chancellor Thorneycroft in 1958 over what he considered to be excessive government spending.
29. S. BRITTAN, *The Economic Consequences of Democracy*, Temple Smith, 1977, p. 59.
30. *The Times*, 8 March 1973.
31. *The Times*, 15 March 1973.
32. The *Economist*, 31 March 1973.
33. *Hansard*, 22 May 1973, Vol. 857, Col. 218.
34. Interview, Treasury Adviser.
35. S. BRITTAN, op. cit. (Ref. 29), p. 61.
36. According to one Treasury Minister, 'there was no dash for growth and no 5% target. We wanted to increase the level of demand above the growth of productive capacity and then to bring it in line with the growth of productive capacity'. Interview, Treasury Minister.
37. ALAN BUDD, *The Politics of Economic Planning*, Fontana, 1978, p. 122.
38. *The Times*, 18 May 1973.
39. *Hansard*, 12 May 1973, Vol. 855, Col. 1388.
40. *Hansard*, 28 June 1973, Vol. 858, Col. 1723.
41. Interview, Cabinet Minister.
42. *The Times*, 2 May 1973.
43. R. BACON and W. ELTIS, op. cit. (Ref. 22), p. 59.
44. *Hansard*, 7 May 1973, Vol. 856, Cols. 60–63.
45. *The Times*, 22 May 1973.
46. *Hansard*, 5 July 1973, Vol. 859, Col. 711.
47. *Hansard*, 18 July 1973, Vol. 860, Col. 1199.
48. The 'Heath boom' would have been a more accurate and appropriate description, given the rationality of the 'Heath dilemma' approach.
49. LORD ROBBINS, *Political Economy Past and Present*, Macmillan, 1976, p. 96.
50. *The Times*, 9 November 1973.

Chapter 7

# Stage III, the miners' strike and the February 1974 election

*'Until the present crisis hit the country, the living standards of the British people, since we took office in 1970, had been rising more than twice as fast as they did during the period of the former Labour Administration. One of the cruellest consequences of inflation is the unfair way in which it hits some groups in the community far harder than others. But despite the hardship caused by rising prices, for the great majority of the people of this country the pronounced rise in living standards was a reality . . . .*

*This prosperity has now, for the time being, been blighted by the effects of the three-day week, forced upon us by the need to ration electricity so as to prevent our power stations from running out of coal altogether as a consequence of the industrial action taken by the National Union of Mineworkers.'*

Conservative Party Manifesto
February 1974

## 7.1    The secret Downing Street meeting

The question of the miners' attitude was crucial to Stage III. Following their success in 1972 the miners realized that despite the relative decline of the coal industry in the 1960s they held enormous industrial strength, which, given the level of trade union militancy, they were expected to – and prepared to – use. As Mr Gormley told the NUM conference on 2 July, the miners 'must be at the head of the wages league'[1]. Both the Government and the miners' leaders were under no illusion. They knew that unless they could agree to permit the miners a substantial 'special case' increase within the terms of Stage III, the Government's counter-inflationary strategy would prove to be abortive. Indeed, it can be argued that the attempt to identify 'special cases', '. . . indicated the increasing preoccupation of the Conservative incomes policy with the whole question of income distribution'[2]. At their July conference the miners had submitted a new claim for further increases of between £8.21 and £12.71 a week, bringing the minimum basic weekly rate up to £33 for surface workers, £40 for underground workers and £45 for coalface workers, against the current rates of £25.29, £27.29 and £36.79, respectively, and this only 3 months after accepting pay increases effective from 1 April.

At this early stage, with the Stage III negotiations by no means complete, a private meeting took place on 16 July, in the garden of Number 10, between the Prime Minister, Joe Gormley and Sir William Armstrong, the Head of the Civil Service and the official in charge of the counter-inflation policy, to work out a mutually acceptable Stage III deal[3]. The idea of the meeting was 'to find out the miners' mood in private . . . and maybe have another chat later'[4]. For this reason secrecy was maintained so that 'the "team" knew about the meeting but the Cabinet was not told'[5]. This very fact, which individual Cabinet Ministers have confirmed[6], demonstrated how influential Sir William Armstrong had become, not only as the official in charge of the incomes policy but as the chief political adviser to Mr Heath. Indeed, an opponent of statutory incomes policy argued that Mr Heath 'was talked round to incomes policy by Armstrong'[7]. One back bench MP stated that 'Armstrong was an evil influence . . . obsessed with absurdities like selling a scheme to Gormley'[8], and a former Minister commented that 'Armstrong had a Salvation Army mentality . . . totally dedicated to incomes policy . . . and a personality mould attractive to Heath'[9].

That the secret meeting bore the stamp of Sir William Armstrong's influence is undeniable, but the question at the time revolved around whether a deal had been made by which Stage III could make a special concession to the miners based on their unsocial working hours, thus giving them more money than other workers in the forthcoming wage round. In return Joe Gormley would convince the NUM executive that they should approve the bargain, thus preventing industrial action. As Brittan and Lilley note 'Convinced that the Government's defeat by the miners in 1972 had destroyed his previous pay policy, Mr Heath was determined to avoid another confrontation with this seemingly invincible group'[10].

Mr Heath and Sir William Armstrong thus felt able to conduct the Stage III operation with considerable confidence, especially as Stages I and II had survived, in the language of incomes policy, battered but intact. Furthermore, the counter-inflation policy could be regarded as politically successful given the potential handicaps it had overcome and the fact that public opinion was resolutely behind the statutory incomes policy approach[11]. On 8 October a Green Paper, the consultative document on the Price and Pay Code, was published, outlining the Stage III proposals to run from November 1973 to the autumn of 1974. As regards prices, the broad effect of the proposals was to continue generally unchanged the reporting and approval arrangements and the existing restraint measures; the maximum permitted pay increases over a given 12-month period of £1 a week plus 4% under Stage II, however, was replaced by a more complex formula giving a choice between a 7% increase (maximum £350 per annum) or an increase of £2.25 a week, together with various other possible improvements that might reflect particular circumstances and might bring the average increase to 8–9%, with special 'threshold' increases if the retail price index rose by more than 7%. The origins of the 'threshold' approach deserve further explanation. The concept had origi- nally been put forward in 1971 by the TUC's economic committee and was further discussed in November 1971 at the NEDC sub-committee meeting of the 'four wise men' or 'group of four', Sir Frank Figgures, Vic Feather, Campbell Adamson and Sir Douglas Allen. At the meeting it was decided that union leaders and employers would consider a new form of wage deal, the 'threshold agreement', linking pay rises directly to the cost of living, thus eliminating the need for unions to seek rises in anticipation of future price rises. At the time the idea had not attracted much enthusiasm and Sir Frank Figgures himself had cautiously ventured that '. . . we are not on the eve of finding a panacea for present problems, but we want to see if such agreements can help'[12]. However, it was not until Mr Heath's Stage III stipulations were announced that the 'threshold' plan – despite its obvious drawback of generating inflationary expectations – was translated into policy form.

Among the other Stage III proposals, New Year's Day was declared a public holiday in England and Wales and in Northern Ireland, with an alternative additional day in Scotland. The Green Paper contained a draft revision of the Price and Pay Code, which governed the operation of Stage II, although this was subsequently modified before final parliamentary approval and implementation. As with Stage II, wide ranging controls on dividends and profits were stipulated, but it was the proposal concerning the payment for 'unsocial hours' that was soon to become crucial. The origin of the proposal went back to the secret meeting in the garden of Number 10 on 16 July, and as such, was designed to accommodate the miners within Stage III. The Green Paper simply stated that:

> Premium payments outside the pay limit might be made or increased to compensate for 'unsocial hours' worked which did not themselves attract overtime rates, so as to encourage the introduction and maintenance of shift working for the fuller utilization of existing plant and to help attract into employment people who were not available for work in normal hours. Periods covered by such arrangements were basically Saturdays and Sundays and the hours between 8 p.m. and 6 a.m. on other days. These premium payments might not be added to basic rates on which overtime was calculated[13].

Despite the now familiar sound of Mr Powell's dissenting voice the Government swiftly received parliamentary approval for the Stage III code. With certain amendments, the Price and Pay Code was incorporated into a Counter-Inflation Order that was published on 30 October 1973, together with other Orders relating to pay, prices and charges and dividends. Among the principal amendments made to the Code compared with the draft issued on 8 October were as follows.

(1) That, where the operative date of a group's principal increase was deferred by the Stage I standstill, the average pay bill for the group over the previous 12 months might now be calculated as if that increase had been paid from the normal operative date.
(2) That a limit was placed on profits-linked payments whereby these should be limited to £350 above the average benefit for the best two of the last five years (thus preventing large increases to certain employees such as had recently been announced in the case of a number of senior executives).
(3) Allowing threshold compensation to be payable on a *pro rata* basis to all part-time workers (i.e., not only those working 21 or more hours a week)[14].

The Order embodying the revised Code was approved by the House of Commons on 7 November by 270 votes to 231 and by the House of Lords on 20 November[15].

As Fay and Young observe, 'Anyone who missed the Coal Board's offer to the miners on 19 October could have been forgiven. The Yom Kippur war was at a crucial stage [and] Vice-President Spiro Agnew's resignation was announced'[16]. The Board's offer, only two days after the publication of the Green Paper, and within the Stage III guidelines, was equivalent to £44 m a year and comprising increases of £2.20 to £2.57 on basic rates from 1 March 1974, together with additional payments under the provisions for 'unsocial hours' of work and other improvements which, the Board estimated, might in some cases give a further sum of up to £7 a week. This represented a 13% increase in the NCB's wage bill, while an efficiency scheme might be negotiated giving another 3½% from 1 January 1974 – an overall improvement of 16½%.

Norman Siddall, the Board's Deputy Chairman, making the offer in the absence of Sir Derek Ezra who was ill, openly stated that '. . . we have tried to see how best the union's claim can be accommodated with the [Stage III] constraints'[17]. However, by lumping together the basic 7% allowed by the policy, with a shift allowance (i.e., the crucial 'unsocial hours' payment) amounting to 4.5% and an extra 1.5% for odds and ends, Siddall offered the miners 13%, immediately raising the miners' expectations. As Fay and Young state: 'The Minutes describe the NUM's response drily, not naming speakers, but it is immediately clear that the expectations of the miners were inflated beyond the capability of management to satisfy them'[18]. The Board's offer was thus rejected with Gormley claiming that the Downing Street deal had backfired two days earlier when the loophole allowing unsocial hours was written into the Green Paper. This enabled any union, not just the miners, to convince the Pay Board that it was a special case. One Minister commented that '. . . as a result of what we understood from Gormley and Ezra we had every reason to believe we would be all right'[19]. Clearly the Board had offered everything at once, leaving nothing further to bargain for, which was a tactical error the left-wing of the NUM, led by Mick McGahey, quickly exploited. Given such a course of events it was not surprising that Conservative critics would claim that all along it had been 'naive to believe that Gormley would deliver the goods'[20].

Brittan and Lilley have noted that:

The moderates on the Union negotiating team had expected a period of shadow boxing during which they would extract concessions to satisfy their militant colleagues. Deprived of this traditional negotiating process, they were unable to persuade enough of the uncommitted members to accept the terms, against opposition from the militants. The latter were only too anxious to provoke another showdown. Moreover, the mood in the pits had hardened considerably. The Arab oil embargo and first major OPEC price rises which were both announced in mid-October had made the men increasingly aware of their heightened bargaining power. After acquiescing to declining relative earnings for nearly twenty-five years because their bargaining power had been progressively eroded by cheap oil, they saw no reason not to take advantage of this reversal of fortunes. In addition, the 1972 strike, the first official strike for nearly half a century, had whetted their appetite[21].

Similarly, one Minister at the centre of the negotiations conceded that '. . . one of the problems of rigid pay controls is that trade union leaders don't seem to have a function – they like the period of negotiations'[22].

Gormley was thus unable to deliver a majority of his executive as promised and following a delegates' meeting on 26 October, the NUM Executive on 8 November instructed its 270000 members that from 12 November they should work no overtime including weekend work. One adviser to the Prime Minister admitted that 'there was too much reliance on Gormley, who was astonished an agreement could not be reached'[23]. Although the course of the dispute was by no means inevitable at this stage the strategy of the Downing Street deal had failed. Nor had the secrecy of the Downing Street deal helped the situation as the day-to-day running of the miners' pay claim operated without Departmental co-ordination, especially between the Department of Industry and the Department of Employment.

## 7.2    The miners' dispute escalates

In accordance with the NUM decision, miners began an overtime ban on 12 November, with the result that output was sharply reduced. While only a relatively small proportion of coal output is actually produced in overtime hours, a large part of maintenance, safety and repair work is done in such hours, particularly at weekends. Although certain essential safety work was carried out by management, supervisors and other staff not belonging to the NUM, output was largely lost during those week-time hours when normal maintenance was being carried out.

In view of the rapidly deteriorating fuel situation, a State of Emergency was proclaimed on 13 November, together with regulations involving severe restrictions on the use of energy. Douglas Hurd noted that by the middle of November 'it was becoming clear that things were badly wrong. The oil crisis and the coal crisis could not be kept distinct. Together they were shaking the whole strategy of economic expansion'[24]. One former Minister bemoaned that '. . . if there hadn't been the miners' strike and oil crisis we could have continued with our growth policy'[25].

The State of Emergency, the fifth in just over three years, announced in the House of Commons by Robert Carr, the Home Secretary, was declared under the 1920 and 1964 Emergency Powers Act and was based on 'the present industrial dispute affecting persons employed in the coal mines and the electricity supply industry'[26]. John Biffen, one of the Government's most effective back bench critics, argued that:

> The reality is that we will see the Counter Inflation Act 1973 put to the test. It is important that we should know clearly what is the law in respect of that Act. It is as dangerous for the Executive and for statutory bodies such as the Pay Board to exceed the authority they possess as it is dangerous for participants in industrial disputes to do so[27].

Jeremy Thorpe, the Liberal Leader, questioned whether there had ever before 'been a precedent for a State of Emergency being declared for a threatened ban on overtime'[28] and further criticized the Government for allowing the situation to deteriorate to such a serious extent.

Certainly, the drastic cuts in production and 70% increase in the price of oil by the Arab states were strengthening the miners' hand. On its own, action by the Arab states would have destroyed the Government's 5% growth strategy, but with the effects of the miners' overtime ban the Government was faced with the most severe crisis since Suez in 1956[29]. One Minister noted that 'the 5% growth target had become unrealistic because of the 300% rise in commodity prices'[30]. Another Senior Minister recalled that 'we were really aiming for 3½% growth – the talk of 5% was only for a short period. But Heath kept banging the 5% down when it was really 3½%'[31].

On 28 November, Mr Heath with the Chancellor, Maurice Macmillan (Employment Secretary), Tom Boardman (Industry Minister) and Sir William Armstrong met the whole NUM Executive at Number 10 to discuss the situation – a contrast in approach to the secret meeting on 16 July. Mr Heath spelled out the consequences of the Middle East war and appealed to the Executive to call off their industrial action for the sake of the nation. The meeting was far from peaceful; there were reports that Mick McGahey had advocated the downfall of the Government through industrial action as Mr Heath later asserted on television[32]. But Mr Heath's appeal to the Executive in the national interest was far from successful as Lord Armstrong has stated:

[The Meeting] hadn't been going very long before it was obvious that Joe Gormley, to put it kindly, was going to lead from behind. He virtually said, knowing it all himself, he just said he would like to leave it to the lads. And the lads more or less spoke as they felt inclined. In fact, I remember very well, one little man, in the third row, right at the very back, almost out of the window, sort of putting up his hand and eventually getting a hearing, and saying:
'Prime Minister, what I can't understand is this: You have told us that we have no option but to pay the Arabs the price they're demanding for the oil. Now, as far as I know, the Arabs never helped us in World War I, and in World War II, and we flogged our guts out in all of that. Why can't you pay us for coal what you are willing to pay the Arabs for oil?' And although that was put in that way, not put as an economist would put it, that in fact, was bang on the economic nose. And the Prime Minister really had no answer to that[33].

Having considered Mr Heath's appeal the Executive voted, in a room set aside for the purpose at Downing Street, by 20:5, with two abstentions, not to call off the overtime ban. An important opportunity to end the dispute had been allowed to slip by. The Arabs' decision to increase oil prices had occurred after the rudiments of Stage III had been worked out. A new situation had been created allowing '. . . a realistic, if not heroic, pretext for the Prime Minister to say that further concessions to the miners were necessary in order to boost coal supplies as a substitute for oil'[34].

In early December Mr Heath replaced Maurice Macmillan by William Whitelaw, an appointment that brought the comment from the *Economist* that 'As Mr Whitelaw shapes up to the miners it must seem a bit like Ulster all over again'[35]. As Mr Whitelaw himself admits he was ill-prepared for his new role; 'I was quite exhausted . . . and emotionally affected by all that I had been involved with in Ireland. I was not mentally conditioned for home politics [and] made several mistakes'[36]. One Conservative back-bencher commented on the appointment that 'Ted had a curious idea Willie Whitelaw understood the common man'[37].

On 13 December a three-day working week was introduced[38]. Such a move was an essential saving measure to the Government but to the miners, and the supporters they had gained as the dispute had escalated, it appeared to be a political device to rally public opinion around the Government's stand. Mick McGahey has argued that:

> ... it was a political move by the Government. The introduction of the three-day week, in my opinion, was an attempt by the Government to alienate opinion from the miners and, in fact, in my opinion, has boomeranged on them. Because, after all, they've introduced the three-day week. The miners at that stage were on overtime ban. And after all, it's a bad day for miners say, to work a normal week, and normal hours, and the country goes on a three-day week. And I think it was a political manoeuvre on the part of the Government that mis-fired[39].

On 17 December Mr Barber produced another mini-budget that cut public spending programmes by £1200 million, emphasizing that during the past two months '. . . a series of deliberate acts have been taken both abroad and at home which are at present starving this country of energy'[40]. Brendon Sewill, Mr Barber's special Treasury adviser, has described the December 1973 mini-budget as '. . . one of the most deflationary budgets every introduced . . . in real terms the biggest reduction in public expenditure ever announced'[41]. While such a description is not inaccurate it does not give the whole picture. The December measures were only deflationary in view of the massive and unparalleled growth in public expenditure between 1971 and December 1973. Given the extent of the disproportionate increase in public expenditure Mr Barber's action was a testimony to the extent of previous deficit-financed expenditure. However, although the Chancellor's measures were necessary, if somewhat overdue, political attention was focused more on the TUC's attempts to end the miners' dispute.

Len Murray, Alf Allen, David Basnett, Sir Sidney Greene, Jack Jones, and Hugh Scanlon, i.e., the six TUC representatives on the National Economic Development Council, had talks with the Prime Minister and Mr William Whitelaw on 19 December, prior to a meeting on 21 December of the full NEDC under the chairmanship of Mr Heath. Before the 19 December meeting, the general council of the TUC issued a statement that said *inter alia*:

> Workpeople know full well that the blame for the three-day week lies with the Government, who are prepared to lose hundreds of millions of pounds of industrial production rather than let the National Coal Board pay what it knows is necessary to ensure maximum production of coal and to attract men back to the pits. The cost to the nation of adopting this approach, which most employers and all workers know is the only sensible attitude, would be infinitely less than the costs which the

Government are imposing. Nor do they accept that a compromise settlement of the miners' dispute would have wide repercussions in other areas of industry[42].

During December one of the major points at issue that it was thought might enable the NCB to increase its overall offer still within the Stage III limits was the question of 'waiting time' – i.e., those periods before and after each shift when the miner was carrying out preparatory work or washing, but for which he received no pay – and for the second of the two daily 'winding times' of travel between the surface and the underground working area. Payment for these periods, as suggested by Mr Harold Wilson[43] in a letter to the Prime Minister dated 23 November (published on 27 November) was thought to increase considerably the NCB's total wage bill, but while the NCB were prepared to negotiate on such payments, if allowed within the Stage III criteria relating to a reduction of the standard working week of 40 hours, it estimated that they could only marginally increase the offer by 45–70p a week and would fall short of the NUM's demands. This calculation was based on an increase in the daily 7½-hour shifts by 40 minutes for waiting time plus only an average of 30 minutes for winding time, less 20 minutes for a meal break – a total time of eight hours and five minutes; a five-shift week would amount to 40 hours and 25 minutes, of which only the final 25 minutes could be paid as allowable overtime. However, consideration of this aspect of the negotiations was ended on 3 January 1974 when the Pay Board informed the NCB that, as the latter had produced evidence that preparatory waiting and winding time were regarded as standard working hours by custom and practice, the Pay Board could not consider such payments as falling within the terms of Stage III.

## 7.3   The TUC initiative

Attempts by the TUC to circumvent the Stage III restrictions were renewed again on 9 January despite Mr Heath's apparently intransigent attitude that to break the Stage III would be to break faith with the workers who had already settled within its guidelines. Indeed it was this very sticking point that the TUC hoped to overcome. At a NEDC meeting Sir Sidney Greene, the Chairman of the TUC's economic committee, presented a policy statement drawn up by the TUC's economic committee recognizing the 'exceptional situation ' in the coalmining industry and proposing that 'if the Government are prepared to give an assurance that they will make possible a settlement between the miners and the NCB other unions will not use that as an argument in negotiations for their own settlements'[44]. The TUC proposal was, however, rejected by Anthony Barber, the Chairman of the meeting, who said at a press conference after the meeting that 'no assurance had been given that other groups, who might also consider themselves to be essential to the running of the nation, would not also demand settlements outside the Stage III limits' and that the Government could not accept any such settlements[45]. The failure to accept the way out of the dispute which the TUC offer proposed was crucial. One senior CBI negotiator remembered that 'the crisis day was the NEDC meeting. Vic Feather and I used to phone before NEDC meetings, and warn each other. But Len Murray was by then General Secretary and we were taken by surprise'[46]. Indeed, Mr Heath suspected the TUC offer '. . . because it was not made in private'[47]. But this can be explained by Len Murray's relative inexperience as 'a new boy, a man nobody knew because of the TUC's strange habit of keeping the No. 2 down in favour of No. 1'[48]. Clutterbuck has postulated that had Vic Feather still headed the TUC the dispute would have been handled differently, arguing that Len Murray '. . . had not yet built up the necessary power to influence the situation '[49].

One Minister thought that 'Barber unwisely threw out the TUC initiative'[50]. Douglas Hurd thought the TUC proposal '. . . struck and still strikes me as flimsy . . . . The TUC would not in fact be able to hold back individual unions once the miners breached the policy'[51]. Mr Hurd may have been right and the TUC would have been powerless to contain the enthusiasm of rebel unions. But the TUC offer was certainly genuine and as such it allowed a solution to be found that shifted the onus of proof away from the Government and on to the TUC's own shoulders. The problem facing the Government was that it was 'using the law as a weapon in wage restraint . . . which boxed the Government in'[52]. This aspect of bringing the law into disrepute should a compromise outside the statutory limits be agreed was the chief difference between 'N minus 1' and the statutory counter inflation provisions. Such statutory restrictions are in themselves likely to cause 'confrontation', having suspended the forces of supply and demand and, as has been argued, are a prime reason for not having prices and incomes policies on the statute book.

The genuine TUC offer was thus brushed aside. Len Murray's view was that:

> This was a very genuine offer. This wasn't a ploy. It wasn't a tactic . . . . I'm sure we could have made it stick. Absolutely sure. The fact that we got an overwhelming vote in that special conference on the sixteenth of January, made that absolutely copper bottomed. There was no doubt in our mind, but there was doubt in Mr Heath's mind, and this was the factor that bugged it all the way through[53].

One union leader recalled that:

> We were prepared to deal with the miners as a special case. The TUC economic committee decided that we wouldn't quote the miners' settlements in negotiations. But Tony Barber was in the Chair. He's not a progressive sort of chap and he turned us down flat[54].

Similarly, another union representative pleaded that '. . . We were prepared to let the miners be a special case. We kept promising this. Barber in the Chair rejected it and the following morning Heath didn't want to repudiate him'[55]. But Anthony Barber recalled that 'I phoned Ted, who agreed with the line I had taken'[56]. One CBI official thought that the offer was genuine partly because 'the TUC were frightened of the miners'[57].

So the TUC proposal was allowed to slip and was further rejected by Mr Whitelaw, the Secretary of State for Employment, in the course of a speech during the two-day debate in the House of Commons on 10 January, when he asked 'If one group is treated as a special case, can other union leaders undertake not to press their claim for their members outside the limits of Stage III, and can the TUC assure the support and consent of its member-unions to act in this way?'[58]. The proposals drawn up by the TUC economic committee were approved almost unanimously by a special conference of general secretaries and presidents of trade unions affiliated to the TUC held in London on 16 January, it being agreed that if the NUM was allowed to reach a settlement outside the Stage III limits other unions would not use that 'special case' as an argument in negotiations for their own settlements. Addressing the conference Mr Murray said that the 1973 Counter-Inflation Act gave the Secretary of State for Employment the explicit right in exceptional circumstances to approve negotiations and settlements outside Stage III, and that what the TUC were asking the Government to do was to use powers that it took specifically to deal with the sort of situation arising from the miners' claim. What the miners were seeking was exceptional treatment, and the TUC was satisfied that the Government should make negotiations possible on an exceptional basis. In the Commons the Shadow Employment spokesman, Reg Prentice, commented that the TUC's intiative 'gives Ministers the chance if they want it – that is the key question – to take a new initiative in trying to solve the miners' dispute without repercussions on other wage claims . . . . If they do not take the opportunity the country will know who is to blame for the current situation'[59].

After a further meeting on 21 January to discuss the TUC initiative agreement seemed no nearer. Fay and Young state that:

> The occasion is remembered mainly for its long silences. Heath sat for minutes on end, head sunk deep on chest, pondering gloomily but saying nothing . . . . With desperate urgency Hugh Scanlon addressed an ultimate question to him. 'Is there anything, anything at all, that we can do or say which will satisfy you?' The question hung in the air for many seconds. Union men agree that the question was not altogether spontaneous, but insist it was sincerely put. Heath did not answer and left the silence to be broken by the cavilling Barber[60].

Len Murray recalls that, at the moment before Mr Barber replied, '. . . if Mr Heath had leaned back across the table and said: all right, I'll take you on trust, then I believe he'd got the solution right in his hands'[61]. However, the doubts in Mr Heath's mind were sufficient to prevent agreement. Mr Heath was unable to take the TUC 'on trust', fearing that the miners would not end up being the sole 'special case'. As Mr Heath saw it:

> We set out to treat them as a special case and Stage III was deliberately designed to meet their particular needs. I had long talks with Joe Gormley the previous summer, and we thought we had reached an arrangement which was suitable for them. Now, when it came to the point of discussion with the other trade union leaders, they asked us to accept the miners as a special case. Very well – we were prepared to do that; but I said, does this mean that there'll be no other special cases?

You see you can say the miners have special circumstances, therefore they are a special case – now suppose special circumstances of a different kind come along, will you not agree that that is not a special case? And they were perfectly frank and I made no criticism of them at all; they said: 'No we couldn't give the undertaking that circumstances of a different kind should not be a special case'[62].

Similarly, one Minister commented that 'I was at one with Heath over the handling of the crisis. We could not have given way and retained authority. Privately some union leaders pleaded with us not to pull the rug from under their feet'[63]. An alternative view has since been put forward by Sir Ian Gilmour who argues that, with the benefit of hindsight, '. . . one can see the Government might have been wise to accept the TUC's offer to treat the miners as a special case and only hold the election when the unions did not keep their word'[64].

The following day, 22 January 1973, Mr Heath told the Commons that the Government 'recognized the significance of the undertaking offered by the TUC and unreservedly accepted its sincerity and genuineness', but nevertheless maintained that the offer made to the NUM was 'in our view fair and, in the economic situation facing us, as generous as we could afford'[65].

On 24 January the miners' executive decided by 16:10 to recommend the members to strike, but before the miners' acceptance of the recommendation was declared on 4 February, the Government's attention was caught by two separate events.

Firstly, allegations of Communist Party influence within the NUM followed a speech at Aberdeen on 27 January by Mick McGahey, the union's Vice-President, who was reported as having said that if troops were brought in to move the coal 'troops are not all anti-working class – many of them are miners' sons, sons of the working class', and he would, if necessary, appeal to them to assist the miners. After saying that 'the day of the cheap miner is over', Mr McGahey continued:

Not only will we organize the miners . . . we will do it with the confidence and support of other sections of the Labour and trade union movement . . . .We are confident of the support of transport, railway and power station workers in the effort . . . . I believe it is necessary to have a recall of the TUC to mobilize the miners, to burst Stage III, to defeat the Tory Government and to elect a Labour Government committed to Left, progressive policies[66].

The following day in a television interview the Prime Minister criticized Mr McGahey for regarding the dispute as a political matter. Mr McGahey and others had made it quite clear, Mr Heath said, that their objective was not a wage negotiation or a settlement within Stage III or even outside it, but 'to smash Stage III and . . . get rid of the elected Government of the day'. That was 'entirely a political approach', and Mr McGahey had 'said quite plainly that he was prepared to do it in order to get a left-wing Government that would toe the line as far as he is concerned'[67]. The spectre of a 'communist scare' clearly worried the Labour Party and over 100 Labour MPs signed a motion attacking Mr McGahey. As far as the Government was concerned the episode only strengthened the belief that the left-wing of the NUM executive had been politically motivated to prolong the dispute. Sir Alec Douglas Home has argued that:

> 1973 was successfully navigated and it was only at Stage III that the economic package began to come undone. That it did so was largely due to the determination of Mr McGahey, the Communist leader of the Scottish Mineworkers' Union and Mr Scargill of the Yorkshire coal-fields. Both saw the chance to break a Conservative Government by strike action which, by withholding vital supplies of power for industry, would bring the economy of the nation near to a standstill[68].

But, although there was evidence of the involvement of individual Communists, a 'Communist plot' to bring down the state was conspicuous by its absence. The intricacies and rigidity of compulsory wage control, more than any Communist influence, had brought the Government to such a state of crisis. The *Economist* was soon to argue that 'Mr McGahey, the Vice-President and chief choreographer of the NUM executive, has emerged as the Conservatives' greatest election ally since Zinoviev'[69], but the electorate was to be less inclined to view the dispute in such McCarthyite terms.

Secondly, on 24 January the Pay Board's report on relativities was published arguing, as were the miners, that if a group of workers was paid unfairly compared with other groups, they should be made a special case. But the report by the Pay Board's Vice-Chairman, Derek Robinson, himself a miner's son, did allow a way out of the dispute (as had the waiting and winding time considerations and the TUC's initiative), which was, again, allowed to pass.

## 7.4    The February 1974 election

Finally with the miners' decisive vote to strike already made public, Mr Heath opted for the General Election his advisers had advocated throughout January. The *Economist's* reaction was fairly typical of the Press in general, declaring that, 'The chief election issue is the irresponsible use of trade union power, and it is one on which the Conservatives are right to let the country decide'[70]. Mr Barber, uncharacteristically melodramatic, told the House that the alternative to the rule of reason by the rule of Parliament was '. . . chaos, anarchy and a totalitarian or Communist regime'[71].

Although it is not the purpose of this account to chart the detailed course of the Election campaign, it is widely believed that had Mr Heath opted for, say, an election on 7 February, the Conservatives would have won[72]. In the event, on 7 February Mr Heath announced the dissolution of Parliament on the following day and the calling of a General Election for 28 February. The decision to call the election at such a late stage in the crisis was, and has remained, controversial. Two close advisers have noted that Mr Heath was exhausted '. . . not only with the miners but with the Sunningdale talks on power-sharing in Northern Ireland'[73], which 'had him up at three and four in the morning making the pressures on him worse'[74].

Mr Heath's failure to take a holiday during 1973 has also been mentioned as a factor that contributed to the pressures upon him[75]. And it can be easily argued that the nervous breakdown on 2 February and subsequent convalescence of Sir William Armstrong, 'added to the strain on Heath'[76]. A large body of opinion had urged an early election and felt that the delay had not helped the Conservatives' chances. Jim Prior has noted that:

> The mood of the Party was showing itself pretty strongly in letters and messages coming up from most of the area Chairmen and, the advice they were getting from their constituency organizations and so on, that if an election was called, that this would have a good deal of support. It wasn't unanimous, the view that there ought to be an election, but I think that most people within the party organization on the voluntary side were saying, if you're going to have an election, have it early rather than late[77].

One Cabinet Minister explained that 'I wanted the election three or four weeks earlier but Ted felt that the dish wasn't cooked'[78]. Similarly, another Minister was in favour of the election 'a bit earlier when the party machine was in gear and ready to go. But there came a point when the Government lost credibility and its authority was in the process of decline'[79]. One adviser recalled that 'everything was set for a 7 February election. But at the 59th minute of the 11th hour Heath decided not to press the button. He then didn't want an election at all'[80]. Douglas Hurd felt that 'although it cannot be proved I believe that we would have won an election on 7 February. It would have taken place against the background of an overtime ban, not a strike. The three weeks which we lost brought with them, as we predicted, a steady ebb of the Government's authority'[81]. One back bench MP favoured '. . . an early election or no election at all . . . . I felt the mood change during the campaign'[82]. The timing of the election was defended by one Cabinet Minister who was 'not in favour of an election. Only when we were convinced we could not solve it did we have to have an election'[83]. It is also worth noting that 'the options to Heath were limited as the Party was seething with discontent. The grass roots thought that the 1972 defeat by the miners should be avenged'[84]. The feeling 'among the Conservative grass roots that democracy was at stake'[85] was not far removed from that of the 'hawks' at the centre of the stage. Sir William Armstrong was known to take a tough line and according to one critic, 'impressed on Heath a disaster scenario of emergency'[86]. One Cabinet Minister recalled that Mr Heath 'came to rely on Armstrong when Armstrong was becoming a man not to rely upon. He was too apocalyptic and then had to go on leave following his breakdown'[87]. But two other Cabinet Ministers disagreed that Sir William Armstrong's influence has been considerably exaggerated[88].

The decision to call an election as a way of settling the crisis of authority surrounding the dispute was not taken lightly by Mr Heath who had resisted the calls for an earlier election in more favourable circumstances. Douglas Hurd states that 'Mr Heath did not believe that a modern Conservative Party should fight an election battle aimed mainly against the trade unions'[89]. Given the willingness of Mr Heath to negotiate with the trade unions and to pursue policies of which they approved, e.g., the 5%

growth policy, there is no reason to dispute Mr Hurd's assertion. Similarly, Fay and Young concluded that Mr Heath '. . . did not want an election "against" the miners. The possible post-electoral legacy of a class-based Tory victory repelled him'[90]. It is therefore all the more remarkable that in February 1974 Mr Heath chose the general election option knowing that the theme of the Government versus the unions would dominate the campaign. As a senior CBI official recalled: 'I couldn't conceive that any Government would go towards a confrontation without a way out. I couldn't believe they had no other plan apart from an election'[91]. Ultimately, it was not the desire for a confrontation election that forced Mr Heath to go to the country as Mr Hurd has pointed out. Rather it was the utter determination to stick to the letter of the Stage III guidelines without regard for the political consequences. The supreme irony of the situation was that the Stage III guidelines to which Mr Heath so tenaciously held were intended to control the inflation that the Government's deficit financing and 'dash for growth' had produced.

Butler and Kavanagh noted that there was '. . . no little irony in the fact that the Government was forced into an election by its defence of policies that it had repudiated when it was elected more than three years earlier'[92]. Mr Heath was also split between disliking the notion of the election at all, having regarded an election as a last resort, and between the necessity to win the election hopefully by an appeal to 'fairness' rather than the exploitation of the issue of authority that most Conservatives, for electoral reasons, had little alternative but to prefer. As Fay and Young point out, Mr Heath's address to the 1922 Committee of back-benchers on the day the election was announced, 7 February, emphasized moderation not confrontation[93]. When Conservative Party special election advisers suggested an intense crisis campaign Mr Heath vetoed such an approach. The Conservative Party Manifesto, however, entitled 'Firm Action for a Fair Britain' did contain an aggressive concluding section contrasting the Conservatives' moderation with the extremism of Labour, especially Labour's left-wing, and 'a small group of power-hungry trade union leaders'[94]. Unlike in 1970, the 1974 Manifesto was not a radical policy document. Its main proposals were a stronger Price Commission, the amendment of the Industrial Relations Act, a twice-yearly review of pensions, the right of council tenants to purchase their property and, oddly enough for a Conservative document, strict penalties on property profiteering. Labour, meanwhile, in its Manifesto, 'Let us Work Together – Labour's Way Out of the Crisis', offered several radical solutions with the aim of transferring significantly the balance of wealth and power in favour of working people and promoting greater economic and social equality. As expected, Labour promised to repeal both the Industrial Relations Act and the Housing Finance Act, and to fundamentally renegotiate Britain's Common Market position. The Liberal Manifesto, 'Change the Face of Britain. Take Power and Vote Liberal', as expected, criticized the two-party system and recommended decentralization, devolution and greater popular participation, themes that the Liberals had successfully exploited in their by-election successes under the label of 'community politics'.

The General Election campaign itself proved a difficult one for the Conservatives. When it was announced on 7 February, Mr Heath sent a letter to Joe Gormley asking the NUM executive committee 'in the national interest very seriously to consider suspending the national coal strike during the period of the election campaign' so that 'people should be able to concentrate their attention, in an atmosphere as undisturbed as possible, on the issues upon which they will be asked to cast their votes'[95]. This appeal was, however, rejected by the NUM on 8 February by 20 votes to 6, reportedly against the advice of Mr Gormley himself. At the same time it was announced that pickets consisting of not more than six men each would be stationed at pits, open-cast sites, large dumps of coal, ports, docks, steelworks and power stations, but that domestic deliveries would not be affected (including schools and hospitals). In view of some unhappy memories of the 'flying pickets' during the 1972 strike this constituted a shrewd move by the miners, who rejected an appeal from Mr Heath to call off their strike but organized their picketing with great care to avoid the highly unpopular violence of two years previously. The miners, however, as in 1972 were greatly assisted by other unions. One union leader, who was not directly involved in the dispute, argued that '. . . the cards were stacked in favour of the Government with the mildest of winters and plentiful coal stocks. The co-operation of the trade union movement was the crucial thing – not to transport or move the coal'[96].

The NUM's decision to turn down the Prime Minister's request and proceed with the strike despite the election campaign was on the same day strongly criticized by Mr Heath, who furthermore described as 'astonishing' the fact that Mr Wilson had not supported his request. However, Mr Heath was grateful for the efforts of Mr Gormley and 'some of his moderate colleagues on the executive'[97] to prevent the strike. On 8 February, Mr Whitelaw had referred the miners' claim to the Pay Board for examination under the new relativities procedures and had asked the Board to report 'as urgently as is consistent with thorough examination of all the interests and factors involved'. The Board was asked to make recommendations on 'the extent to which an exceptional increase would be justified, in relation to other groups, in pay for mineworkers as from 1 March' (the due date of implementation of the offer originally made by the NCB), taking into account the views of 'others who would be affected by improvement of the miners' relative position' and giving full opportunity for the interests of those other groups to be expressed and considered. In its reference to the Pay Board, the Department of Employment said that in selecting this case for examination Mr Whitelaw had 'had regard to the *prima facie* evidence for the NUM's contention that the coal industry is undergoing a change in its relative importance to the economy as a result of developments in relation to the supply and price of oil'[98].

But a damaging setback to the Conservatives' electoral prospects occurred on 21 February[99]. Statistical evidence prepared by Derek Robinson was leaked from the Pay Board that indicated that the miners were entitled to at least 8% more than the Government had allowed the National Coal Board to offer. The clear implication was that if the Board was right the election was unnecessary and the 'Who runs Britain, the Government or the Unions?' theme was bogus. As Fay and Young note, some Cabinet Ministers, including the Prime Minister, thought that Derek Robinson had conspired against the Government for political reasons[100].

Although Robinson denies this strongly, the Board's disclosures only a week before polling served to weaken Mr Heath's hand. Mr Wilson regarded the disclosures as the crucial turning point in the campaign and exploited the situation with customary political acumen. One Labour MP thought that the leaked figures cost Mr Heath the election[101]. Sir Alec Douglas Home felt that '. . . this incident made the difference between a Conservative victory and defeat'[102]. As John Gummer, a Vice-Chairman of the Conservative Party (who was to lose his seat) put it: 'I personally believe the Pay Board Report was very, very important indeed. But it was important not because of its direct effect, but because it was one in a series of things which gave people the impression that events were taking hold of us rather than we controlling events'[103]. Douglas Hurd thought the relativities episode to be:

> . . . the worst moment of the campaign. For the first time a national event made itself locally felt. 'A glum day till evening. We are cruelly savaged by Pay Board putting out entirely new figures on relative pay for miners, much more favourable to their case. EH retires in a cloud of stubborn and unconvincing negatives. A very difficult moment'[104].

Similarly, one Minister recalled that 'as a candidate I felt it slip through our fingers. The relativities figures showed the crisis of authority in the Government and Enoch had a critical effect on the crucial Midlands marginals'[105]. One former Minister thought the Conservatives did not come over to the electorate as a united team because of Mr Heath's dominance:

> Heath was against ministers having any limelight. If you were asked by the BBC to appear he would later be critical. He had no team and this was obvious in the 1974 [February] election. I was in hospital and listening to the radio; only Heath and sometimes Barber were heard while Labour had several well-known people broadcasting[106].

Sir Harold Wilson has noted that while the Conservatives '. . . sought to narrow the issue, [Labour] sought to follow the traditional election approach of fighting on the whole record of the Government and our alternative policies of every issue of importance to the electorate'[107]. This approach clearly helped Labour far more than the Conservatives. Thus, the fact that food prices had risen by 20% in the previous year and 40% since the Conservatives took office could not be easily explained away, especially to those who had voted Conservative in 1970 as a protest against rising prices under Labour. Alt, in his study of public opinion and Britain's economic problems, noted that:

> . . . after 1970 rising prices or inflation came to be seen by a plurality of the electors as the most important problem facing the country; a plurality which grew, apart from brief periods of concern with industrial relations and unemployment in 1971–2, into a substantial majority by the end of 1973. At the time of the election of February 1974, between 60% and 70% of the electorate felt that prices were the most important problem facing the country and about one-third felt that the issue had been the 'single most important thing' on their minds when voting[108].

Only hours before the polls closed on 28 February, the Relativities Board's report was completed, conceding more to the miners than they would have hoped for at any stage since their conference in early July 1973, but the election campaigning was by then over[109]. The Conservatives lost 33 seats, leaving Labour the largest party in Parliament by a majority of four. Mr Heath's hopes of retaining office with a Liberal coalition proved to be abortive and on 4 March Harold Wilson became Prime Minister for the second time. The Liberals had achieved their best result since 1945 with 14 seats and a greatly increased share of the popular vote, and the SNP gained 6 seats to give them a total of 7. But even if Mr Heath had managed to come to an agreement with Mr Thorpe, the Liberal leader, the two parties combined would have had only 310 seats in the Commons, still short of an overall majority. It would have been by no means certain that such a coalition could have survived. In any case Mr Heath was not prepared to pay the price of some form of proportional representation that the Liberals demanded as a pre-condition for a parliamentary pact. The election result itself, like the circumstances that brought about the election in the first place, was freakish and bizarre. The swing from Conservative to Labour was merely 0.8%, yet nearly 40 seats had changed hands. The Liberals with 24% of the vote emerged with only 14 seats, an aspect of the British electoral system that produced much controversy in following years. The Conservatives also suffered as a result of the complete break-up of the Northern Ireland parties, with 11 out of 12 seats won by the United Ulster Unionist Coalition, effectively eliminating the Conservatives' traditional Unionist allies, which in normal circumstances would have enabled Mr Heath to have won the election. Similarly, the Conservatives could count themselves unfortunate that although polling a higher total of all votes than Labour, it was Labour who emerged with 4 seats more.

Mr Heath's reluctant decision to fight the election on the issue of trade union power had narrowly failed. A close adviser to Mr Heath has written that the Conservatives lost in spite of the fact that the polls 'continued to show clear evidence that most people favoured the Government rather than the miners and believed that the Conservatives rather than Labour would deal better with the worsening crisis'[110]. That the Government chose to fight an election on the theme of 'Who runs the country?' and not on the Government's records, as the Conservatives had done after periods in office in 1955, 1959 and 1964, emphasizes how acute the political crisis had become. The Government's record was hardly enviable even to its most convinced supporters, despite Mr Heath's belief that a statutory incomes policy 'had considerable success over the three phases'[111]. Lord Blake has noted that 'The Heath Government had not got much of a record to present to its supporters in 1974'[112], which, it may be argued, is a considerable understatement. One former Minister, who was against the election, thought that:

> Heath was stupid to take on the miners. The mining industry is so sheltered that miners are not amenable to public opinion. Anyway, the public likes miners and think all miners work at the coal-face. Also they did have an overwhelming case for being at the top of the blue collar wages league[113].

Crouch has argued that the post-war consensus 'won' the February 1974 election in that 'victory was registered in the votes of the minor parties which historically had little to do with it'[114]. This is not altogether convincing, given the massive defection to the Liberals by Conservative voters as the by-election Liberal gains had demonstrated during 1973, when 'confrontation' was conspicuous by its absence. However, it would be accurate to say that the electorate took the attitude of 'a plague on both your houses' and rejected outright victory for either Conservative or Labour. As Crewe *et al.* have pointed out '. . . the electorate felt that there was not much difference between Conservative and Labour'[115]. This may partly help to explain why the Conservatives were unable in 1974 to keep the issue of trade union power at the centre of the electorate's attention. One Cabinet Minister recalled that:

Heath gave the impression of being stubborn and not really capable of handling the miners. Enoch, Adamson and the Relativities all sapped our morale. People were disenchanted with the Conservatives but they didn't want to go the whole hog and vote Labour so they voted Liberal instead[116].

Even in the seats which the Conservatives held, the increase in the Liberal vote was substantial so that '. . . in seat after seat especially in the south of England [the Liberals] swept Labour into third place'[117]. This disaffection in the Conservative heartland was not simply a question of 'ducking' the confrontation nature of the election campaign, but rather it represented a continuation of the by-election defections to the Liberals by traditional Conservative voters. However, as Steed pointed out[118] the Liberal upsurge was not at the expense of one party rather than the other. The disillusionment among Conservative voters mentioned above was matched by disillusionment with Labour voters which, similarly, could be traced back during 1970–74 and was not simply a function of the 1974 Election campaign. Steed also explains the apparent paradox of the net swing to the Conservatives recorded in many Tory seats as reflecting the effect of tactical switches from Labour to Liberal[119]. He notes that:

. . . it did not require a totally hopeless outlook for their Party to make some Labour voters more prone to go Liberal than in a Labour or marginal seat. Some of this switching may well have reflected the reaction of Labour voters to a local atmosphere of Conservative preponderance and to the policital environment of the countryside, market towns, sea-side resorts, and middle-class suburbs, rather than a careful calculation of the real chances of Conservative defeat[120].

In the end, the Heath Government left office with a high rate of inflation, unemployment, a sinking pound aggravating a vast balance of payments deficit, public expenditure at an unprecedented level, and the most comprehensive prices and incomes policy hitherto devised, after defeat in a General Election that the Prime Minister had been most reluctant to call. It was not surprising that to some observers 'what was unique about Mr Heath's administration was that failure was total'[121]. Although it has been unconvincingly argued that it was the external influence of the Yom Kippur war that really destroyed the Government's growth strategy[122] and that the original intention of the secret meeting in the garden at Downing Street had been explicitly to avoid a 'confrontation', it remains true that the circumstances of the Heath Government's downfall produced the country's biggest peace-time crisis since the 1926 General Strike. As Brittan and Lilley have accurately pointed out:

> . . . even had all gone smoothly in the case of the miners, the incomes policy, by its very nature, made the sort of confrontation which occurred possible at any time and inevitable in the long run. If laws are passed, sooner or later someone will break them, even though the laws have overwhelming public support. To establish a legal code which cannot be enforced yet cannot be breached without provoking a constitutional crisis puts both respect for the law and the authority of the state at risk[123].

Fay and Young conclude that 'neither Gormley, nor Mr McGahey, nor the miners beat Heath. Ted Heath beat himself'[124], which in many ways is true. The 'Heath dilemma' therefore was never finally resolved and the responsibility for Britain's economic fortunes within the wider European framework had ended up in the hands of Mr Wilson. But the crucial point remains that Mr Heath galvanized himself, and the country, into the crisis for the sake of Stage III of his counter-inflation strategy[125]. This strategy itself had been overtaken by events; some self-inflicted, like the inflationary increases in public expenditure and others external, like the oil crisis resulting from the Yom Kippur war. In this sense Ted Heath did beat himself – with the implicit logic of his own incomes policy[126]. Douglas Hurd admits that it could have been avoided by abandoning the incomes policy although 'the political consequences of that would have been disastrous'[127]. The Government, he argues, would have limped on, broken-backed for a year or so, possibly under a different Prime Minister. Mr Hurd may be right or he may be exaggerating the political consequences of abandoning the incomes policy. After all, Mr Heath's Government had abandoned a series of policies by February 1974 and the option of continuing in office with another year and a half before a General Election was necessary gave some considerable scope for a political revival. But these are mere speculations.

The fact remained that a comprehensive statutory prices and incomes policy had produced the crisis of the winter of 1973/74. As Parkin points out there was '. . . a clear case in which [prices and incomes] controls led to a massive reduction in economic welfare as a result of lost output'[128]. In political terms, too, the breakdown of Mr Heath's incomes policy resulting from the winter crisis and subsequent election defeat for the Conservatives confirmed the fact that, as Scott has noted '. . . successive incomes policies have all broken down, both here and in other countries, shows that it is not easy to devise a permanent workable incomes policy in a free democratic country [they exist all right behind the Iron Curtain]'[129]. It may be argued that such an interpretation was critical to the February 1974 election and the crisis preceding it. The mistakes made during that crisis were implicit in the U-turn on incomes policy that was completed in November 1972 when the statutory policy was initiated. It was not the consequence of the

Wilberforce award to the miners in 1972, as Mr Hurd claims[130], that was crucial to the events of 1973/74, but rather it was the return, at the time widely believed to be imperative in the battle against inflation, to the rigidities of statutory incomes policy that was decisive. Without the inflexibilities of the statutory pay policy there would have been no restrictions on an early settlement and, consequently, no general election. A close political adviser to Mr Heath has pointed out that:

> One of the myths is that the miners brought the Government down. It was the people who did that at the polls. The miners didn't force the election. Ted Heath called the election because he thought he could win[131].

However, Mr Heath's lack of enthusiasm for an election in the first place and lack of enthusiasm for the 'crisis election' approach suggest that winning the election was not entirely the reason for calling it. Mr Heath had staked his own reputation and his Government's electoral strategy on a statutory incomes policy and once that decision had been made the likelihood of a prolonged industrial confrontation had increased. Thus, despite the secret attempts to allow the miners to be a 'special case', which were initiated at Downing Street in July 1973 and despite Mr Heath's reluctance to call an election at all, the ultimate decision to call the 28 February General Election rested with Mr Heath's personal commitment to the Stage III incomes policy guidelines. Without the Stage III restrictions the crisis of authority that emerged from the miners' industrial action would not have involved the calling, however reluctantly, of a 'who rules; Government or unions' General Election[132]. The irony was not essentially that Mr Heath had introduced a statutory incomes policy in contradiction of the 1970 Election Manifesto, but that statutory incomes policy, a cornerstone to the 'Heath dilemma' alternative to the 'Quiet Revolution', was so instrumental in bringing Mr Heath's removal from office[132].

## References

1. *The Times*, 3 July 1973.
2. C. T. SANDFORD and M. S. BRADBURY, *Case Studies in Economics: Economic Policy*, Macmillan, 1977, p. 228.
3. For a more detailed, and dramatic, account see *The Fall of Heath* by STEPHEN FAY and HUGO YOUNG, Sunday Times Publication, 1976, p. 7.
4. Interview, Lord Armstrong.
5. Interview, Lord Armstrong.
6. Interviews, with four Cabinet Ministers.
7. Interview, Conservative Party Adviser.
8. Interview, Conservative MP.
9. Interview, Cabinet Minister.
10. S. BRITTAN and P. LILLEY, *The Delusion of Incomes Policy*, Temple Smith, 1977, pp. 170–71.
11. Thus a Gallup Poll in October 1973 found 39% believing the Government's approach to be good for the country and 32% taking the opposite view. *Gallup International Public Opinion Polls (GB) 1937–75*, p. 1284. However, a National Opinion Poll survey on the Stage III proposals found that only 24%, as opposed to 52%, thought that Stage III would work, *NOP Political Bulletin*, October 1973, p. 12.
12. *The Times*, 4 November 1971.
13. Cmnd 5444, *The Price and Pay Code for Stage 3*, HMSO, 1973.

14. The *Economist*, 24 October 1973.
15. *Hansard*, 17 October 1973, Vol. 861, Col. 234.
16. S. FAY and H. YOUNG, op cit. (Ref. 3), p. 13.
17. Ibid. p. 13.
18. Ibid. pp. 13–14.
19. Interview, Cabinet Minister.
20. Interview, Conservative Party Official.
21. S. BRITTAN and P. LILLEY, op. cit. (Ref. 10), p. 171.
22. Interview, Cabinet Minister.
23. Interview, Conservative Party Adviser.
24. D. HURD, *An End to Promises: Sketch of a Government 1970–74*, Collins, 1979, p. 117.
25. Interview, Junior Minister.
26. *Hansard*, 13 March 1973, Vol. 864, Col. 257.
27. *Hansard*, 15 November 1973, Vol. 864, Col. 702.
28. *Hansard*, 13 November 1973, Vol. 864, Col. 263.
29. During December the Government secretly alerted the Civil Contingencies Unit, the alternative to Government set up following the 1972 miners' strike to maintain essential services.
30. Interview, Cabinet Minister.
31. Interview, Cabinet Minister.
32. Mr McGahey was referring to a change of government through the ballot box as he told Fay and Young.
33. Thames Television transcript of 'Miners: State of Emergency', 15 March 1978.
34. T. F. LINDSAY and M. HARRINGTON, *The Conservative Party 1918–79*, Macmillan, 1979, p. 276.
35. The *Economist*, 8 December 1973.
36. S. FAY and H.YOUNG, op. cit. (Ref. 3), p. 18.
37. Interview, Conservative MP.
38. A further complicating factor in the industrial situation was the decision on 3 December by the executive of the Amalgamated Society of Locomotive Engineers and Firemen (ASLEF) to ban Sunday, overtime and rest-day working from 12 December in support of improved terms for a restructuring of pay throughout the industry, which was additional to the normal annual round of pay negotiations.
39. Thames Television transcript, op. cit. (Ref. 33).
40. *Hansard*, 17 December 1973, Vol. 866, Col. 952.
41. R. HARRIS and B. SEWILL, *British Economic Policy 1970–74: Two Views*, IEA Hobart Paperback No. 7, 1975, p. 46.
42. *The Times*, 20 December 1973.
43. According to the Thames TV transcript Gormley thought the Wilson initiative was a political ploy which hindered the chance of a settlement. Op.cit. (Ref. 33).
44. *The Times*, 10 January 1974.
45. *The Times*, 10 January 1974.
46. Interview, Senior CBI Official.
47. Interview, Lord Armstrong.
48. Interview, Lord Armstrong.
49. R. CLUTTERBUCK, *Britain in Agony: The Growth of Political Violence*, Penguin Books, 1980, pp. 120–21.
50. Interview, Cabinet Minister.
51. D. HURD, op. cit. (Ref. 24), p. 126.
52. Interview, Conservative Party Adviser.
53. Thames Television transcript, op. cit. (Ref. 33).
54. Interview, Trade Union Leader.
55. Interview, Trade Union Leader.
56. Interview, Lord Barber.
57. Interview, Senior CBI Official.
58. *Hansard*, 10 January 1974, Vol. 867, Col. 187.
59. *Hansard*, 10 January 1974, Vol. 867, Col. 198.
60. S. FAY and H. YOUNG, op. cit. (Ref. 3), pp. 21–22.
61. Thames Television transcript, op. cit. (Ref. 33).
62. 'A Record Defended', Shirley Williams talking to Edward Heath, *Listener*, 25 October 1979.

63. Interview, Cabinet Minister.
64. SIR IAN GILMOUR, *Inside Right: A Study of Conservatism*, Quartet, 1978, p. 259.
65. *Hansard*, 22 January 1974, Vol. 867, Col. 1446.
66. *The Times*, 28 January 1974.
67. *The Times*, 29 January 1974.
68. LORD HOME, *The Way the Wind Blows: an Autobiography*, Fontana, 1979, p. 271.
69. The *Economist*, 2 February 1974.
70. The *Economist*, 9 February 1974.
71. *Hansard*, 6 February 1974, Vol. 868, Col. 1242.
72. For a comprehensive account see D. E. BUTLER and D. KAVANAGH, *The General Election of February 1974*, Macmillan, 1974.
73. Interview, Conservative Party Adviser.
74. Interview, Conservative Party Adviser.
75. Ibid.
76. Interview, Conservative Party Adviser.
77. Thames Television transcript, op. cit. (Ref. 33).
78. Interview, Cabinet Minister.
79. Interview, Junior Minister,
80. Interview, Conservative Party Adviser.
81. D. HURD, op. cit. (Ref. 24), pp. 127–28.
82. Interview, Conservative MP. An added advantage of an early election would have been that the new register would not have been in force. The Labour Party was thus considerably relieved that the election was not fought before 16 February, the date when the new register came into operation.
83. Interview, Cabinet Minister.
84. Interview, Cabinet Minister.
85. Interview, Junior Minister.
86. Interview, Conservative Party Official.
87. Interview, Cabinet Minister.
88. Interview, two Cabinet Ministers.
89. D. HURD, op. cit. (Ref. 24), p. 130.
90. S. FAY and H.YOUNG, op. cit. (Ref. 3), p. 26.
91. Interview, Senior CBI Official.
92. D. E. BUTLER and D. KAVANAGH, op. cit. (Ref. 72), p. 43.
93. S. FAY and H. YOUNG, op. cit. (Ref. 3), p. 27.
94. Conservative Party Manifesto, February 1974.
95. *The Times*, 8 February 1974.
96. Interview, Trade Union Leader.
97. *The Times*, 9 February 1974.
98. *The Times*, 9 February 1974.
99. As well as the leaked statistical evidence the Conservatives were not helped during the campaign by Campbell Adamson's adverse comments on the Industrial Relations Act, Enoch Powell's advice to vote Labour, the publication of high Bank profits, a record £383 m January trade gap, and a controversial Party Political Broadcast by Mr Barber on 19 February.
100. S. FAY and H. YOUNG, op. cit. (Ref. 3), pp. 29–30.
101. Interview, Dick Leonard.
102. LORD HOME, op. cit. (Ref. 68), p. 273.
103. Thames Television transcript, op. cit. (Ref. 33).
104. D. HURD, op. cit. (Ref. 24), p. 134.
105. Interview, Junior Minister. The swing to Labour from the Conservatives was 16% in Mr Powell's former seat and between 5% and 10% in the industrial constituencies west of Birmingham.
106. Interview, Junior Minister.
107. SIR HAROLD WILSON, *Final Term: The Labour Government 1974–76*, Weidenfeld & Nicolson and Michael Joseph, 1979, p. 5.
108. J. E. ALT, *The Politics of Economic Decline: Economic Management and Political Behaviour in Britain since 1964*, Cambridge University, p. 157.
109. Thus having demanded 25% the miners wound up with 29% – the very outcome the statutory incomes policy had been designed to prevent.

110. WILLIAM WALDEGRAVE, *The Binding of Leviathan: Conservatism and the Future*, Hamish Hamilton, 1978, pp. 65–66.
111. 'A Record Defended', Shirley Williams talking to Edward Heath, The *Listener*, 25 October 1979.
112. LORD BLAKE and J. PATTEN (Eds.), *The Conservative Opportunity*, Macmillan, 1976, p. 3.
113. Interview, Junior Minister.
114. COLIN CROUCH, *The Politics of Industrial Relations*, Fontana, 1979, p. 88.
115. I. CREWE *et al*, Partisan Dealignment in Britain 1964–74, *British Journal of Political Science*, Vol. 7, 1977.
116. Interview, Cabinet Minister.
117. IAIN MACLEAN, *Elections*, Longmans, 1976, p. 8.
118. In the Appendix to D. E. BUTLER and D. KAVANAGH, op. cit. (Ref. 72), pp. 314–16.
119. Ibid. pp. 319–322.
120. Ibid, p. 321.
121. R. BACON and W. ELTIS, *Britain's Economic Problems: Two Few Producers*, Macmillan, 1976, p. 56.
122. e.g., TERENCE HIGGINS' article, *Sunday Times*, 10 July 1977.
123. S. BRITTAN and P. LILLEY, op. cit. (Ref. 10), p. 172.
124. S. FAY and H. YOUNG, op. cit. (Ref. 3), p. 31.
125. It must be stated however that a Gallup Poll in February 1974 recorded that the public still considered the Government's policy to be good for the country by a 38% majority. However, the same poll found that the public thought that the Government's handling of the emergency situation to be good, 30% and bad, 56%. *Gallup Opinion Polls*, op. cit. (Ref. 11), p. 1312.
126. Mr Heath's Government had, ironically, come to power rejecting the philosophy of compulsory wage control.
127. D.HURD, op. cit. (Ref. 24), p. 135.
128. MICHAEL PARKIN, *The Illusion of Wage and Price Control*, The Fraser Institute, 1976, p. 129.
129. MAURICE SCOTT, *Can we get back to Full Employment?*, Macmillan, 1978, p. 84. BRITTAN and LILLEY, op. cit. (Ref. 10), Ch. 5 and 6, cite Holland, Sweden and the USA as countries where incomes policy has, contrary to general belief, been unsuccessful in controlling inflation. For an alternative view see A. JONES, *The New Inflation: The New Politics of Prices and Incomes*, André Deutsch and Penguin Books, 1973, Ch. 9.
130. D. HURD, op. cit. (Ref. 24), p. 135.
131. Interview, Conservative Party Adviser.
132. It may be argued, with the benefit of hindsight, that the crisis of the winter of 1973/74 marked the end of *statutory* incomes policy as a political panacea. The Labour administration 1974–79, unlike its 1964–70 predecessor, did not enact statutory controls. Similarly, the hostility towards statutory controls shown by Mrs Thatcher in Opposition has not been reversed in Government.

Part III

# Conclusions

Chapter 8

# Policy reversals and Prime Ministerial power

*'What had transformed Cabinet government into Prime Ministerial government has been the unique integrating roles of a British Prime Minister . . . there are three fields in which he exerts central authority: the Cabinet with its base in Parliament, the Civil Service, and [to a lesser but still significant extent] the party machine outside. It is because he is the only man who wields central authority in all these fields that we can rightly describe the British system as Prime Ministerial.'*

R. H. S. Crossman, *Inside View:*
*Three Lectures on Prime Ministerial*
*Government*, Jonathan Cape, 1972

## 8.1   Mr Heath's style of government

Mr Heath's Prime Ministerial style of Government in relation to back bench dissent had been effectively analysed by Philip Norton. But in the context of the policy changes so far discussed the question of personalities had been deliberately played down. Policy decisions, especially policy U-turns, are never simply a matter of external factors or historical forces controlling the policy makers. Each external factor, for example a rise in unemployment, affects each policy maker differently according to the political priorities and personality of the policy maker. Prime Ministers have long since been associated with policies which reflected their personal approach to politics and their personal ideological preferences or lack of them. The Munich policy reflected Neville Chamberlain's personality; the style of war-time leadership suited Sir Winston Churchill's personality and the mood associated with affluent society in the days of 'you've never had it so good' was the personal projection of Harold Macmillan's premiership. Edward Heath's premiership 1970–74 reflected his personal style through two directly connected features of policy reversals and the pursuit of almost total Prime Ministerial power. As one former Minister noted 'no member of the Cabinet was identified with a policy different from Mr Heath's'[1].

Political opponents have often described Mr Heath as stubborn or inflexible. In a personal sense this may be true but in the context of the policies pursued by his Government the opposite is the case. Mr Heath was the Prime Minister who changed his mind. The platform on which he was elected in 1970 was not only repudiated but put into reverse. The 'Quiet Revolution' was short lived; the Industrial Relations Act was put 'on ice'; disengagement from industry was turned into the most active interventionist policy hitherto devised in Britain; the abandonment of statutory incomes policy was the prelude for its return in the most comprehensive peace time form; public expenditure cuts in October 1970 foreshadowed an enormous increase in deficit-financed public spending; the control of inflation was replaced by the reduction of unemployment as the economic priority; and floating exchange rates, which had been previously scorned, were introduced. All these changes of policy reflected the change in Mr Heath's mind, a change of mind previously analysed as the 'Heath dilemma', the search for a rational alternative to the 'Quiet Revolution'. It was the way he pushed through so many policy changes that made his premiership the classic textbook case of Prime Ministerial government. One former Minister thought that 'Iain Macleod's death had a lot to do with how Ted Heath came to operate. Had there been a figure of stature and intellect to argue policy through this would have made a great difference'[2]. Iain Macleod's death certainly deprived Mr Heath of a senior figure of political standing, but it is doubtful whether Macleod, a consensus 'Butskellite' politician, would have proved a stout defender of the 'Quiet Revolution' policies with which Mr Heath took office. In this context it is worth mentioning the role of the Chancellor, Anthony Barber, in Mr Heath's policy reversals. Mr Barber has often been blamed for his handling of the economy and in particular that he was responsible for the so-called 'Barber boom'. One Junior Minister recalled that 'Barber was a disaster managing the economy'[3], a popular view among both Conservative monetarist critics and the Labour Opposition.

A closer examination of the evidence, however, suggests otherwise; although a close personal friend of Mr Heath, he was far from being Mr Heath's closest ally in the retreat away from the 'Quiet Revolution'. Unlike Mr Heath, Mr Barber was never a believer in incomes policy, voluntary or statutory, as a permanent solution to inflation but, once a statutory policy was introduced, he took the view that the Government had to see it through. During the period of negotiations during 1972 aimed at voluntary policy Mr Barber was the toughest negotiator on the Government's side, the least willing to accept that the TUC was actually able to deliver the goods. One union leader commented that 'Barber was the nigger in the woodpile – I don't think he actually wanted an agreement'[4]. Another union leader thought that Barber '. . . in my opinion was reluctant [to reach an agreement] in the first place'[5]. But Mr Barber's reputation has been most tarnished by the phrase 'the Barber boom', used to describe the measures associated with the 'dash for growth'. In reality the 'dash for growth ' and the deficit-financed package were part of the 'Heath dilemma' alternative policy imposed on the Treasury from Number 10 to Mr Barber's considerable disapproval. Thus as Samuel Brittan has put it, 'Mr Barber . . . was less responsible than almost any other senior member of the Cabinet for the so-called 'Barber boom'[6]. The 'boom' and 'dash for growth' were examples of Prime Ministerial power not Treasury 'influence'.

Given Mr Barber's unpublicized lack of enthusiasm for Mr Heath's policy reversals the obvious question is why did Mr Barber not resign, as Peter Thorneycroft had done in 1958, on a matter of principle? After all, Mr Thorneycroft had resigned over a mere £50m of excess government spending and Mr Barber was deeply concerned by a spending level far greater. Mr Barber's main reason for not resigning was loyalty both to the Prime Minister and to the Conservative Party. He did not want to be seen rocking the boat amid already stormy seas. As Mr Barber recalled:

I was very frustrated over the level of public expenditure – I thought it excessive. But I had decided that I was to retire at the next election, that I was going to go anyway, so I thought I ought to soldier on. If the Chancellor of the Exchequer resigns over public expenditure it can have a very bad effect on sterling and is a poor thing for the country. It should also be remembered that Mr Heath and the Cabinet had supported me on a number of matters which were not particularly to their liking. I was not prepared to throw in the towel and let my colleagues down[7].

Thus, having considered resignation, Mr Barber felt that his own personal circumstances and the political effects of his resignation as the Chancellor, obliged him to continue in office. It is speculation to suppose that had Mr Barber resigned Mr Heath would have re-considered his 'dash for growth' policy. The more likely outcome would have been the appointment of a Chancellor far more committed to Mr Heath's policies than was Mr Barber. For although Mr Barber made little headway in resisting Mr Heath's 'reflationary' enthusiasm, a Chancellor who shared Mr Heath's approach would have been even less likely to appreciate the dangers of inflation that such a policy created. As it was Mr Barber did make public spending cuts of £1200m on 17 December 1973. While it can be argued that Mr Barber ought to have taken the option of resignation, as Peter Thorneycroft did in 1958, it can no longer be argued that Mr Barber was responsible for the so-called 'Barber boom' and the worst excesses of deficit financing. That policy was Mr Heath's and as such was reluctantly carried out by a Chancellor who was prepared to lay down his reputation for the sake of loyalty to his Party. It may, therefore, be argued that Mr Barber's loyalty was a testimony to the complete control over policy making that Mr Heath possessed.

Mr Heath's control was so total that he dominated his Cabinet, his Party, and his back-benchers as well as the Treasury. One senior Conservative has written that as Prime Minister 'his style of leadership was military'[8]. To one adviser part of the problem was that Mr Heath 'had no close friends in politics'[9]. While it may be argued that Mr Heath showed an interest in electoral popularity by adopting the traditional post-war Keynesian politics of demand management to reduce unemployment, it may also be pointed out that he did not seek popularity as such with his own Party – indeed the Liberal revival was a consequence of his unpopularity among Conservative voters. He was also ill at ease with the media. As one senior lobby correspondent of the time has since noted:

. . . As Prime Minister he disliked journalists and distrusted newspapers. Political correspondents he felt had been willing parties in their seduction by the arch-villain Harold Wilson. He never expected a good Press and was always wary of journalists . . . . He kept in his own hands all the levers of power and information and of the latter precious little was allowed to escape. When he became enmeshed in his confrontation with the National Union of Mineworkers in late 1973 the people were totally uninformed, and confused[10].

Similarly, Douglas Hurd has tactfully observed that Mr Heath '. . . was rarely angry with the media . . . but he rarely warmed towards them'[11].

It is not surprising that it was a Civil Servant, Sir William Armstrong, who became his closest adviser in the running of the Incomes Policy, rather than a Cabinet Minister. Indeed, the role of the Cabinet as such would appear to have been one of quiescence or acquiescence. A former back bench MP remarked that Mr Heath 'did not regard the Cabinet as central to policy making'[12] and another back bench critic regarded 'the 1970 Cabinet as the most Prime Ministerial since Chamberlain'[13]. Norton claims that apart from Mrs Thatcher and very occasionally one or two other Members such as Mr Davies and Mr Rippon[14], Cabinet Ministers were not prepared to argue with the Prime Minister. One Conservative MP thought that Heath 'excluded from the Cabinet men of ability – particularly John Biffen'[15]. But it is important to remember, as one former Cabinet Minister has written, that 'As Prime Minister there was never an item on the Cabinet agenda upon which he personally was not exceptionally well briefed'[16]. Mr Heath's command of detailed information tended to make him impatient with those who had been more selectively briefed. One close adviser recalled that:

Heath always had very good documentation but he didn't listen to his Cabinet colleagues and didn't have a high opinion of them. He is a lonely, thoughtful man, an intellectual bully. He was socially insecure because of his background[17].

A particular critic of Mr Heath's administration noted that '. . . dissent was treated as treason and within the Cabinet there was little debate. Those who didn't go along with Heath were manoeuvred out'[18]. One Cabinet Minister who was critical of Mr Heath's U-turns, recalled that 'I was just too involved in what I was doing in my Department – that was part of the problem. But after February 1974, I was able to reflect'[19]. Indeed, Mr Heath's personal style was not that of the politician, the debater or the communicator but that of the civil servant. In strictly policy terms this could have turned out to be an advantage but evidence suggests otherwise. One Junior Minister observed that 'the Prime Minister turned to Civil Servants not political colleagues for advice'[20]. Other critics thought Mr Heath 'an autocrat and civil servant at heart'[21], 'a natural autocrat who treated people in a regal fashion and regarded criticism as treason'[22], and even a '2nd rate Civil Servant with no intellectual mind'[23]. Many Conservatives also became dissatisfied with the way in which Mr Heath appeared to use Conservative Central Office as a way of suppressing dissent within the Party by increasing centralization so that the Party machine resembled even more closely the Leader's private office.

Mr Heath's natural preference for Civil Service rather than political advice greatly assisted his Prime Ministerial style of government. This was particularly the case after the introduction of the statutory prices and incomes policy in November 1972 when Mr Heath came increasingly to rely on Sir William Armstrong, the Head of the Civil Service and the official in charge of the running of the policy. Although one trade union leader regarded Armstrong as 'more than a deputy Prime Minister – he was a co-Prime Minister'[24], this is an exaggeration of his role. Thus, rather than a deputy or co-Prime Minister, Armstrong was 'more a Chief of Staff'[25]. One adviser thought Mr Heath 'came to rely more than usually on

Armstrong but the phrase of Vic Feather's that he was a Deputy Prime Minister was unfortunate and unfair'[26]. What is beyond dispute is that Sir William Armstrong became Mr Heath's closest adviser and as such was playing a political role. As the architect of the incomes policy, on which Mr Heath thought his Government's success depended, Sir William Armstrong's advice was bound to be continually sought. In another sense 'Armstrong was a natural reflection of Mr Heath's character'[27], which meant that other advisers, such as Cabinet Ministers, were kept in the background. One Senior Minister recalled that:

> Armstrong was a political civil servant. He often went behind my back and we had several rows. It was difficult for a Minister to object to Armstrong playing such a big part. Government was carried on not by Ministers but by a small mixed group of civil servants and Ministers on an *ad hoc* basis. This enabled Armstrong to reduce the people on the committee to himself and Ted[28].

Thus at the start of the dispute with the miners in 1973, according to one Cabinet Minister, 'Mr Heath didn't pay much attention to his Secretary of State for Employment [then Maurice Macmillan]. He preferred to consult Armstrong'[29]. Mr Heath's over-reliance on the Civil Service was a central feature of his Prime Ministerial style of government, in effect the antithesis of Cabinet government.

Certainly this aspect of Mr Heath's premiership may be seen in the wider context of modern British government. Without wishing to re-state the familiar arguments relating to the institutional growth of Prime Ministerial power, Mr Heath's style of government certainly lends weight to those who, like Richard Crossman, argue that British government is prone to Prime Ministerial rather than collective cabinet government. In Mr Heath's case, however, it may be argued that the institutional trappings of Prime Ministerial power – kitchen cabinets, rigorous control of Cabinet agenda, the by-passing of full Cabinet by Cabinet committees, and the exalted political status of the Prime Minister presented in the media – were essentially secondary to Mr Heath's total control. While some Prime Ministers become more Prime Ministerial as they pick up the levers of power during their periods of office, e.g., Mr Wilson, in Mr Heath's case this does not apply. Mr Heath's pursuit of power and the ultimate extent to which he was prepared to use that power, was entirely personal rather than institutional. James David Barber has argued in relation to President Nixon that '. . . power is a core need . . . concentrated in the White House and within [the White House] in the hands of the President himself'[30]. The same may be argued in relation to Mr Heath. As with President Nixon, Mr Heath brought to his office a personality that sought, as a matter of course, to concentrate power ultimately in the hands of Mr Heath himself or the trusted William Armstrong. The emergence of Prime Ministerial government in Britain certainly facilitated Mr Heath's concentration of power.

But apart from his domination of his Cabinet Mr Heath also dominated parliamentary management. The Chief Whip, Mr Francis Pym, would inform Mr Heath [himself a former Chief Whip] who would often ignore this information[31]. One Cabinet Minister regarded Mr Heath as '. . . straightforward and honest, but he didn't indulge in the niceties a Prime

Minister ought to indulge in'[32]. Mr Heath's domination of his parliamentary party is, in consequence, central to an understanding of British government in this period. Conservative back-benchers were accorded no higher status than that of lobby fodder. Mr Heath, once persuaded of the correctness of a measure, apparently decided to introduce it without consultation with back-benchers, and regardless of anticipated back bench reaction. Norton has explained that:

> This failure of Mr Heath's to communicate adequately with his back-benchers helped generate a feeling of unease within the parliamentary party as a whole (particularly in the latter half of the Parliament), and to further alienate back bench dissenters in particular. Members disliked or were ambivalent toward certain measures being introduced and passed through the House in a manner that seemed to take little account of their disquiet, but also found the Prime Minister apparently unresponsive to their objections on the matter, the cumulative effect of which was to help precipitate the Members towards opposition in the division lobbies[33].

The influences upon Mr Heath in determining new policies during the Parliament – such as the U-turns on aid to industry and the economy – were extra-parliamentary and extra-Cabinet. There appears to have been no prior consultation before the introduction of measures with back-benchers, nor indeed, in some cases with Junior Ministers as, for example, with the U-turn on aid to industry. One Junior Minister recalled that:

> Poor John Eden had scarcely got rid of the IRC [Industrial Relations Court] when Heath initiated a replacement which went even further and instructed Civil Servants not to inform ministers about the change of policy. Ministers just weren't kept informed[34].

Similarly, the Cabinet was not consulted over the U-turn on incomes policy nor informed of the secret meeting in July 1973 between Mr Heath, Sir William Armstrong and Joe Gormley. It may be argued convincingly that Mr Heath was a man to change his mind. However, once the change had taken place the necessary measures were introduced and swiftly carried through. Norton shrewdly comments that Mr Heath was a 'manager of measures not men'[35]. In the same context it has been argued that Mr Heath

> never adjusted himself in style, conviction and person to being Party Leader. He commanded the troops from on high with an authoritative smack to which they were not accustomed. He was never a comfortable, chummy leader. He found it almost impossible to unbend[36].

The considerable parliamentary dissent against Mr Heath's measures has been extensively documented[37]. One back-bencher favourable to the policy reversals of the Government explained that 'Heath is a shy man and gives the impression of being more dogmatic than he really is. It never bothered me that he never stopped to talk'[38]. But Mr Heath's aloofness from his back-benchers was not surprising given his downgrading of the Cabinet. In this way, 'Heath couldn't understand why back-benchers could dissent. He wasn't prepared to mix or talk to back-benchers either at a personal or an intellectual level'[39]. Behrens has noted that:

No Conservative appeared immune from the effects of Mr Heath's chilly disposition. Younger members complained of not being acknowledged in the House, senior back-benchers were dealt with in a high-handed fashion, and loyal colleagues treated with a curt incivility. Even dedicated Heath supporters compared Mr Heath's visits to the House of Commons smoking room with an inspection of the troops by the commander-in-chief[40].

In a similar way one former Minister noted that:

Heath takes on soldiering, politics, music, sailing and he's a fantastic success. But you only communicate with him when you work with him – an extraordinary person. He is a man of integrity but he can't nurture friendships[41].

Although Mr Heath's dominant personality led to the Prime Ministerial style of government that antagonized many Ministers and back-benchers, it is worth noting that members of his personal staff have been less eager to criticize. This may well be the result of effective communication between them and Mr Heath. Douglas Hurd, Mr Heath's political secretary, has praised his 'sensitive kindness to those whom he knew well' and the 'comradeship at Number 10 during this time'[42]. Another close personal adviser praised Mr Heath as a 'warm and generous man to work for. He had the ability to be rude and to command respect. He was very dominant and we didn't stand up to him enough'[43]. One Minister felt that 'Heath learned a lot in three and a half years – the policies pursued in the last eighteen months seemed about right'[44].

But to those with whom Mr Heath did not work closely or those who disapproved of the U-turns were less likely to be as complimentary. One former adviser thought that 'Ted Heath had no political antennae'[45], and a former Conservative Central Office official criticized Heath as 'not in the Tory tradition . . . he remained a Balliol Conservative'[46]. Whatever the arguments concerning Mr Heath's policy reversals it is crucial that they are seen as part of Mr Heath's Prime Ministerial style of government. So, without the total control over his Cabinet and his Party in the House, the dissent that did exist would have been far greater. It was because of Mr Heath's control that so many policy U-turns were carried through in such a short period of time. As well as the limited criticism within the Conservative Party regarding the U-turns – the overall view was that Mr Heath was doing the right thing for the right reason. Mr Heath's Government faced criticism from political opponents. Most of the criticism from the Labour Opposition centred around Mr Heath's alleged desire for 'confrontation'.

## 8.2    The politics of confrontation?

While it is true that there were five States of Emergency declared in three and a half years and that industrial relations disputes often caught the headlines there is little evidence that Mr Heath actually sought, or enjoyed, industrial confrontation. However, critics, not necessarily on the Left, have referred to Mr Heath's administration as the 'politics of confrontation'[47]. The charge of 'confrontation' as Douglas Hurd has rightly pointed out is often made without recourse to reasoned argument:

> . . . confrontation has already become a word of abuse, like 'appeasement' in the 1940s, a word you hurl at your opponent without pausing to consider if it has any meaning. No-one need be particularly worried about this temporary version of history, because history will quickly dispose of it[48].

'Confrontation', moreover, is rarely a one-sided business; government or trade unions can hardly confront themselves. Certainly, Mr Heath's Government did 'confront' the unions on some issues in a way that made matters worse. The rigid insistence on the Stage III guidelines exacerbated the fateful dispute in the winter of 1973/74 when the irrelevance of such guidelines was already quite plain to see. The Industrial Relations Act, despite its honourable intentions, did actually make 'confrontation' worse by increasing the number, and the seriousness, of industrial disputes. But even the Industrial Relations Act was abandoned by the Government as a political panacea as the tripartite talks began in the summer of 1972. The charge of 'confrontation' can be more easily levelled at the trade unions. It is the prerogative of trade unions, in a free society, to take strike action. The use of this prerogative, however, is entirely voluntary. The inconvenience caused to the public, as well as to employers, by strike action is a consequence of the unions' monopoly powers as suppliers of labour. Mr Heath's Government, of course, had to deal with such crises as they affected the nation, but was not responsible for them. It was the Government's responsibility to manage the economy as a whole; the responsibility for strike action was that of the trade unions. So if the charge of 'confrontation' is to be made, it can be more easily hurled at the unions than at Mr Heath's Government. In this sense Mr Heath's Government was unlucky in that it coincided with the massive increase in trade union militancy that had originated in the 1960s but which only reached its peak of destructiveness after 1970. The problems of the abuse of trade union power dominated every aspect of Mr Heath's domestic economic policy-making, putting a tremendous strain on an industrial economy already in decline. Whatever the rights or wrongs of Mr Heath's policy reversals there is no doubt that Mr Heath never abdicated or avoided the problems that trade union power were causing, or exacerbating.

Furthermore, although such measures as the 'amendment of the law to outlaw strikes against the community [or strikes which exploit monopoly power]'[49] have since been proposed by Brendon Sewill, formerly Mr Barber's Chief Treasury adviser, Mr Heath and his Ministers did not consider this to be a viable strategy. Nor were social security benefits to strikers' families restricted despite calls, largely from the Conservative Right, to do so. Far from using the power of the Government to undermine the collective growth of trade union influence, Mr Heath's own Prime Ministerial style of government helped to add to the status and importance of nationally-known trade union leaders. As well as adopting such policies as the 'dash for growth', which the unions had been urging for many years, Mr Heath, by seeking direct agreement with trade union leaders through the tripartite talks, elevated the status of trade union leaders to the Prime

Ministerial level. The union leaders were accorded a position somewhat akin to visiting Heads of State dealing directly with the Prime Minister who would later, as has been noted, present a *fait accompli* to the Cabinet and Parliament. The exercise of Mr Heath's Prime Ministerial power thus reinforced the corresponding growth of trade union status and power at the expense of the public's representatives (MPs), in Mr Heath's case, and at the expense of the disruption caused to the public (by strike action), in the trade unions' case. But it would be wrong to draw the conclusion that such developments of Mr Heath's Prime Ministerial style of government became increasingly identifiable with a corporate state. This accusation, usually from the Right, like the accusation from the Left that Mr Heath sought confrontation, missed the point that Mr Heath's policies, while often similar to those advocated by the trade unions, such as higher levels of public expenditure, were not based on any agreed consensus. The Government was quite prepared to go it alone over statutory prices and incomes policy to the displeasure of both the TUC and CBI, a determination in the context of Stage III that was to precipitate the fall of the Government. Thus if, as Lehmbruch argues, '. . . a high degree of collaboration among [interest] groups themselves in the shaping of policy'[50] is the distinguishing trait of corporatism, Mr Heath's post 'Quiet Revolution' policies cannot be called corporatist in that sense. Only in the loose context, as defined by Grant and Marsh (see page 81) can Mr Heath's policies be defined as corporatist and as such no more (or less) corporatist than those of other post-war governments[51]. Similarly, it may be argued that Mr Heath's Government was no more (or less) desirous of confrontation than any other post-war government.

On another level the Heath Government can be criticized as the Government that ran away from 'confrontation', that was too eager to change its policies in the face of opposition. It failed to carry through the necessary state disengagement from industry, completely reversing its original policy; it failed to stand firm against rising unemployment, despite evidence that it was not the Government's fault, and launched a high programme of deficit-financed public spending; and it failed to face up to the problem of inflation by resurrecting the incomes policy delusion and 'dash for growth' package. Such failures were the consequences of not 'confronting' certain problems for fear of political or industrial opposition. So that even when the correct analysis was at hand – for example that the Government was not to blame for rising unemployment – the political will was lacking to back it up. It is ironic that the Heath Government was thought of as constantly confronting the trade unions when its policy reversals and the adoption of a high growth policy were the very policies which the unions – not business or traditional Conservative voters – had consistently urged successive governments to adopt.

This aspect of Mr Heath's administration has since come into even clearer context, given the monetarist approach of Chancellor Denis Healey in the 1974–79 Labour Government following Britain's resort to the IMF in 1976. Similarly, Mrs Thatcher's Government, continuing the broadly monetarist policies of public spending controls initiated by Mr Callaghan after 1976, has proved far less responsive to TUC remedies than did Mr Heath. With the benefit of hindsight that such a context allows it may be argued that Mr Heath's Government, in the pursuit of the 'Heath dilemma' alternative strategy, came closer than any other government in modern times to accommodating the policy priorities of Britain's trade union leaders. It is not surprising, as previously mentioned, that the trade union leaders came to admire and respect Mr Heath when his policy reversals had moved in the direction the unions found most congenial. In the overall context the use of the term 'confrontation ' to describe relations between the government and the unions is positively misleading. Only in certain specific cases, e.g., the Government's commitment to the Stage III guidelines, is the term relevant and applicable.

## 8.3    The criticisms of the Conservative Right

If the criticism of 'confrontation' has come mainly, though not exclusively, from the Left, the criticism for the major policy U-turns of the Heath Government has come mainly from the Right. The extent of the U-turns and the swiftness of their execution depended, as already discussed, on Mr Heath's dominant Prime Ministerial style of government. Mr Heath, in effect, led the policy about-turns from above, with the Cabinet, the parliamentary party, industry and most important the Conservative electorate, all being presented with a *fait accompli*. The 'Quiet Revolution' policies of reducing the role of the state in industry, in wage and price decisions, and of reducing government expenditure were all abandoned by Mr Heath and eventually reversed. The crucial reason for this was the over-reaction to rising unemployment, which caused a shift of political emphasis in the opposite direction to the 'Quiet Revolution' programme, and which made the 'Heath dilemma' alternative a rational attraction. Keegan and Pennant-Rea note that '. . . wholesale panic in the ranks of the Government . . . was such that the Government resorted to every reflationary device in sight'[52]. Mr Heath personally led those who feared a return to the 1930s levels of unemployment and the labelling once again of the Conservative Party as the party of unemployment. The key point is that, with the best of intentions, Mr Heath acted according to the post-war Keynesian orthodoxy '. . . at the point at which the Keynesian model was falling apart'[53]. One special Treasury adviser recalled that:

> Most of us – the economic establishment that is – were guilty of not knowing enough about monetary policy. We were shipwrecked in 1970–74. It was the last death throes of the post-war consensus – the end of social engineering and demand management[54].

Not surprisingly, it is those who deny the end of the Keynesian era who have emerged as Mr Heath's stoutest defenders. Frank Blackaby of the National Institute for Economic and Social Research (NIESR) has praised Mr Heath's 'viable strategy', adding that '. . . nobody will come before the cameras and say "Ted was right" . . . . He was though'[55]. Apart from the obvious point that Mr Heath's strategy ended in electoral defeat and that on leaving office the purely economic indicators showed record inflation, unemployment, trade imbalance and levels of deficit-financed public expenditure, Mr Blackaby's praise, coming as it did in 1980, sounded less convincing that it might have done in, say, 1974. The main reason for this lay in conventional Keynesian policies that had proved so unsuccessful under Mr Heath, although this was not as evident at the time of their adoption. Again, in the wider context provided by hindsight it may be argued that Mr Heath's reliance on crude Keynesianism has proved an object lesson to successive governments of both major parties. If 'Butskellism' has been replaced by 'Howleyism', then Mr Heath's Government may be regarded as instrumental to such a fundamental change in British political economy. In effect the failure of the Keynesian remedies of the 'Heath dilemma' alternative brought the Keynesian era to an end.

The Heath Government's policies in effect came to depend on the '. . . endless preoccupation with demand as the keystone to economic policy'[56], at a time when such a policy was losing economic and electoral appeal[57]. Mr Heath's over-reaction to the unemployment that his administration had neither welcomed nor created was central to each U-turn. It led to the downgrading of inflation control as a policy priority; the rescue of Upper Clyde Shipbuilders; the interventionist Industry Act; the massive increase in public expenditure by deficit financing; 'the dash for growth' and statutory prices and incomes policy; the effective suspension of the Industrial Relations Act as a prerequisite for trade union co-operation; the abandonment of the 'liberalism' of the 'Quiet Revolution' in favour of the leftward direction of the – admittedly well-intentioned – 'Heath dilemma' approach from the spring of 1972.

But these specific criticisms should be placed in the context of a more general criticism that they merely exemplify. The underlying theme of Mr Heath's Government according to the Right was that it misunderstood the function of government. It tended to think that the role of government was to manage, to administer and to solve specific problems. It forgot that the purposes for which government is most needed, and which is the most it can successfully achieve, is to uphold and develop the rules within which individuals, families, companies and voluntary groups can manage their own affairs. The temptation to try to manage everything, rather than to uphold the rules within which others do so, *ipso facto* deprives individuals and voluntary groups of their former responsibilities in that sphere. They then behave in a different and literally 'irresponsible' manner. This creates new problems, which a managerial government is by nature bound to try to solve – by further extending its responsibilities[58]. There is no logical end to this process. The Conservative Right have claimed that this is not mere abstract political theory inapplicable to the real world, and that it applies in particular to Mr Heath's over-reaction to rising unemployment. Certainly, no politically desirable level of unemployment was set by Mr Heath's Government. Instead, a whole series of *ad hoc* measures were taken until the rate had fallen substantially but the political priorities had changed. The electorate's main concern was inflation not unemployment and the Liberal revival based on disaffected Conservative voters was well under way.

Ultimately the policy reversals of Mr Heath's Government led neither to economic power nor political salvation. On leaving office most economic indicators were pointing in the wrong direction. Inflation and unemployment (despite the measures taken) were at record levels. The balance of payments deficit was vast and the value of the pound declining. Public expenditure was at an unprecedented level and the prospects for sustainable economic growth had ceased to exist. Budd has pointed out that the chief characteristic of Mr Heath's policy '. . . was the attempt to over-ride or deny the existence of market forces. Inflation, in particular, became something that could be negotiated away'[59]. On the political level the Conservative Party had forfeited office after only three and a half years, despite the electorate's lack of enthusiasm for the official Labour Opposition. Conservative voters disillusioned above all with the increasing rate of inflation, had abstained, or voted Liberal, in sufficient numbers to leave Labour *inter alia* the largest party in the House of Commons. These economic and political failures, it may be argued, were the direct consequence of the policy reversals, however rational and well-intentioned, which Mr Heath had initiated as political pressure caused the abandonment of economic policy objectives.

## References

1. Interview, Cabinet Minister.
2. Interview, Junior Minister.
3. Interview, Junior Minister.
4. Interview, Trade Union Leader.
5. Interview, Trade Union Leader.
6. S. BRITTAN, *The Economic Consequences of Democracy*, Temple Smith, 1977, p. 9.
7. Interview, Lord Barber.
8. NIGEL FISHER, *The Tory Leaders*, Weidenfeld and Nicolson, 1977.
9. Interview, Conservative Party Official.
10. JAMES MARGACH, *The Abuse of Power*, W. H. Allen, 1978, p. 157.
11. D. HURD, *An End to Promises: Sketch of a Government 1970–74*, Collins, 1979, p. 83.
12. Interview, Conservative MP.
13. Interview, Conservative MP.
14. See P. NORTON, op. cit. (Ref. 31) p. 88 for a more detailed account.
15. Interview, Conservative MP.
16. PETER WALKER, *The Ascent of Britain*, Sidgwick and Jackson, 1977, p. 58.
17. Interview, Senior Civil Servant.
18. Interview, Conservative MP.
19. Interview, Cabinet Minister.
20. Interview, Junior Minister.
21. Interview, Treasury Adviser.
22. Interview, George Hutchinson.
23. Interview, Former Conservative MP.
24. Interview, Trade Union Leader.
25. Interview, Senior Treasury Official.
26. Interview, Senior Civil Servant.
27. Interview, Treasury Adviser.
28. Interview, Cabinet Minister.
29. Interview, Cabinet Minister.
30. J. D. BARBER, *The Presidential Character*, Prentice-Hall, 1972, p. 422.
31. P. NORTON, *Conservative Dissidents: Dissent within the Parliamentary Conservative Party, 1970–74*, Macmillan, 1978, p. 166.
32. Interview, Cabinet Minister.
33. P. NORTON, op. cit. (Ref. 31), p. 166.
34. Interview, Junior Minister.
35. P. NORTON, op. cit. (Ref. 31), p. 229.
36. J. MARGACH, op. cit. (Ref. 10), p. 162.
37. P. NORTON, op. cit. (Ref. 31), Ch. 3–5.

38. Interview, David Knox.
39. Interview, Philip Norton.
40. ROBERT BEHRENS, *The Conservative Party from Heath to Thatcher: Policies and Politics 1974–79*, Saxon House, 1980, p. 32.
41. Interview, Junior Minister.
42. D. HURD, op. cit. (Ref. 11), p. 138.
43. Interview, Cabinet Minister.
44. Interview, Cabinet Minister.
45. Interview, Conservative Party Official.
46. Interview, Conservative Party Official.
47. A. SKED and C. COOK, *Post-War Britain: a Political History*, Penguin Books, 1979, Ch. 10.
48. D. HURD, op. cit. (Ref. 11), pp. 139–40.
49. R. HARRIS and B. SEWILL, *British Economic Policy 1970–74: Two Views*, IEA Hobart Paperback No. 7, 1975, pp. 62–64.
50. G. LEHMBRUCH in P. C. SCHMITTER and G. LEHMBRUCH, *Trends towards Corporatist Intermediation*, Sage, 1979, p. 150.
51. See also T. RAISON in *The Corporate State: Myth or Reality*, by R. E. PAHL *et al*, Policy Studies Institute, 1976, pp. 101–2, for the view that corporatism should not be confused with state control or nationalization, and p. 106 for a useful dual definition of corporatism.
52. W. KEEGAN and R. PENNANT-REA, *Who Runs the Economy? Control and Influence in British Economic Policy*, Temple Smith, 1977, pp. 199–200.
53. Interview, Senior Treasury Official.
54. Interview, Treasury Adviser.
55. FRANK BLACKABY, 'In Praise of Edward Heath', The *Listener*, 21 February 1980.
56. Interview, John B. Wood.
57. See p. 81.
58. For a particularly illuminating analysis of the process in the context of Keynesian political economy, see N. JOHNSON, *In Search of the Constitution*, Methuen, 1980, Ch. 1 and particularly pp. 12–13.
59. A. BUDD, *The Politics of Economic Planning*, Fontana, 1978, p. 123.

# Chapter 9
# Policy reversals and contemporary Conservatism

*'. . . one of the abiding assets of the Conservative Party is its flexibility – it can absorb wide discrepancy of views among its members and still remain a coherent and unified entity.'*

Lord Butler, *The Art of the Possible*
Hamish Hamilton, 1971

## 9.1   The context of Conservatism

Mr Heath's policy reversals and the loss of office after only three and a half years caused a major upheaval in the Conservative Party. Mr Heath himself, when stripped of the Prime Ministerial title by which he dominated his Party, was removed as Conservative Party Leader less than a year after the February 1974 Election defeat. Once Mr Heath was no longer Prime Minister the Conservative Party, particularly the back bench MPs, could strike back without fear of disloyalty or 'rocking the boat'. His successor, Mrs Thatcher, began the process of returning the Party to policies in most cases similar to those of the 'Quiet Revolution'. Interventionism and statutory incomes policy were again eschewed. Indeed, Mrs Thatcher publicly warned that statutory pay policy put the state into confrontation with major sectional interests in society and hence should be avoided, a view consistent with the argument that the interventionist policies of the Conservative Left, not the non-interventionism of the Right, are more likely to lead to social discord. Furthermore it may be argued, with the benefit of hindsight, that Mrs Thatcher's first two and a half years of monetarist political economy have seen a decrease in numbers of working days lost to strikes, which compares favourably with Mr Heath's overall record. Similarly, Mrs Thatcher's Government has avoided the blind alley of statutory incomes policy that caused the precipitous downfall of Mr Heath's Government. In the context of such a comparison is it fair, therefore, to regard Mr Heath's policies as essentially unconservative, or alien to post-war Conservative philosophy?

The answer must, of course, be an ambiguous one since the very philosophy of Conservatism is ambiguous and the Conservative Party itself, probably more so than the Labour Party, especially after the formation of the Social Democrats into a formal party, is a 'broad church' party combining a number of ideological and interest groups. In electoral terms this blend has proved remarkably successful though in terms of defining what Conservatism actually is, even the most objective of observers is likely to become lost in the mists of time searching for historical alleyways which, for contemporary purposes, lead nowhere.

140

In the specific case of Mr Heath's Government, 1970–1974, most Conservatives experienced some discomfort over the policy priorities being pursued at some stage of the period. Those who supported the 'Quiet Revolution' approach regarded the Government's policy reversals as unnecessary, perhaps even ideologically perverse, while those close supporters of Mr Heath's U-turns usually regarded the 'Quiet Revolution' phase as an embarrassment, ill-advised and ill-considered. Without becoming bogged down in the largely bogus dilemma of defining 'left-wing' and 'right-wing' it is convenient to characterize the defenders of the 'Quiet Revolution' as belonging to the Conservative Right and the supporters of the policy reversals as belonging to the Conservative Left. For all their faults the terms 'Right' and 'Left' are marginally preferable to such euphemisms as 'neo-liberals' and 'paternalists' or, as Behrens has suggested, 'diehards' and 'ditchers'[1].

The ablest defender of Mr Heath's policy reversals on the Conservative Left is Sir Ian Gilmour, a member of Mr Heath's Cabinet. Sir Ian has denied that Mr Heath betrayed true Conservatism by moving too far to the Left and offers a well-argued case that all Conservative leaders face charges from the party's right-wing of drifting leftwards. As Sir Ian puts it, 'There is nothing new in right-wing accusations that Conservative leaders have forsaken Conservative principles. The leadership of the Conservative Party has nearly always been criticized by party zealots for conceding too much'[2]. But the point that Sir Ian misses is that Mr Heath's Government went further than any other Conservative government in adopting interventionist solutions, having in 1970 deliberately vowed to reduce the state's role in the economy and society. The references to other post-war Conservative leaders facing a discontented right-wing may be valid but the real question is how valid the criticisms of the Right were. In this context the Heath administration indeed stands out on its own as moving drastically, not gradually, in a leftward direction. It can be further argued that Mr Heath's post 'Quiet Revolution', 'Heath dilemma' policies, particularly the 1972 Industry Act and statutory incomes policy, paved the way for what many Conservatives have regarded as the excesses of the Labour Government 1974–1979, including the decline in governmental respect for the rule of law.

Sir Ian also argued that the Conservative Party should be a '. . . moderate non-ideological party . . . the more Labour moves to the Left, the more relentlessly should the Conservative Party cling to moderation and the Centre'[3]. But the problem was that the Conservative Party, by drifting to the Left under Mr Heath, actually made it easier for Labour, the natural party of the Left, to enact more left-wing measures than it might otherwise have done. Curwen and Fowler have noted that with the rescue of Rolls-Royce and UCS by Mr Heath '. . . the barrier was broken [and] the way opened for the left-wing of the Labour Party to press for a widespread extension of the public-enterprise sector'[4]. This is an important point in the context of British political economy from the mid-1970s, which explains why the Left of the Labour Party has increased its strength. Thus, as Mr Heath's move to the Left pushed the overall centre of gravity in British politics to the Left, the policies of Labour's left-wing that hitherto the Labour Right had resisted, were accredited a legitimacy they had previously failed to find. Although it may be argued that the Callaghan/ Healey control over policy, 1976–1979, successfully frustrated Labour's left-wing, and that the electorate, by voting-in Mrs Thatcher's Government in May 1979, also rejected the solution of the far Left, it still remains the case that the Left have made the running, in the Labour Party, since the early 1970s. Mr Heath's move leftwards in substantially expanding the public sector both directly and indirectly is a policy that is now clearly associated with the Labour Party and particularly its left-wing. So that although the Conservative Party under Mrs Thatcher has repudiated huge increases in public spending and state control, the Labour Party, since 1979, has not, and as such is in a strikingly close position to adopting the policy priorities inherent in the 'Heath dilemma' alternative. At least while Mrs Thatcher remains Conservative Party Leader the heirs to the 'Heath dilemma' approach are more likely to be found in the Labour Party. But even within the 1970–1974 context the argument that Mr Heath's policy reversals were examples of pragmatic Conservatism, as opposed to the ideological commitments of the 'Quiet Revolution', is a far from convincing argument. It is, in any case, a poor definition of pragmatism to equate it with the absence of ideology. There is no more dangerous ideology than not having an ideology. In practical terms Mr Heath's policy reversals may be viewed as being far from pragmatic, even though quite rational at the time, in the context of the 'Heath dilemma'.

The real solutions – for example, sound money as the cure for inflation – were rejected. Statutory incomes policy proved to be distinctly unpragmatic particularly when the Stage III limits prevented a solution up to the 1973/74 miners' crisis. It may also be argued that it was hardly pragmatic to pour millions of pounds of public money into the subsidization of declining industries merely to postpone the inevitable day of reckoning. Claims to pragmatism, like claims to ideological preference, must have their roots in the practicalities of the real world. Conservative philosophy is neither obsessively 'ideological' nor indiscriminately 'pragmatic'.

It may, of course, be pointed out that Conservatism has a history of both individualism, the belief in free enterprise, and paternalism, involving the state provision of welfare benefits. Both these strands of contemporary Conservatism were present in the 'Quiet Revolution' policies that were not a return to *laissez-faire* in the sense of dismantling the National Health Service or wholesale de-nationalization. The whole 'Quiet Revolution' approach was an attempt to reduce the role of government within the context of a mixed economy. The 'Quiet Revolution', particularly after six years of leftward-moving Labour government, represented the 'middle way', 'government from the centre', and the 'balance and moderation' that Sir Ian Gilmour puts at the heart of contemporary Conservatism[5]. But the reversal of the 'Quiet Revolution' policies was in an explicitly leftward direction, moving beyond the leftward trend of the preceding Wilson administration. Ultimately, it was not the replacement of the mixed economy by *laissez-faire* that Mr Heath bequeathed but the downgrading of the individualist, free enterprise facet of Conservatism and its replacement by considerable state intervention.

This is the central paradox of the 'Heath dilemma' itself. Mr Heath was not prepared to wait for private industry, and the private sector as a whole, to invest a sufficient degree to bring about the economic revival that Mr Heath believed to be essential to Britain's entry into the EEC. Similarly, Mr Heath was not prepared to wait for unemployment to fall by workers pricing themselves back into jobs. In short Mr Heath was not prepared, either ideologically or personally, to wait for the 'Quiet Revolution' to bear fruits. The resultant move to the Left implicit in the 'Heath dilemma' alternative, although couched in non-ideological terms such as 'growth', was thus a very considerable strain on the individualist, free-enterprise beliefs of contemporary Conservatism. Thus, as Budd had argued, under Mr Heath the Conservatives '. . . moved closer to . . . [the] pursuit of administrative and collective solutions to economic problems rather than reliance on markets'[6]. Thus, for example, Mr Heath's U-turn on incomes policy led to the most complex legislative attempt to control individual incomes, prices, profits and dividends hitherto devised. As Patrick Cosgrave points out:

> Every previous incomes policy, Mr Wilson's as much as Mr Macmillan's, was justified as a temporary expedient, designed to meet a crisis, a British Conservative Prime Minister [Mr Heath] was the first to introduce an essentially collectivist measure of major importance as a permanent feature of government life[7].

It is hardly surprising that the policy reversals that brought such a transformation about have demonstrated the Conservative Party's need '. . . from time to time [to] spell out the fundamentals of its creed as coherently as possible'[8]. Contemporary Conservativism had largely shed its aristocratic, landowning, Church of England orientated, Empire-preserving attitudes when Edward Heath became leader in 1965. Mr Heath, himself, represented meritocracy and the increasingly classless nature of British society. The problem that such a modernization of Conservatism brought about was that Conservative philosophy became wedded more than ever before to economic matters. In the sense that British politics now revolved around economic issues, the Conservatives simply had to orientate themselves to the economic requirements that a mass electorate demanded. Issues of foreign policy, administrative or constitutional change, including the importance attached to the EEC by the 'Establishment', increasingly had tended to find the electorate simply apathetic. Issues of taxation, social welfare benefits, inflation, unemployment and the fostering of economic growth had come to dominate political controversy largely because such issues have an electoral appeal and can be translated by the major parties into terms that Britain's mass electorate can identify with, if not thoroughly comprehend.

## 9.2   Economic priorities and political pressure

In successive elections since the Second World War the Conservative Party has been forced by this process to rely more on an appeal to the electorate in economic terms and less on its previous identification as the party of Empire, Church and a 'ruling elite'. Beloff and Peele have argued that:

. . . the rise of the Labour Party to national-party status has meant that for much of the twentieth century the political agenda of the United Kingdom has been set by that Party while the Conservative position has in general been a defensive one[9].

Certainly the reformist Labour administration 1945–1951, during which the modern Welfare State was born, put an emphasis on economic matters that had hitherto not dominated policy making. It may also be argued that during the Conservatives' 13 years in office, 1951–1964, 'Keynesian', 'consensus' politics were pursued that involved the acceptance and encouragement – not the repudiation – of much of the work of the 1945–1951 Labour Government. Thus, as Labour's political priorities were economic, in terms of socialism, nationalization and greater social equality, the Conservatives' counter arguments became increasingly economic in terms of the 'property-owning democracy' and efficient economic management, which reached its apogee in the 'you've never had it so good' days of Harold Macmillan. But the Labour Party, too, particularly after Harold Wilson became Leader in 1963, had to come to terms with the fact that an appeal simply to working class solidarity would be insufficient to persuade the floating voters whose vote would be vital in order to return Labour to office. Maclean has noted that '. . . before the last war [the economy] was rather like the weather – it might be bad or good but politicians did not think they could do anything about it, or about its effects on their election chances'[10]. The growth of the importance of the economy in electoral strategy revolutionized both parties in the post-war era. But in terms of the affluent society that Britain has become – despite the arguments about comparative economic decline – the Conservative Party faced an easier task than Labour, whose own historically socialist views seemed largely irrelevant to the mid-1960s. The economic nature of the political debate left – and still leaves – many Conservatives uneasy. But by 1970, when the Conservatives returned to office, the 'Quiet Revolution' programme provided an ideological framework compatible both to Conservative philosophy and to the practical matter of maintaining office in an age when economic considerations are, by their nature, political[11].

It is ironic that Mr Heath abandoned this approach to government in the 1970s by exaggerating the problems of rising unemployment, which he mistakenly interpreted as being in the dimensions of the 1930s. As has been agreed, that single misconception led to the chain of events that replaced the policies of the 'Quiet Revolution' by policies virtually their opposite. The political panic over the rising unemployment figures made the policy reversals on incomes and industry easier to put into effect. Mr Heath's Prime Ministerial style of government enabled such U-turns to be made swiftly with the minimum of opposition from the Conservative Party at the time. Those who argue that Mr Heath was in keeping with traditional Conservatism by acting pragmatically must be prepared to counter the criticisms that Mr Heath's Conservatism became increasingly interventionist both intellectually and in terms of actual policies. In this sense it may be argued that Mr Heath rejected his own party long before it rejected him. He had no time for philosophical theorizing by nature and did not think in terms of Conservatism as a series of basic principles. He saw himself more of a statesman than a politician; as a Prime Minister in a hurry, putting country well before party. It did not bother him that the 'Heath dilemma' alternative might be classified as moving the Conservative Party too far to the Left.

Among the popular misconceptions about policy-making 1970–1974, e.g., that Anthony Barber was responsible for the 'Barber boom', that the Wilberforce settlement of the 1972 miners' strike necessitated the end of 'N minus 1', and that the 'Quiet Revolution' was about to return to nineteenth century *laissez-faire* – the most ironic is that Mr Heath was anti-trade union, a man of 'confrontation'. In reality Mr Heath's patient hours of talks with representatives of the trade unions, with the resulting mutual respect on both sides, present the clearest image of Mr Heath's determination to tackle the problems of an economy beset with a high level of trade union militancy. Mr Heath's move leftwards to attempt to defuse this militancy is, of course, open to criticism from the Right, but Mr Heath's integrity of motive is not open to question. That Mr Heath was often closer to the trade union leaders than to the representatives of the CBI showed the extent of the drift to the Left that Sir Ian Gilmour denies. Dorfman has put it that 'Mr Heath staked his own reputation on the U-turn towards collectivism'[12]. Similarly, it may be convincingly argued that the 'Conservatives did not go into battle [in February 1974] convinced that they were standing for something different from socialism'[13].

It may be argued that, unlike other Conservative leaders, Mr Heath's main ideological error was in not realizing the limitations of the state and the dangers of state intervention in matters best left to individuals or groups of individuals. Critics have claimed that it is no coincidence that Mr Heath's policies led to an increase in the number of civil servants by 98 000. Mr Heath's civil service background and his reliance on civil service rather than party political advice – for example, the role of Sir William Armstrong – no doubt facilitated this development. While such recruitment may have been good for the unemployment statistics it created further problems for the economy. Bacon and Eltis note that:

> A Conservative Government like Mr Heath's which failed to cut the rate of public expenditure to marketed output, and actually increased the number of civil servants by 98 000 in three years, failed to ease any of the economy's real pressures because it failed to improve the underlying structure in which business and workers have to operate[14].

Furthermore, it may be argued, the high increase in numbers in the Civil Service, both centrally and locally, under Mr Heath placed a very heavy burden on the British economy beyond the period 1970–1974. Thus the Thatcher Government has had to tackle this inherited problem by reducing the gross overmanning in the Civil Service, resisting wholly unjustified civil service pay claims, which led to strike action, and reconsidering the clearly unfair and inequitable situation of index-linked civil service pensions, originally introduced by Mr Heath.

Apart from the legacy of Civil Service expansion the reform of Local Government initiated by Mr Heath, as well as the reorganization of the National Heath Service, brought about, as Lord Blake points out, no obvious benefits[15], although at tremendous expense to the Exchequer.

One former Minister recalled that 'the local government reorganization was totally ridiculous. The expense was terrible – all the salaries went shooting up'[16]. Britain's entry into the EEC, with its long-term burden of a high economic price, and the schemes for an airport at Maplin and a tunnel under the English Channel[17] are other examples that critics have cited of the prestige-project style favoured by Mr Heath, with the costs to the nation seemingly of less importance. But to one Conservative critic Mr Heath was '. . . on the surface a high spender and at bottom a managerial collectivist'[18].

It is not surprising as the critics on the Conservative Right have pointed out that all the above schemes helped to produce massive levels of public expenditure, backed only by the printing of money with the all too obvious inflationary implications. Mr Heath's Government has thus been held responsible, more than any other, for Britain's accelerating rate of inflation comparative to other industrialized competitors. Ironically it was this fear that originally helped to inspire the 'Quiet Revolution' programme aimed at reversing Britain's poor economic and industrial performance. Furthermore, the adoption of policies based on the idea that government intervention can always 'solve' problems was not in keeping with the Conservative philosophical tradition, which, as previously explained, held little interest to a Prime Minister deeply concerned with 'practical' problems and committed to Britain entering Europe with as strong an economy as possible. While it may be explained away that EEC entry, Local Government reform, and NHS reorganization policies were products of the fashionable thinking of the time – that 'modernizing' administrative structures leads to better government[19] – it is impossible to overlook the fact thay many of Mr Heath's policies were simply unconservative.

The Government was committed, following its policy reversals, to regulate individual prices, wages, rents, profits and dividends, maintain 'full' employment, and supervise the construction of prestige projects, drafting in 98 000 more civil servants to assist the process. Such policies did not really belong to the Conservative tradition, including the consensus Conservatism of the post-1945 era, nor even to the tradition of 'Tory paternalism' belonging to the days when '. . . the Liberal Party of Cobden and Bright was the enemy [but] is largely irrelevant now'[20]. One particular adverse consequence of Mr Heath's policies according to the Right was that respect for the rule of law – itself central to the Conservative tradition – was undermined by the impractical intricacies of statutory prices and incomes control.

William Waldegrave, although not associated with the Right, has argued that:

It has become clear that the use of the law to lead opinion in an effort to keep pay to sensible levels falls into the category of the unenforceable and dangerous [law]; no consensus about the general platitude that pay should be sensibly limited will stand up against the impassioned argument for the inevitable special case to the extent of approving enforcement; breaches are spectacular, cannot be ignored and therefore damage the whole fabric of the law. To mean anything the law has either to enter into such detail about figures and percentages as to be hopelessly unwieldy, or delegate such sweeping powers to bodies of experts as to raise serious questions about the accountability of these boards, panels and tribunals[21].

Sir Ian Gilmour admits that the 'Heath Government . . . tried to do too much'[22] but the reason for this lay in Mr Heath's belief that government could achieve virtually any policy objective simply by benevolent legislation, regulation and control. The Conservative Right has argued that this naïve trust in the capacity of government is not the hallmark of Conservatism, a criticism that has also been made to explain the disillusionment among Conservative voters with Mr Heath's Government, which in February 1974 was *inter alia* sufficient to return Labour to office.


## 9.3    Final assessment

The ideological implications of Mr Heath's policy reversals are relevant to the arguments of the Right that the Conservative Party did not fight the February 1974 election on a platform of Conservatism. The 1970 manifesto which sought to roll back the infringements of the state in economic and social matters offered a clear alternative to the interventionist policies of Harold Wilson's Labour Government, 1964–1970. But the 1970 manifesto, not the 'Quiet Revolution' revealed at Blackpool in October 1970, sought to deny the state its proper role – a role historically defended by Conservatism in such matters as social welfare, defence and educational reform. Thus, for example, Disraeli legislated against blatant abuses of nineteenth century capitalism and '. . . Salisbury and Balfour did not hesitate to put the state's power into the scales on the side of better organization of education and defence'[23]. The 'Quiet Revolution' did not challenge this traditional role of the state; and its commitment to the 'mixed economy' was unequivocable. What the 'Quiet Revolution' did seek was rather the curtailment of the socialist, not the traditional Conservative, version of the role of the state. Thus as Jock Bruce-Gardyne has pointed out, for example:

> The Government . . . was prepared to act on the assumption that neither it nor its dedicated civil servants always knew best about a whole variety of matters ranging from day to day management of the nationalized industries to the correct geographical location of the mousetrap industry and even individual mousetrap factories; from the proper relationship between the wages of a dustman and those of a High Court Judge to the optimum number of houses to be built by every local authority in the land[24].

The 1970 'Quiet Revolution' approach embodied the philosophy, described by Lord Robbins, that there is:

> . . . without in any way denying the importance of the essential functions of the state and their necessary increase in modern industrial societies . . . much good sense in the presumption that the state action should be

confined to those spheres in which it is doing things, which if they are not done by government, are not done at all[25].

But by February 1974 after the 'Quiet Revolution' policies had been reversed the Conservative Party contested a general election defending policies – particularly statutory incomes control – that it had vowed to disregard as philosophically and practically abhorrent only three and a half years previously. Although among Conservatives there was considerable debate as to the merits of Mr Heath's policy changes, there was less disagreement that the policy reversals themselves had been imposed on the Conservative Party by virtue of Mr Heath's total control over policy making and distinctly autocratic style of leadership. Ministers, back bench MPs and the party in the country were often presented with a *fait accompli* in terms of policy reversals and were reluctant to rock the boat too violently for fear of appearing disloyal. Nevertheless as Norton has argued, back bench dissent was more in evidence than in any other post-war Conservative administration.

While it may be argued that Enoch Powell and the small groups of Conservative economic liberals kept the flame of traditional Conservatism burning the fact remained that it was Mr Heath not Mr Powell who was officially Leader of the Conservative Party. 'Powellism' in economic matters thus tended to be viewed as akin to disloyalty, if not outright treason, given the personal animosity between Mr Powell and his Party Leader. But fighting the February 1974 election under Mr Heath's leadership was contrary to Mr Powell's principles though he, more than anyone else, had sought to keep the party on the lines intended in 1970. The failure in February 1974 therefore stemmed not so much from short-term effects of the miners' crisis that precipitated the election but from the long-term disillusion of Conservative voters who, during 1973, had served notice on Mr Heath's Government by voting Liberal in the series of Conservative by-election defeats. The further irony is that by moving leftwards (from the mythical 'middle ground') Mr Heath came to adopt the solution of statutory prices and incomes control which, as the Right have argued, led to the wholly unnecessary confrontation with the miners in the winter of 1973/74.

In both practical and electoral terms, therefore, Mr Heath's policy reversals on incomes and industry are, with hindsight, susceptible to the criticisms of the Right in terms of Conservative philosophy or tradition, even if allowance is made for the lightness of Conservative ideological luggage. Similarly, as the Right were quick to point out, the policy reversals cannot be justified as politically necessary as opposed to econo-mically necessary. Sir Ian Gilmour argues that 'For a Tory, politics are more important than purely economic considerations'[26]. However, as a result of the political pressure that caused the changes in economic policy, Mr Heath's Government gained neither political, social nor economic benefits from its policy reversals, despite the fact that no Prime Minister more than Mr Heath had held such a deep commitment to economic progress and rising living standards. Furthermore, arising from Mr Heath's policy failures, the subsequent election defeat in February 1974 denied the credibility of the Conservatives to be the natural party of government, their previous tenure in office lasting 13 years compared to Mr Heath's three and a half[27]. What also galled many Conservatives accustomed to the Party being in office was that under Mr Heath's leadership the Conservative Party fought four elections and only once gained a majority of seats. Behrens notes that many Conservatives '. . . saw a close relationship between this electoral failure and Mr Heath's own personality. It was said that he could excite the enthusiasm of neither the electorate nor his own party workers'[28]. However, in terms of the Right's criticism , this failure of personality was secondary to the failures of policy.

While it is correct to describe the Government's and particularly Mr Heath's reaction to the rising unemployment figures in 1971 as a 'political panic', the Government did not reap any political or electoral benefit. The political panic over rising unemployment that is central to the policy reversals was not an example of Conservative pragmatism, according to the Right, but the lack of political will to carry through the traditional Conservative approach of the 'Quiet Revolution'. This criticism, as previously mentioned, is one that has usually been made with hindsight and while the Government's reaction to rising unemployment was certainly a panic, there existed reasons, historically based and genuinely believed, that the modern Conservative Party could not afford to be labelled as a party of unemployment. However, the Right have argued that it was neither politically expedient nor pragmatic to rescue UCS, introduce an Industry Act and impose a prices and incomes policy if the known result was a massive extension of state intervention involving public expenditure at a higher inflationary level. For in terms of obligations, as William Waldegrave points out, the state undertakes '. . . in writing, on every banknote to maintain a stable currency . . . '[29]. The failure of Mr Heath's Government to fulfil this obligation contrasts with the desire to do so with which it took office. The 1970 election was won largely by promising to reduce the rate of inflation and having originally adopted the necessary measures, it was politically unwise rather than pragmatic to inflate the economy to its highest level on record. Although in terms of the 'Heath dilemma' this policy was rational and at the time widely regarded as beneficial the net result heralded the end of the Keynesian era of expansionary demand management. In the final analysis the policy reversals of the Conservative Government 1970–1974, left to the Conservative Party, to the economic policy makers, and ultimately to the British people, only the lessons of failure.

## References

1. R. BEHRENS, *The Conservative Party from Heath to Thatcher: Policies and Politics 1974–79*, Saxon House, 1980, Ch. 2.
2. SIR IAN GILMOUR, *Inside Right: A Study of Conservatism*, Quartet Books, 1978, p. 17.
3. SIR I. GILMOUR, op. cit. (Ref. 2), p. 142.
4. P. J. CURWEN and A. H. FOWLER, *Economic Policy*, Macmillan, 1976, p. 60.
5. SIR I.GILMOUR, op. cit. (Ref. 2), p. 167.
6. A. BUDD, *The Politics of Economic Planning*, Fontana, 1978, pp. 121–22.
7. PATRICK COSGRAVE, *The Failure of the Conservative Party 1945–75*, p. 122 (see p. 157).

8. GILLIAN PEELE in *The Conservative Opportunity* (Ed. by Lord Blake and J. Patten), Macmillan, 1976, p. 14.
9. MAX BELOFF and GILLIAN PEELE, *The Government of the UK: Political Authority in a Changing Society*, Weidenfeld and Nicolson, 1980, p. 149.
10. I. MACLEAN, *Elections*, Longmans, 1976, p. 76.
11. For an interesting interpretation of the relevance of economic considerations to Conservative philosophy, see R. SCRUTON, *The Meaning of Conservatism*, Penguin Books, 1980, Ch. 5.
12. GERALD A. DORFMAN, *Government versus Trade Unions in British Politics since 1968*, Macmillan, 1979, p. 86.
13. PATRICK COSGRAVE, op. cit. (Ref. 7), p. 123. A Gallup Poll found that the electorate took a similar view: only 49% as opposed to 45% thought there were major differences between the parties, *Gallup International Public Opinion Polls (GB) 1937–75*, p. 1312.
14. R. BACON and W. ELTIS, *Britain's Economic Problems: Two Few Producers*, Macmillan, 1976, p. 80.
15. LORD BLAKE and J. PATTEN (Eds), op. cit. (Ref. 8), p. 3.
16. Interview, Junior Minister. See also B. CASTLE, *The Castle Diaries 1974–76*, p. 450 for a similar analysis regarding the NHS reorganization.
17. Maplin and the Channel Tunnel were subsequently abandoned by the Labour Government 1974–79.
18. PATRICK COSGRAVE, op. cit. (Ref. 7), p. 116.
19. This is in itself an anti-conservative approach; it may be argued that EEC entry, by downgrading the sovereignty of Parliament, was a profoundly radical unconservative policy. Similarly, the dismemberment of the long-established local government system was unconservative in that it sought to destroy traditional regional loyalties in the name of administrative modernization.
20. LORD BLAKE and J. PATTEN (Eds), op. cit. (Ref. 8), p. 8.
21. W. WALDEGRAVE, *The Binding of Leviathan: Conservatism and the Future*, Hamish Hamilton, 1978, p. 67.
22. SIR I. GILMOUR, op. cit. (Ref. 2), p. 128.
23. W. WALDEGRAVE, op. cit. (Ref. 21), p. 49.
24. J. BRUCE-GARDYNE, *Whatever Happened to the Quiet Revolution?*, Charles Knight, 1974, pp. 165–66.
25. LORD ROBBINS, *Political Economy Past and Present*, Macmillan, 1976, p. 179.
26. SIR I. GILMOUR, op. cit. (Ref. 2), p. 229.
27. Mr Heath's lack of electoral appeal is in marked contrast to most twentieth century Conservative Leaders. Out of four General Elections in 1966, 1970, February 1974 and October 1974, Mr Heath won only one, in 1970.
28. R. BEHRENS, op. cit. (Ref. 1), p. 35.
29. W. WALDEGRAVE, op. cit. (Ref. 21), p. 110.

Part IV

# Appendixes

# Appendix I

| March | – | Postmen's strike ends; vindication of 'N minus 1' strategy. |
| | – | Anthony Barber cuts taxation by £546m in budget. SET and Purchase Tax to be abolished. |
| April | – | Unemployment figures up to 774000. |
| June | – | Upper Clyde Shipbuilders put into liquidation. |
| July | – | £100m public works scheme announced in mini-budget to reflate the economy. |
| | – | UCS 'work-in' begins. |
| August | – | Industrial Relations Act receives Royal Assent. |
| | – | Thomas Cook and State pubs denationalized. |
| | – | CBI price initiative begins. |
| September | – | NUM lodges a 47% pay claim. |
| November | – | Giro reprieved to save 2500 jobs. |
| | – | Unemployment figures up to 970000. |

*1972*

| January | – | Miners' strike begins. |
| | – | Seasonally unadjusted unemployment total over one million. |
| February | – | Upper Clyde Shipbuilders relaunched with £35m aid. |
| March | – | Wilberforce settlement granting 21% accepted by miners. Ministers regard 'N minus 1' as finished. |
| | – | Budget reduces taxation by £1200m; industrial grants reintroduced. |
| | – | T&GWU fined £55000 for contempt of National Industrial Relations Court. |
| April | – | Ministerial reshuffle: Sir John Eden, Nicholas Ridley and Frederick Corfield removed from the DTI. Christopher Chataway and Tom Boardman appointed Ministers of Industrial Development and Industry, respectively. |
| | – | Railwaymen's work-to-rule begins. |
| May | – | Railwaymen ballot 6:1 in favour of strike action, following a cooling-off period, under the Industrial Relations Act. |
| | – | Industry Act introduced. |
| June | – | Mr Heath informs House of Commons that the rate of wage increases since the Wilberforce settlement is still 9%. |
| | – | Docks dispute worsens. |
| | – | The Pound floated. |
| July | – | National dock strike following the imprisonment of the 'Pentonville five'. |
| | – | Extension of the CBI's price initiative until the end of October. |
| | – | Tripartite talks begin in earnest; the Industrial Relations Act effectively 'put on ice'. |
| September | – | TUC rejects proposals for a voluntary agreement of a £2 limit to pay increases and a 5% price limit. |
| | – | TUC suspends 32 unions for failure to deregister. |
| November | – | Tripartite talks reach impasse. |
| | – | Statutory prices and incomes policy introduced beginning with a 90-day freeze. (Stage I.) |

December  –  Unemployment falls to 744 000.
          –  Liberals gain Sutton and Cheam from the Conservatives.
          –  £175 m subsidy provided for the coal industry. NCB debts written off.

## 1973

February  –  Stage II introduced; £1 per week, plus 4%. Price Commission and Pay Board established. Freeze extended 60 days. Controls on profits and dividends.
March     –  'Neutral' budget at net cost to the Exchequer of £120 m; emphasis on growth policy.
          –  £5 m Government subsidy to the motor cycle industry.
May       –  Official TUC May Day demonstration against the incomes policy.
          –  £500 m public expenditure cuts.
          –  Unemployment falls to less than the 600 000 the Conservatives had inherited from Labour.
          –  Mr Heath attacks the 'unacceptable face of capitalism'.
July      –  Liberals gain Ely and Ripon from the Conservatives.
          –  Secret meeting at Downing Street between Mr Heath, Joe Gormley and Sir William Armstrong.
September –  20 unions expelled from the TUC for failure to deregister.
October   –  Outbreak of the Arab-Israeli war and consequent oil crisis.
November  –  Liberals gain Berwick-upon-Tweed from the Conservatives.
          –  Stage III introduced; 7% or a maximum of £2.25 per week plus partial indexation.
          –  NUM begin overtime ban.
December  –  William Whitelaw replaced Maurice Macmillan as Employment Secretary.
          –  Three-day week introduced.
          –  Measures announced by Anthony Barber to cut public spending by £1.2 billion in 1974/75.

## 1974

January   –  TUC proposal to treat the miners as a special case rejected by the Government.
          –  NUM Executive votes 16:10 to recommend strike action.
February  –  Miners' strike begins.
          –  Mr Heath calls a General Election for 28 February.
          –  NUM rejects by 20:6 an appeal to call off the strike during the election campaign.
          –  Enoch Powell advises the electorate to vote Labour.
          –  Statistical evidence leaked from the Pay Board suggests that the miners are entitled to a further 8%.
          –  Conservatives defeated in the General Election, losing 33 seats.
March     –  Edward Heath resigns; Harold Wilson becomes Prime Minister.
          –  Miners' settlement agreed.

# Appendix II

**Select Bibliography**

1. J. E. Alt.  *The Politics of Economic Decline: Economic Management and Political Behaviour in Britain since 1964,* Cambridge University Press, 1979.

2. R. Bacon & W. Eltis.  *Britain's Economic Problems: Too Few Producers,* Macmillan, 1976.

3. J. D. Barber.  *The Presidential Character,* Prentice-Hall, 1972.

4. D. Barnes & E. Reid.  *Government and Trade Unions: The British Experience 1964–79,* Heinemann PSI, 1980.

5. R. Behrens.  *The Conservative Party from Heath to Thatcher: Policies and Politics 1974–79,* Saxon House, 1980.

6. M. Beloff & G. Peele.  *The Government of the United Kingdom: Political Authority in a Changing Society,* Weidenfeld & Nicolson, 1980.

7. F. T. Blackaby (Ed.)  *British Economic Policy 1960–74: Demand Management,* Cambridge University Press, 1979.

8. Lord Blake & J. Patten (Eds.)  *The Conservative Opportunity,* Macmillan, 1976.

9. B. Bracewell-Milnes.  *Pay and Price Control Guide,* Butterworths, 1973.

10. S. Brittan.  *Steering the Economy,* Penguin Books, 1971.

11. S. Brittan.  *Capitalism and the Permissive Society,* Macmillan, 1973.

12. S. Brittan.  *Second Thoughts on Full Employment Policy,* Centre for Policy Studies, 1975.

13. S. Brittan.            *The Economic Consequences of Democracy*,
                           Temple Smith, 1977.
14. S. Brittan &           *The Delusion of Incomes Policy*,
    P. Lilley.             Temple Smith, 1977.
15. J. Bruce-Gardyne.      *Whatever Happened to the Quiet Revolution?*,
                           Charles Knight, 1974.
16. J. Bruce-Gardyne.      *Meriden: Odyssey of a Lame Duck*,
                           Centre for Policy Studies, 1978.
17. A. Budd.               *The Politics of Economic Planning*,
                           Fontana, 1978.
18. D. E. Butler &         *The General Election of February 1974*,
    D. Kavanagh.           Macmillan, 1974.
19. D. E. Butler & M.      *The General Election of 1970*,
    Pinto-Duschinsky.      Macmillan, 1971.
20. B. Castle.             *The Castle Diaries 1974–76*,
                           Weidenfeld & Nicolson, 1980.
21. H. Clegg.              *How to run an Incomes Policy and Why We
                           Made Such a Mess of the Last One*,
                           Heinemann Educational Books, 1971.
22. H. Clegg.              *Trade Unions under Collective Bargaining*,
                           Blackwell, 1976.
23. H. Clegg.              *The Changing System of Industrial Relations in
                           Great Britain*,
                           Blackwell, 1979.
24. R. Clutterbuck.        *Britain in Agony: The Growth of Political
                           Violence*,
                           Penguin Books, 1980.
25. P. Cosgrave.           'The Failure of the Conservative Party
                           1945–75',
                           from *The Future that Doesn't Work: Social
                           Democracy's Failures in Britain*,
                           Doubleday, New York, 1977.
26. R. H. S. Crossman.     *Inside View: Three Lectures on Prime Ministerial
                           Government*,
                           Jonathan Cape, 1972.
27. R. H. S. Crossman.     *The Diaries of a Cabinet Minister: Vols I–III*,
                           Hamish Hamilton & Jonathan Cape, 1975–77.
28. C. Crouch.             *Class Conflict and the Industrial Relations Crisis*,
                           Heinemann Educational Books, 1977.
29. C. Crouch.             *The Politics of Industrial Relations*,
                           Fontana, 1979.
30. C. Crouch &            *The Resurgence of Class Conflict in Western
    A. Pizzorno (Eds.)     Europe since 1968. Vol. II, Comparative
                           Analysis*,
                           Macmillan, 1978.
31. P. J. Curwen &         *Economic Policy*,
    A. H. Fowler.          Macmillan, 1976.

32. G. A. Dorfman.     *Government versus Trade Unions in British Politics since 1968*, Macmillan, 1979.

33. S. Fay & H. Young.     *The Fall of Heath*, Sunday Times Publication, 1976. (Originally printed in the *Sunday Times* on 22 and 29 February and 7 March 1976.)

34. P. Ferris.     *The New Militants: Crisis in the Trade Unions*, Penguin Books, 1972.

35. N. Fisher.     *The Tory Leaders*, Weidenfeld & Nicolson, 1977.

36. A. Gamble.     *The Conservative Nation*, Routledge & Kegan Paul, 1974.

37. Sir I. Gilmour.     *Inside Right: A Study of Conservatism*, Quartet Books, 1978.

38. W. Grant & D. Marsh.     *The CBI*, Hodder & Stoughton, 1977.

39. J. A. G. Griffith.     *The Politics of the Judiciary*, Fontana, 1977.

40. N. Harris.     *Competition and the Corporate State*, Methuen, 1972.

41. R. Harris & B. Sewill.     *British Economic Policy 1970–74: Two Views*, IEA Hobart Paperback No. 7, 1975.

42. R. J. Harrison.     *Pluralism and Corporatism: The Political Evolution of Modern Democracies*, George Allen & Unwin, 1980.

43. K. Hawkins.     *Unemployment*, Penguin Books, 1979.

44. F. Hirsch & J. H. Goldthorpe (Eds.)     *The Political Economy of Inflation*, Martin Robertson, 1978.

45. Lord Home.     *The Way the Wind Blows: an Autobiography*, Fontana, 1979.

46. J. Hughes & R. Moore (Eds.)     *A Special Case? Social Justice and the Miners*, Penguin Books, 1972.

47. L. C. Hunter & D. J. Robertson.     *Economics of Wages and Labour*, Macmillan, 1969.

48. D. Hurd.     *An End to Promises: Sketch of a Government 1970–74*, Collins, 1979.

49. G. Hutchinson.     *Edward Heath*, Longmans, 1970.

50. N. Johnson.     *In Search of the Constitution*, Methuen, 1980.

51. A. Jones.     *The New Inflation: The Politics of Prices and Incomes*, André Deutsch and Penguin Books, 1973.

52. W. Keegan & R. Pennant-Rea.     *Who Runs the Economy? Control and Influence in British Economic Policy*, Temple Smith, 1977.

53. M. Laing.            *Edward Heath: Prime Minister*,
                         Sidgwick & Jackson, 1972.
54. Z. Layton-Henry      *Conservative Party Politics*,
    (Ed.)                Macmillan, 1980.
55. R. Lewis.            *Enoch Powell: Principle in Politics*,
                         Cassell, 1979.
56. T. F. Lindsay &      *The Conservative Party 1918–79*,
    M. Harrington.       Macmillan, 1979.
57. I. Maclean.          *Elections*,
                         Longmans, 1976.
58. W. A. P. Manser.     *Britain in Balance*,
                         Penguin Books, 1973.
59. J. Margach.          *The Abuse of Power*,
                         W. H. Allen, 1978.
60. J. McGill.           *Crisis on the Clyde*,
                         Davis Poynter, 1973.
61. M. Moran.            *The Politics of Industrial Relations*,
                         Macmillan, 1977.
62. P. Norton.           *Dissension in the House of Commons 1945–74*,
                         Macmillan, 1975.
63. P. Norton.           *Conservative Dissidents: Dissent within the
                         Parliamentary Conservative Party 1970–74*,
                         Macmillan, 1978.
64. R. E. Pahl *et al*.  *The Corporate State: Myth or Reality?*,
                         Policy Studies Institute, 1976.
65. M. Parkin.           *The Illusion of Wage and Price Control*,
                         The Fraser Institute, 1976.
66. G. T. Pepper &       *Too Much Money?*,
    G. E. Ward.          IEA Publication, 1976.
67. J. Ramsden.          *The Making of Conservative Party Policy: The
                         Conservative Research Department since 1929*,
                         Longmans, 1980.
68. Lord Robbins.        *Political Economy Past and Present*,
                         Macmillan, 1976.
69. A. Roth.             *Heath and The Heathmen*,
                         Routledge & Kegan Paul, 1972.
70. T. Russell.          *The Tory Party: Its Policies, Divisions and
                         Future*,
                         Penguin Books, 1978.
71. C. T. Sandford *et al*  *Case Studies in Economics: Economic Policy*,
                         Macmillan, 1977.
72. P. C. Schmitter &    *Trends towards Corporatist Intermediation*,
    G. Lehmbruch.        Sage, 1979.
73. D. E. Schoen.        *Powell and the Powellites*,
                         Macmillan, 1977.
74. R. Scruton.          *The Meaning of Conservatism*,
                         Penguin Books, 1980

75. A. Sked &        *Post-War Britain: a Political History*,
    C. Cook.          Penguin Books, 1979.
76. M. Stewart.      *The Jekyll and Hyde Years: Politics and
                     Economic Policy since 1964*,
                     Dent, 1977.
77. R. Taylor.       *The Fifth Estate: Britain's Unions in the Modern
                     World*,
                     Pan Books, 1980.
78. W. Thompson &    *The UCS Work-in*,
    F. Hart.          Lawrence & Wishart, 1972.
79. W. Waldegrave.   *The Binding of Leviathan: Conservatism and the
                     Future*,
                     Hamish Hamilton, 1978.
80. P. Walker.       *The Ascent of Britain*,
                     Sidgwick & Jackson, 1977.
81. B. Weekes *et al.*  *Industrial Relations and the Limits of Law:
    (Eds.)            Effects of the Industrial Relations Act 1971*,
                     Warwick Study on Industrial Relations,
                     Blackwell, 1975.
82. E. Wigham.       *Strikes and the Government 1893–1974*,
                     Macmillan, 1976.
83. Sir H. Wilson.   *Final Term: The Labour Government 1974–76*,
                     Weidenfeld & Nicolson and Michael Joseph,
                     1979.
84. J. B. Wood.      *How Little Unemployment*,
                     IEA Hobart Paper No. 65, 1975.

# Index